Vicky Balabanski is Lecturer in New Testament at Parkin-Wesley College, Adelaide College of Divinity, Flinders University, South Australia. This is her first book.

If the expectations of the early church concerning the return of Christ and the End of the World were disappointed, the magnitude of the disappointment and the form in which it was expressed do not seem to fit with the expectations of modern scholars. This study questions both the idea that the delay of Christ's return – the parousia – was the primary factor shaping the development of eschatological expectation in the early church, and the linearity of the models used to understand the development of early Christian eschatology. Vicky Balabanski argues that Matthew's Gospel shows a more imminent expectation than Mark's, and that there were fluctuations in eschatological expectation caused by factors within these early communities and those of the Didache. She traces these fluctuations and offers some new interpretative keys to Mark 13, Matthew 24 and 25 and Didache 16, as well as some vivid and original historical reconstructions.

SOCIETY FOR NEW TESTAMENT STUDIES

MONOGRAPH SERIES

General editor: Richard Bauckham

97

ESCHATOLOGY IN THE MAKING

Eschatology in the making

Mark, Matthew and the Didache

VICKY BALABANSKI

*Parkin-Wesley College, Adelaide College of Divinity,
Flinders University, South Australia*

CAMBRIDGE
UNIVERSITY PRESS

PUBLISHED BY THE PRESS SYNDICATE OF THE UNIVERSITY OF CAMBRIDGE
The Pitt Building, Trumpington Street, Cambridge, CB2 1RP, United Kingdom

CAMBRIDGE UNIVERSITY PRESS
The Edinburgh Building, Cambridge CB2 2RU, United Kingdom
40 West 20th Street, New York, NY 10011–4211, USA
10 Stamford Road, Oakleigh, Melbourne 3166, Australia

First published 1997

Printed in the United Kingdom at the University Press, Cambridge

Typeset in Times 10/12 pt

A catalogue record for this book is available from the British Library

Library of Congress cataloguing in publication data
Balabanski, Vicky.
Eschatology in the making : Mark, Matthew and the
Didache / Vicky Balabanski.
     p. cm. – (Monograph series/Society for New Testament Studies 97)
Revision of the author's thesis (doctoral) – University of Melbourne, 1993.
Includes bibliographical references (p.   ) and indexes.
ISBN 0 521 59137 6
1. Eschatology – Biblical teaching.
2. Bible. N.T. Mark XIII – Criticism, interpretation, etc.
3. Bible. N.T. Matthew XXIV–XXV – Criticism, interpretation, etc.
4. Eschatology – History of doctrines – Early church, *c.* 30–600.
5. Didache. I. Title.
II. Series: Monograph series (Society for New Testament Studies) : 97.
BS2585.6.E7B35   1997
236′.09′015–dc21   96–48934   CIP

ISBN 0 521 59137 6 hardback

Radi and Helene Balabanski

CONTENTS

PREFACE

This study is a revised version of my doctoral thesis which was submitted to the University of Melbourne in February 1993, a week before I took up my lecturing responsibilities at Parkin-Wesley College, South Australia, and some eight weeks before the birth of my second child. I wish to acknowledge my gratitude to my supervisors, examiners, colleagues and, not least, to my family for enabling both the study itself to come to fruition, and the present revision to be undertaken.

It was with the encouragement of my supervisors Professor Frank Moloney and Dr Geoff Jenkins that I embarked on this project after the completion of my honours degrees in Arts and Theology. I am most grateful for their guidance, insightful criticisms and confidence in me. The choice of this area of studies came about through my fascination with the Gospels and a sense that the shape of the earliest Christianities was much more diverse than meets the eye. My studies took me to Göttingen, Germany, where I particularly appreciated the stimulation of the 1987 SNTS Conference. In 1987/88 I spent five months in Jerusalem, studying in the fine library of the Ecole Biblique et Archéologique Française, supported by a Robert Maddox Award. My thanks in this period are due particularly to the late Revd Dr Gilbert Sinden SSM and Revd Tom Brown SSM who welcomed my husband and me into their home for the duration of our stay in Jerusalem and offered us insight into the Holy Land. In 1988/9 a Swiss Government Scholarship enabled me to pursue my studies in Berne, Switzerland, under the very capable and gracious supervision of Revd Professor Ulrich Luz. It was there that the present study took shape, and I am particularly grateful to Professor Luz and to the Revd Isabelle Noth for their encouragement, insight and friendship.

On returning to Melbourne with our daughter Anna only a few weeks old, it took another three and a half years to complete the study. Towards the end of that period, and expecting our daughter Laura, I took up a lectureship in New Testament at Parkin-Wesley College. I am very grateful to my colleagues for their unfailing support, and to the College Council for enabling this period of study leave in Jerusalem.

The thesis was examined by Professors Graham Stanton and Jerome Murphy O'Connor, for whose encouraging and helpful comments I am very grateful. My thanks are also due to Dr Margaret Thrall, former General Editor of the SNTS Monograph Series, whose perceptive criticisms have brought about many improvements to this book.

My final acknowledgement is to the incalculable contribution of my family. Anna and Laura have helped me focus my energies, and have kept me firmly anchored to the joys and challenges of life. My sister, Dr Joanna Barlow, read the manuscripts and offered every encouragement along the way. And most gratitude of all is due to my husband, Peter, without whose support, patience and practical assistance this study would not have been written. I dedicate this book to my parents, who both died while I was still a child, but whose mark is tangible in all that I do.

ABBREVIATIONS AND NOTE ON TEXTS

All abbreviations conform to the standard set out in the 'Instructions for Contributors', *Journal of Biblical Literature* 107/3 (1988), 579–96. This covers periodicals, reference works, serials, and names of biblical and other ancient writings. Where titles occur that are not covered in that article, I write them out in full. I have also followed its guidelines for transliteration of ancient languages. All citations from the Bible in English are from the New Revised Standard Version except where stated otherwise.

AB	Anchor Bible
AnBib	Analecta Biblica
AusBR	Australian Biblical Review
BAGD	W. Bauer, W. F. Arndt, F. W. Gingrich, and F. W. Danker, *Greek–English Lexicon of the New Testament*
BDR	F. Blass, A. Debrunner, and F. Rehkopf, *Grammatik des neutestamentlichen Griechisch*
BETL	Bibliotheca ephemeridum theologicarum lovaniensium
BGBE	Beiträge zur Geschichte der biblischen Exegese
Bib	*Biblica*
BibLeb	*Bibel und Leben*
BJRL	*Bulletin of the John Rylands University Library of Manchester*
BR	*Biblical Research*
BZ	*Biblische Zeitschrift*
BZAW	Beihefte zur Zeitschrift für die alttestamentliche Wissenschaft
CBQ	*Catholic Biblical Quarterly*
ConBNT	Coniectanea Biblica, New Testament
EKKNT	Evangelisch-katholischer Kommentar zum Neuen Testament
ETL	*Ephemerides theologicae*

EvT	*Evangelische Theologie*
EWNT	H. Balz and G. Schneider, eds., *Exegetisches Wörterbuch zum Neuen Testament*
ExpTim	*Expository Times*
FRLANT	Forschungen zur Religion und Literatur des Alten und Neuen Testaments
HSS	Harvard Semitic Studies
HTKNT	Herders theologischer Kommentar zum Neuen Testament
HTR	*Harvard Theological Review*
Int	*Interpretation*
JAC	Jahrbuch für Antike und Christentum
JBL	*Journal of Biblical Literature*
JR	*Journal of Religion*
JRelS	*Journal of Religious Studies*
JSJ	*Journal for the Study of Judaism in the Persian, Hellenistic and Roman Period*
JSNT	*Journal for the Study of the New Testament*
JSOT	*Journal for the Study of the Old Testament*
JTS	*Journal of Theological Studies*
LB	*Linguistica Biblica*
LSJ	Liddell–Scott–Jones, *Greek–English Lexicon*
NICNT	New International Commentary on the New Testament
NovT	*Novum Testamentum*
NTAbh	Neutestamentliche Abhandlungen
NTF	Neutestamentliche Forschungen
NTS	*New Testament Studies*
ÖBS	Österreichische biblische Studien
PEQ	*Palestine Exploration Quarterly*
PG	J. Migne, *Patrologia Graeca*
RB	*Revue biblique*
RelSRev	*Religious Studies Review*
ResQ	*Restoration Quarterly*
RQ	*Römische Quartalschrift für christliche Altertumskunde und Kirchengeschichte*
RSR	*Recherches de science religieuse*
RSV	Revised Standard Version
SANT	Studien zum Alten und Neuen Testament
SBL	Society of Biblical Literature
SBLDS	Society of Biblical Literature Dissertation Series

SE	*Studia Evangelica*
SEÅ	*Svensk exegetisk årsbok*
SJT	*Scottish Journal of Theology*
SNTSMS	Society for New Testament Studies Monograph Series
ST	*Studia theologica*
StPatr	*Studia Patristica*
StudBib	Studia Biblica
Tbl	*Theologische Blätter*
TDNT	G. Kittel and G. Friedrich, eds., *Theological Dictionary of the New Testament*
TF	*Theologische Forschung*
THKNT	Theologischer Handkommentar zum Neuen Testament
TLZ	*Theologische Literaturzeitung*
TTZ	*Trierer theologische Zeitschrift*
TU	Texte und Untersuchungen
TynB	*Tyndale Bulletin*
TZ	*Theologische Zeitschrift*
UBSGNT	United Bible Societies *Greek New Testament*
USQR	*Union Seminary Quarterly Review*
Vcaro	*Verbum caro*
WBC	Word Biblical Commentary
WUNT	Wissenschaftliche Untersuchungen zum Neuen Testament
ZNW	*Zeitschrift für die neutestamentliche Wissenschaft*
ZST	*Zeitschrift für systematische Theologie*

INTRODUCTION

It is a most intriguing fact that the delay of Jesus' parousia did not represent much more of a crisis for the first Christians than actually was the case. Though doubtless the earliest community was confronted by a serious problem in the non-fulfilment of their expectation of an imminent end, nevertheless it cannot be denied that the community survived the delay of the parousia without a substantial break. The question as to how the first Christians came to terms with the delay of the end of the world and the parousia without bitter disappointment and without sacrificing their eschatological hope still requires careful historical and theological consideration. [1]

Ever since the 'rediscovery' in the late nineteenth century of the significance of eschatology for Jesus and the early Christian movement, the problem of the delay of the parousia has intrigued scholars. If the eschatological expectations of the early church were disappointed, the magnitude of the disappointment and the form in which it was expressed do not seem to fit with *our own* expectations. Although there are indications within the New Testament canon that Christian communities did grapple with a disappointment in expectation, nowhere are there echoes of the sort of crisis that we of the late second millennium would have expected. It seems that our models for understanding the changes in early Christian eschatological expectation have not yet been adequate to the task of accounting for what is in fact reflected in the documents themselves.

I do not set out to give a comprehensive analysis in this study of the various nineteenth- and twentieth-century models which seek to

[1] Bornkamm, 'Verzögerung', 116 (translation mine).

account for the developments in early Christian eschatological expectation, nor yet to propose a more adequate model and then test its validity. Rather, after taking account of the range of possible interpretations and evaluating several recent contributions (chapter 1), I undertake a series of exegetical studies of material from the Gospels of Mark and Matthew, and from the Didache. I accept as a basis the two-source hypothesis. On this basis, the material selected for chapters 3, 5 and 6 is examined as a 'progression': Mark 13 was used and reshaped in Matthew's eschatological discourse, and Didache 16 in turn (I conclude) knew and reshaped the Matthean discourse. Such a 'progression', or reworking, of a particular set of traditions enables us to trace the way in which the communities reflected upon their eschatological situation. The way in which these various communities received and reinterpreted these traditions gives us some insight into the ways in which eschatological expectation varied and fluctuated.

If one comes to these traditions expecting them to reflect a particular development, such as a progressive waning in the expectation of an imminent End, one may be surprised. What I find in the course of this study is, in fact, more a fluctuation than a linear development: Matthew shows a more imminent expectation of the End than does Mark. Rather than seeking to account for this by concluding that the two-source hypothesis ought to be superseded by the Griesbach or another source hypothesis, I suggest that this calls into question the strong linearity of our models. Although in theory one might expect that the passing of time led to the waning of hopes for an imminent End, in reality the historical contexts of the various communities seem to have led to a greater variation in *Naherwartung* than our theories would suggest.

In addition to the studies tracing the reception and reinterpretation of the eschatological material of Mark 13, I have found it useful to examine two related areas. The first is the eschatological development in the Matthean community as reflected in a special Matthean tradition, Matt. 25:1–13. Because the findings of this study give some insight into the processes of early eschatological reflection well prior to the events of 70 CE, this is included as the first exegetical chapter, chapter 2. The order of the chapters is thus in some sense chronological. The second related area forms the basis of chapter 4, namely the historical implications of my study of Mark 13. My approach is characterized by the endeavour to deal with eschatological development not primarily as a 'history of ideas', but as grounded in historical particularities, the most far-reaching of which were the implications of the Jewish War and the destruction of Jerusalem in 70 CE. Thus chapter 4 pursues the historical circumstances of the Markan material.

Within the scope of this study, it has not been possible to examine all the passages in the two Gospels which bear upon their respective eschatologies. It has been necessary to draw selectively from a range of materials in order to demonstrate that the developments in eschatology in the first century of Christianity cannot be adequately explained by a blanket theory, but must be seen as expressions of the historical particularities of the communities in question.

The intriguing questions of Jesus' own eschatological expectations and the ways in which the early churches upheld or diverged from them would warrant studies in their own right.[2] These questions have been deemed to be beyond the scope of the present monograph.

A variety of methodologies is represented in the following chapters, ranging from source and form criticism, redaction and narrative criticism to questions of historical criticism. The methodologies have, of course, been chosen according to the nature of the questions at hand, and I am confident that the reader will find the range neither baffling nor inconsistent. At a time when historical and literary studies of the New Testament have become polarized, I hope that this study can make a small contribution towards their integration.

---

[2] A recent contribution in this area is Witherington's *Jesus, Paul and the End of the World*.

1

AN IMMINENT END? MODELS FOR UNDERSTANDING ESCHATOLOGICAL DEVELOPMENT IN THE FIRST CENTURY

1. The problem of the delay of the parousia: a modern construct?

There are indications in the canon of the New Testament and in early extra-canonical sources that the delay of the parousia of Christ presented the early church with an eschatological and theological problem.

In modern scholarship the delay of Christ's return and the presumed disappointment it engendered has been seen as a primary factor, and in some cases as *the* primary factor, in the development of Christian eschatology. The systematic theologian M. Werner stated in his work *The Formation of Christian Dogma* that 'the longer the non-fulfilment of the Parousia of Christ and the final events connected therewith continued, the weaker became the conviction that the End of the world would come in the Apostolic Age and that the Death and Resurrection of Jesus had, correspondingly, a fundamental eschatological significance'.[1] The problem is thus seen not simply as one of eschatology, but of the fundamentals of christology.

It is perhaps not surprising, therefore, that this problem has received much attention from biblical and systematic scholars over the past century. I will begin by giving an overview of ways in which modern scholarship has sought to deal with the challenge of this problem: by embracing it as the exegetical and systematic key to developments in the early church, by rejecting it as such, or by seeking alternative approaches.

The modern development of studies in New Testament eschatology began with J. Weiss' work *Jesus' Proclamation of the Kingdom of God*. In it, he sought to make clear the profoundly eschato-

---

[1] Werner, *Formation*, 31.

logical nature of Jesus' proclamation of the Kingdom of God. Although Weiss' position was foreshadowed to some extent by O. Schmoller and E. Issel and, earlier still, by the work of H. S. Reimarus,[2] it was not until Weiss' polemically stated thesis that the significance of a future eschatological Kingdom of God was borne in upon German scholarship which had until then been characterized by Ritschlian liberal humanism. Weiss set out to show that the generally accepted religious-ethical understanding of the Kingdom of God had stripped away its original eschatological-apocalyptic meaning, and that 'the Kingdom of God is a radically superworldly entity which stands in diametric opposition to this world. This is to say that there *can* be no talk of an *innerworldly* development of the Kingdom of God in the mind of Jesus!'[3] Weiss sought to demonstrate exegetically that the Kingdom Jesus expected was not both future and present, but exclusively future. This presented the German theological establishment, which was already struggling with D. F. Strauss' challenge to the historicity of Jesus,[4] with a fundamental problem: if it was indeed Jesus' expectation that the Kingdom of God was exclusively a future entity which was to be established at the latest within a generation,[5] what can faith make of a Jesus who was so radically mistaken? Yet even in posing the problem, Weiss stepped back from the brink, claiming that we do not share this expectation, but can be joyfully confident that this world is the arena in which God's purposes are worked out.[6]

It was Weiss' work that gave A. Schweitzer the impetus to formulate his controversial ideas about the eschatology of Jesus and his disciples,[7] and to advocate a programme which he called 'konsequente Eschatologie', rendered in English as 'consistent' or 'thoroughgoing eschatology'. He defined this programme in his book *Out of my Life and Thought* as follows:

> For the historical understanding of the life of Jesus . . . it is necessary to think out all the consequences of the fact that He did actually live in the eschatological, Messianic thought world of late Judaism, and to try to comprehend His resolutions and actions not by means of considerations

[2] Schmoller, *Die Lehre vom Reiche Gottes;* Issel, *Die Lehre vom Reiche Gottes im Neuen Testament;* Reimarus, *Von dem Zwecke Jesu und seiner Jünger.*
[3] Weiss, *Proclamation,* 114.   [4] See Strauss, *Life.*
[5] Weiss, *Proclamation,* 91.   [6] *Ibid.,* 135.
[7] Schweitzer, *Messianitäts- und Leidensgeheimnis,* and more comprehensively in *Quest.*

drawn from ordinary psychology, but solely by motives provided by His eschatological expectations.[8]

Schweitzer took up not only Weiss', but also Strauss' challenge in his thoroughgoing eschatological reading of the Gospels of Mark and Matthew in particular. In his opinion, this reading made the historicity of these Gospels apparent. Schweitzer set out to show that a historical – that is a thoroughgoing or consistent eschatological – reading of Jesus leaves us with a person who is to our time 'a stranger and an enigma'.[9] Yet he, too, stepped back from the brink which such a conclusion might approach by recourse to a reality which does not belong to historical discourse: 'Jesus means something to our world because a mighty spiritual force streams forth from Him and flows though our time also. This fact can neither be shaken nor confirmed by any historical discovery. It is the solid foundation of Christianity.'[10]

Perhaps not surprisingly, others did not share Schweitzer's confidence that this constituted a solid foundation for Christianity. An ahistorical claim may not be sufficient to recover the Jesus of faith when the historical reality seems to point to a Messiah who was mistaken in his expectation. The problem lay not so much with the apocalyptic expectation *per se* – Jesus was after all part of the thought-world of late Jewish apocalyptic. Rather, the problem lay with the non-fulfilment of the parousia expectation; even if Christians of former centuries could make light of such a delay or indeed fail to recognize it for what it was, modern theology demanded that the problem be reckoned with.

This, then, is the background against which the numerous twentieth-century studies of early Christian eschatology were written. Those theologians who rejected Schweitzer's programme of 'consistent eschatology' argued against the claim, originally made by Weiss, that the Kingdom of God could not be conceived of as both present and future. If Jesus' understanding of the Kingdom was both present and future, the 'mistakenness' of the timing of its future advent is relativized and thus alleviated.

For the theologians who embraced Schweitzer's programme of 'consistent eschatology', the delay (or non-fulfilment) of the par-

[8] Schweitzer, *Life and Thought*, 43.
[9] Schweitzer, *Quest*, 397. The challenge of Schweitzer's position is still with us, as is shown by Witherington, *Jesus*, 20–2.
[10] Schweitzer, *Quest*, 397.

ousia was understood as the overriding issue, not only for the twentieth century, but necessarily also for the whole of church history, and in particular for the development of the early church. Schweitzer gave the lead by arguing that the real driving force behind the whole history of Christianity has been the need to 'de-eschatologize' it in the face of the non-occurrence of the parousia.[11] Thus the non-occurrence of the parousia had become an important issue for twentieth-century theology, but it was not seen in the first instance as a problem specific to the modern age. In fact, as the preceding quotation shows, it was understood as an interpretative tool for examining theological developments of the first century.

M. Werner applied this to the development of doctrine in the early church, first in his volume entitled *The Formation of Christian Dogma* and later in his more detailed work in two volumes entitled *Der protestantische Weg des Glaubens*. Another notable systematic exponent of 'consistent eschatology' was F. Buri, with his work *Die Bedeutung der neutestamentlichen Eschatologie*.

Exegetically, the concept of the centrality of the delay of the parousia in shaping early Christian eschatology was applied by H. Conzelmann to Luke's Gospel.[12] E. Grässer then studied the synoptic Gospels and Acts from this perspective.[13] However, Grässer did not altogether align himself with Schweitzer's reconstruction of Jesus' eschatological development, because he saw it as questionable from a form-critical point of view. Moreover, Grässer was of the opinion that the exponents of 'consistent eschatology' have given too much weight to the factor of the delay of the parousia by overlooking other factors which enabled the early church to come to terms with the delay, such as gnostic ideas.[14] Even so, Grässer proceeded to exegete the synoptic Gospels and Acts using the delay of the parousia as the hermeneutical key to distinguish layers of authentic dominical tradition from early Christian formulations and to determine the age of a particular tradition. In doing so, he created a hermeneutical circle which is very similar to that of Schweitzer and Werner, even if somewhat more agnostic as regards Jesus' own expectation.

Thus it was that much exegetical and systematic study of the

---

[11] *Ibid.*, 358.
[12] Conzelmann, *The Theology of St. Luke*. Conzelmann had taken up the idea as it had been put forward in an article by Vielhauer, 'Zum "Paulinismus" der Apostelgeschichte'.
[13] Grässer, *Das Problem des Parusieverzögerung*.　　[14] *Ibid.*, 9–10.

New Testament proceeded on the basis of the theory that the early church was profoundly shaped by the disappointment it experienced in its eschatological expectation. There were, however, scholars who questioned whether the early church had undergone the sort of 'crisis' in eschatology which modern scholarship sought to trace. One such scholar was G. Bornkamm, with whose words I opened the introduction. In his view, the New Testament documents do not reflect the bitter disappointment in expectation which one might have expected; the fact that the early church survived the non-occurrence of the parousia without a significant break and without relinquishing its eschatological hope seemed to him a puzzle which had not yet been fully solved. Other scholars, such as E. von Dobschütz and C. H. Dodd, saw the problem of the delay of the parousia as only an apparent one, and argued that Jesus' own eschatology was focussed upon the present reality of the Kingdom of God rather than upon a future coming. In Dodd's view, although Jesus used the language of apocalyptic eschatology, this was really meant to describe a higher reality:

> It appears that while Jesus employed the traditional symbolism of apocalypse to indicate the "otherworldly" or absolute character of the Kingdom of God, He used parables to enforce and illustrate the idea that the Kingdom of God had come upon men [sic] there and then. The inconceivable had happened: history had become the vehicle of the eternal; the absolute was clothed with flesh and blood.[15]

To Dodd, then, the historical Jesus was by no means mistaken; rather, he was using the language of symbolism. This was not, in Dodd's opinion, fully understood by the early church, which then reinterpreted the 'apocalyptic' predictions in terms of its own developing eschatology.[16]

By taking as his hermeneutical key the sayings which speak of the Kingdom of God as present reality, he subordinated the future-orientated sayings to his interpretation of Jesus' realized eschatology. Accordingly, he resolved the eschatological tension between the 'already' and the 'not yet' by portraying it as only a seeming tension, a lack of understanding on the part of the early church.

---

[15] Dodd, *Parables*, 197.   [16] *Ibid.*, 102.

There are a number of criticisms which one might level against such a resolution:

(i) The early church is understood to have first re-eschatologized Jesus' Kingdom theology, and then later, given the (misguided) assumption of the delay of the parousia, to have proceeded to reverse the process and de-eschatologize it. This postulates two diametrically opposed tendencies in the early church within a remarkably short space of time, which, though not impossible, is problematic.

(ii) Dodd sought the 'solid foundation of Christianity', to use Schweitzer's phrase, in a Jesus who so transcended his own thought-world that his own understanding of the presence of the Kingdom of God in his own person and ministry was widely misunderstood and reinterpreted.

(iii) Dodd's theory bears some similarity to R. Bultmann's programme of 'demythologizing', which, by means of existentialist (Heideggerian) categories, sought to reinterpret such myths as the apocalyptic world view in terms of human constructs rather than as a scientific representation of external reality. One suspects that what Bultmann endeavoured to do in systematic theology, Dodd attempted exegetically. However, what for Bultmann was a distinction between ancient and modern thought-worlds seems to be for Dodd a distinction between Jesus and his contemporary society, so that Jesus is 'rescued' from the trappings of apocalyptic and placed within the parameters of modern existentially orientated eschatology.

Thus neither the solution offered by Dodd's 'realized eschatology' nor, at the other end of the spectrum, the construct of the exponents of 'consistent eschatology' is entirely satisfactory. Both have perceived an important aspect of the tradition, but each has resolved the tension between the present and future Kingdom sayings by giving precedence to one group over the other. Moreover, both have formulated their theories on the basis of certain modern assumptions. On the one hand, 'realized eschatology' reconstructs an essentially modern Jesus, whose use of the language of apocalyptic was symbolic only, and for whom the presence of the Kingdom made the passing of time insignificant. 'Consistent eschatology', on the other hand, imputes to the early church the sort of crisis in eschatology and theology which modern scholars think it should have had, but which is not reflected in the documents themselves.

I will now turn to the work of three more recent scholars who have found reason to question whether the early church underwent the sort of eschatological crisis proposed by the exponents of consistent eschatology. The first of these studies is by D. E. Aune, 'The Significance of the Delay of the Parousia for Early Christianity', the second is 'The Delay of the Parousia', by R. J. Bauckham, and the third is 'Christ and Time: Swiss or Mediterranean?', by B. J. Malina. After reviewing these studies, I will set out my own approach to the question of the development of eschatology in the early church.

2.   Three recent contributions to the debate

2.1   D. E. Aune.

D. E. Aune's approach in his article 'The Significance of the Delay of the Parousia for Early Christianity' is shaped in part by his earlier comprehensive study *The Cultic Setting of Realized Eschatology in Early Christianity*. The thesis of this monograph was that 'at no time was the experience of salvation placed wholly in the future within the belief system of earliest Christianity',[17] and this has led him to be sceptical of any scholarly attempts (such as A. Schweitzer's) to reconstruct the development of earliest Christianity solely on the basis of the non-occurrence of the expected experience of future salvation, namely the parousia. I will begin by outlining the most significant aspects of the argument of Aune's article, and then draw some directions from it for the present study.

The aim of Aune's article is twofold: first of all, he sets out to question the theory that the delay of the parousia was a causal factor in the theological transformation of early Christianity; secondly, he offers some suggestions as to the structural and functional significance of the parousia hope in the first century of Christianity. He opens with an outline of the widely held model of the 'decline of eschatology' or 'de-eschatolization' in the first century, which postulates that primitive Palestinian Christianity was characterized by early fervent expectation, which fell away in the face of the passage of time and the expansion of Christianity

---

[17] This summary is quoted in his article 'Significance', 105.

into 'Roman Hellenism', and resulted in the lessening of the fervency and significance of the parousia hope. Despite the fact that Aune's study predates the widespread criticism to which the neat distinctions between 'primitive Palestinian' and 'Hellenistic' Christianity have been subjected,[18] Aune already shows himself to be only partially convinced by the 'primitive Palestinian/Hellenistic' distinction.[19]

The second section of the article sets out four 'schools' of thought on the subject of the significance of the delay of the parousia. The first two are the consistent/thoroughgoing and the realized approaches outlined above. The latter two are Bultmann's form-critical/existential interpretation, which accepts the futurity of the Kingdom but emphasizes its existential aspect, and the approach of O. Cullmann and others which focusses on the perspective of salvation-history. This last approach, by emphasizing that the saving event has already occurred in Christ's crucifixion and resurrection, seeks to hold both the temporal and existential aspects of eschatology in tension. Aune himself is most sympathetic to the fourth 'school', and criticizes the others on the grounds of the extent to which theological interests have shaped them (though one might perhaps level this criticism at the 'salvation-history school' as well). Nevertheless, Aune recognizes that Bultmann in particular, as a historian, made some important observations:

(i) that disappointment over the non-occurrence of the parousia did not take place everywhere at the same time;
(ii) that the parousia was never, in the early period, expected to occur at a fixed date, and consequently;
(iii) that adjustment to the continuing non-occurrence of the parousia never occurred in crises, but rather gradually.[20]

These observations are useful guidelines in formulating an approach to the implications of the non-occurence of the parousia.

[18] E.g. Hengel, *The 'Hellenization' of Judea.*
[19] Cf. Aune's statement in 'Significance', 107–8:
    While it would be a falsification of the evidence to suggest that individualism was exclusively Hellenistic while the communal emphasis was exclusively Jewish (since Hellenism had penetrated Judaism beginning with Alexander's conquest of Palestine), nevertheless these two typologies of man-in-himself and man-in-community, and various combinations of the two, are helpful for analyzing the structure of early Christian religious thought, though necessarily divested of their supposed cultural loci.
[20] Aune, 'Significance', 91–2, citing Bultmann's *History and Eschatology,* 51.

In his third section, Aune accepts the argument of W. Thüsing[21] that imminent eschatological expectation characterized the outlook of earliest Palestinian Christianity. He then examines the question of how to define 'imminent expectation' (*Naherwartung*), and, in keeping with his preference for a 'salvation-history' interpretation, suggests that imminent expectation is 'comprised of two interrelated and essentially inseparable aspects, the quantitative (the temporal aspect) and the qualitative (the existential aspect)'.[22] On the basis of a brief overview of Q and synoptic material, he concurs with Bultmann's observations, cited above, that as an exact date of the parousia was never specified, it was impossible for its non-occurrence to become a critical problem.[23]

If the delay of the parousia had caused the sort of anxiety and disappointment that the thoroughgoing eschatology school sought, Aune considers the number of texts in early Christian literature in which the problem comes to expression to be remarkably few. Aune does, however, argue that the experience of sporadic persecution provoked periodic intensifications of the expectation of the parousia, and sees this as making any theory of a gradual and linear decline of the parousia hope problematic.[24]

He concludes this section with a further problem of the 'de-eschatologization' paradigm, and one which he considers the most significant of all: 'there is no demonstrable causal relationship between the oscillating functional significance of the Parousia expectation on the one hand, and various changes and developments in early Christian life on the other'.[25] Given the insights of comparative sociology, Aune considers that assigning such a major function to a single factor betrays a simplistic notion of socio-cultural change. The dynamics of such change are sufficiently complex, he argues, that no one cognitive factor can be isolated as the *sine qua non*.[26]

The final section of his article seeks to ascertain the function of the parousia in early Christianity. In this section, the influence of his earlier monograph cited above is most apparent. The parousia hope represented full bestowal of salvation to early Palestinian Christianity, but that salvation was never perceived as being wholly future. Salvation was also experienced in the presence of

---

[21] Thüsing, 'Erhöhungsvorstellung', 224–5.   [22] Aune, 'Significance', 96.
[23] *Ibid.*, 98.   [24] *Ibid.*, 100.   [25] *Ibid.*, 101.   [26] *Ibid.*, 102.

the Spirit and in cultic ritual at the individual and communal level. The balance between future and present aspects varied according to such factors as the exposure to Hellenistic religious thought and the experience of persecution. Aune ascribes the gradual diminution of emphasis on the parousia to the fact that it was functionally replaced by the conception of personal immortality upon death.

Aune's article thus confirms Bornkamm's insight that the non-occurrence of the parousia does not seem to have had the effect that the proponents of thoroughgoing eschatology expected. Aune rightly questions the model of linear 'de-eschatolization' and calls for a more nuanced, sociologically plausible analysis of the development of early Christian theology. Such an analysis would take into account not only the passing of time and the influence of Hellenistic religious thought, but more importantly the variety of settings of early Christianity, the diverse functions which the parousia hope served, and the role of persecution in heightening the imminence of expectation.

Nevertheless, there are a number of criticisms that can be levelled at Aune's article. The most obvious vulnerability of the study is the brevity of his exegetical work, and his heavy reliance on others in the exegetical underpinning of his position. This is due in part to the constraints of journal-article length. Even so, this leaves him open to the criticism that he is, like his predecessors, imposing certain results on the material.

Second, one cannot assume that the lack of a specific date for the parousia in the New Testament passages in question necessarily means that the effect of the non-occurrence of the parousia was negligible. By the time the Gospels were redacted, the non-occurrence of the parousia may have already been faced and, to a large extent, dealt with. The synoptic materials may only give us echoes of that process. Moreover, though Aune is right that no one factor can be seen as determining the whole development of early Christianity, this does not necessarily mean that, at some point in some communities, the delay of the parousia did not have an important effect.

It will be necessary to bear Aune's positive contribution in mind, as well as these criticisms of his argument, in formulating the approach of the present study. I now move on to the second study, namely that of R. J. Bauckham.

2.2   R. J. Bauckham

R. J. Bauckham, in his article entitled 'The Delay of the Parousia', recognizes that the problem of eschatological delay was not exclusively Christian, but was in some respects the same problem that had long confronted Jewish apocalyptic eschatology. While not denying that the problem of the delay of the parousia has distinctively Christian characteristics, he sets out to explore the largely neglected background of how Jewish apocalyptic tradition dealt with the issue of eschatological delay.[27]

The first section of the article sets out the problem of eschatological delay as 'one of the most important ingredients in the mixture of influences and circumstances which produced the apocalyptic movement'.[28] Most apocalypses are conscious, at least to some degree, of the problem, in that the prophecies had so long remained unfulfilled, and yet maintain the conviction of their imminent fulfilment. The resulting tension, rather than leading to the discrediting of the hope or the lessening of the sense of imminence, was embraced within apocalyptic faith. Bauckham accounts for this by arguing that, alongside the theological factors which promoted the imminent expectation, there were also theological factors accounting for delay, and that these were held in paradoxical tension.

A *locus classicus* for apocalyptic reflection on the problem of delay was Hab. 2:3, which appeals to the omnipotent sovereignty of God, who has determined the time of the End. From this was drawn the notion that apparent delay belongs to the purpose of God, and thus an appropriate response is both prayer that God should no longer delay *and* patient waiting while the sovereign God did delay. In this way, 'the tension was held within a structure of religious response which could contain it'.[29]

However, the problem of delay in apocalyptic is no ordinary problem of unfulfilled prophecy, according to Bauckham. Rather, it is the apocalyptic version of the problem of evil: the problem of God's righteousness in the face of the unrighteousness of the world. In their profound consciousness of the dimensions of the problem

---

[27] Bauckham comments that 'it is remarkable that the school of "Consistent Eschatology" . . . seems not to have asked how Jewish apocalyptic coped with the problem of delay', and cites Werner, *Formation*, in this regard. 'Delay', 4, n.3.

[28] Bauckham, 'Delay', 4.   [29] *Ibid.*, 7.

of evil and its challenge to God's righteousness, the apocalyptic writers looked for the elimination of evil on a cosmic scale.

The appeal to the sovereignty of God was in some instances supplemented by attempts to find some positive meaning in the delay. Such attempts are more evident in later Jewish apocalyptic, especially after the fall of Jerusalem in 70 CE. In this context, Bauckham makes some observations that are of particular significance for this study:

> I think that this fact [of later Jewish apocalyptic seeking positive meaning in the delay] must correspond to a certain intensification of the problem of delay in late first-century Judaism. This was not due to the mere continuing lapse of time: it is a mistake to suppose the problem of delay necessarily increases the longer the delay. The problem is intensified not by the mere lapse of time, but by the focusing of expectation on specific dates or events which fail to provide the expected fulfilment. In the case of Jewish apocalyptic, the Jewish wars of AD 66–70 and 132–135 were disappointments of the most extreme kind, for so far from being the onset of eschatological salvation, they proved to be unprecedented contradictions of all the apocalyptists had hoped for. Consequently the apocalyptic writers of the late first century are engaged in a fresh and agonizing exploration of the issues of eschatological theodicy. The imminent expectation seems if anything to be heightened, but it seems to require that on the other hand some meaning be found in the interval of delay.[30]

On this basis, Bauckham proceeds to examine four examples from the late first century CE in the second section of his study. I will pass over the first example, the rabbinic debates attributed to R. Eliezer and R. Joshua, noting only that the texts link the coming of redemption to Israel's repentance, which God's 'gracious chastisement' will bring about. The second example, the Apocalypse of Baruch (2 Apoc. Bar.), makes the traditional appeal to divine sovereignty, but also relates the delay to another characteristic of God, namely God's longsuffering. In 2 Apoc. Bar. 59:6, this longsuffering is portrayed as the quality by which God bears with sinners and refrains from intervening in judgement as soon as the

---

[30] *Ibid.*, 10.

sinners' deeds deserve it. In Bauckham's view, this theme is not original to the author of this apocalypse, but represents a common strand in apocalyptic reflection, as indeed 4 Ezra 3:30; 7:33, 74 would suggest. God's mercy to the righteous who suffer, which will be expressed on the Day of the Lord, and which led the apocalypticist to trust in the imminence of judgement, is in tension with God's longsuffering, which restrains the expression of divine wrath and prolongs the delay. Both are aspects of God's character. There is, however, a positive aspect to the delay, namely that God's people are graciously granted the opportunity for repentance (2 Apoc. Bar. 44:2–15; 46:5–6; 77:2–10; 78:3–7; 83:1–8; 84:1–85:15). The fall of Jerusalem itself brings the End nearer, in that it is to precipitate a precondition of the End, namely the repentance of Israel (2 Apoc. Bar. 20:2).

The latter two examples are drawn from the New Testament: 2 Peter 3 and the Apocalypse of John. 2 Peter 3 is shown to be a thoroughly Jewish treatment of the problem of delay, and Bauckham concludes that the arguments used here were well known in contemporary Jewish circles.[31]

In his discussion of Revelation, Bauckham does not accept that the problem of eschatological delay was less acute for the early church because of the element of realized eschatology in Christian thinking:

> If the victory over evil has already been won, it seems even more necessary that the actual eradication of evil from the world should follow very soon. The powers of evil loom large in the imagery of Revelation: the problems of theodicy which they pose are, in one sense, not alleviated but intensified by the faith that Christ has already conquered them.[32]

Bauckham considers the way in which, on the literary level, the imminent expectation of a final resolution is frustrated by the long 'parentheses', particularly those that precede the final seal and the final trumpet. It is in these parentheses that John's understanding of the meaning of the delay is to be found. Through martyrdom, Christian discipleship is linked to Jesus' own witness through the cross; the time of delay is the time of identification of Christians with their Lord, the time in which they are 'sealed on their

---

[31] *Ibid.*, 27.   [32] *Ibid.*, 29.

foreheads'. The idea of God's longsuffering, God's restraint, is also present here; it is pictured in chapter 7 by the four angels holding back the four winds to prevent them from harming the earth. The final judgement cannot take place until this 'sealing on their fore-heads' has occurred (Rev. 7:3). Thus the delay is in part for the sake of the church, so that the Lamb may be the leader of a vast new people drawn from every nation and sharing his victory through suffering.

The other aspect of delay, as seen in the parenthesis between the sixth and seventh trumpets (10:1–11:13), is for the sake of the church's witness to the world; God does not simply inflict warning judgements upon sinners, but actively seeks them in the mission of the church. In Bauckham's view, then, John makes no attempt to resolve the tension of imminence and delay, but invites his readers to perceive the positive aspects of being part of Christ's suffering and mission.

The strength of Bauckham's study is that it recognizes the real tension which confronted the early church as the expected parousia of Christ was delayed. He does not need to postulate that the delay was not a real issue within the early church, particularly given the heightened expectations that characterized the period of the Jewish War (and indeed, according to Bauckham, followed it). Instead, in tracing some of the resources that were available to the early church via the apocalyptic tradition, Bauckham plausibly accounts for the way in which writers, both Jewish and Christian, could continue to hold in tension both a conviction of eschatological imminence and consciousness of delay. Given the sort of theological resources available to the early church in Jewish apocalyptic tradition, the delay of the parousia did not cause the sort of crisis which the advocates of consistent or thoroughgoing eschatology sought. In this respect, Bauckham confirms Aune's position, though he does not share the conviction that the cultic and individual experience of present salvation was the primary factor in the avoidance of an eschatological 'crisis' over the delay of the parousia of Christ.

It would of course be a mistake to assume that all Christian writers, or Jewish ones for that matter, took the apocalyptic approach of holding imminence and delay in tension (Bauckham himself does not imply that they did). At various times, such as when a community faced no external pressure, the tension may not have been felt keenly. In certain contexts, the tension between the expectation of future salvation and the present experience of salvation will have shifted in favour of one or the other. This seems to have been the case among at least some people at Corinth, whose consciousness of their present salvation resolved the tension, and prompted Paul to reiterate and stress the future aspect (cf. 1 Cor. 4:8–13).

One need not accept Bauckham's exegetical results in every respect to recognize the usefulness of his approach. Although he does not define what he means by 'the apocalyptic movement',[33] it is clear that he understands this as a broadly based phenomenon rather than a narrow sectarian one; its ideas crossed various social and religious boundaries in the first century CE and left its mark in the literature of Qumran, in the Tannaitic traditions and, of course, in early Christian literature.

Bauckham's approach belongs to the stream of scholarship that examines the history of ideas. Concrete historical conclusions are at best hinted at. Although this study will devote greater attention to historical questions, Bauckham's article, which seeks to anchor the development of Christian eschatology firmly within its Jewish context, makes a worthwhile contribution to my own approach.

I now turn to the third and final study which will be treated in detail in this context, namely that of B. J. Malina.

2.3   B. J. Malina

In his article 'Christ and Time: Swiss or Mediterranean?', B. J. Malina points out that 'among the basic modalities of perception required for interpretation [of sacred writings], time perception is crucial for discovering the meaning of what people say and do'.[34] His thesis is that the ancients were quite different from us in time perception, that circum-Baltic peoples were and are fundamentally different from circum-Mediterraneans, and that it is consequently the first-century Mediterranean appreciation of time that the interpreter of the New Testament must appropriate in order to understand issues of New Testament eschatology.

Malina begins with the question of a society's time orientation, whether past, present or future. Time preference is seen when people are faced with a problem: do they turn initially to the past, the present or the future to find a solution to it? While mainstream

[33] *Ibid.*, 4.   [34] Malina, 'Christ and Time', 2.

middle-class America is future-orientated, Mediterranean societies of the first century, Malina asserts, were classical peasant societies, characterized by a temporal orientation towards the present as their primary preference, with past second and future third.

This raises my first question: can one confidently assert that the documents of the New Testament reflect the mind-set of a classical peasant society, with its temporal orientation heavily biased towards the present? The 'cognitive map', to use Malina's term, of first-century Jews, whatever their social status, cultural bias and affiliation to a religious group, may have been more strongly attuned to the past than Malina allows; to identify oneself as a Jew was to identify oneself with the past, with the history of the Jewish nation and with the God whose past actions were the source for drawing implications for the present. Not only the Hebrew Scriptures but also the cult and the festivals must have reinforced the importance of looking towards the past for comprehending the present. If this is true for first-century Jews, whether rural or urban, it must also have been an important influence on the early Christian movement.

Malina adduces certain proverbs and sayings from the New Testament and related writings to support his thesis of present orientation. The first example is 'Tomorrow will be anxious for itself'; 'Let the day's own trouble be sufficient for the day' (Matt. 6:34, RSV). However, the evidence of such proverbs is by no means unequivocal; while they may *advocate* present orientation, by implication they reflect an opposite tendency.

In seeking to distinguish modern American and ancient Mediterranean time orientation from one another, Malina pushes the evidence to its limit: 'There surely is no expressed concern for the future in the Synoptic story line. And it would appear that the same holds for the entire NT since any time description consisting of this age and a rather proximate age to come has no room for a future of the sort we speak of.'[35] The concern for the future in passages such as Mark 13 *et par.* may not be the same as that of modern America.[36] However, the nature of the Gospels – as texts which are at once concerned with events of the past (the life of Jesus of

---

[35] *Ibid.*, 7.
[36] It would be interesting to pursue the question of the extent to which middle-class America's future orientation actually derives from its theological heritage. Does the modern Western shift towards existential eschatology relativize the future orientation?

Nazareth), events of the present (the community's present experience) and events that are to take place before the advent of the age to come (persecution, mission) – does not allow me to endorse the statement that there is no expressed concern for the future in the synoptic story line.

Malina concludes the first section of his article with the claim that the anxiety about a perceived delay of a parousia was only in the eyes of nineteenth-century northern European biblical scholars and their twentieth-century heirs, and that presumed future-orientated categories of the Bible are in fact present-orientated.[37]

In the lengthy second section of his article, Malina examines a number of models of time perception drawn from the fields of sociology, social anthropology and social psychology. The importance of this approach, in my view, lies in the fact that it requires scholars to become conscious of their own interpretative parameters, and of the possibility that these parameters may be inappropriate tools for the interpretation of ancient texts.

I do not propose to set out the various models with their strengths and weaknesses in detail. Much of it is challenging and provocative, though open to debate. One important insight which should be mentioned is that the present was not conceived of as a quickly vanishing point in ancient societies, but rather covered a broad sweep. The present could be perceived as being of long duration, depending on the process or event involved.[38]

However, the present may not be experienced as continuous in times of crisis, such as war. Malina does not seem to take into account that experienced time can be based not simply upon procedures (agricultural or social), but may itself have political or ideological implications. While he acknowledges that procedures or processes may be cut short, he does not explore the possibility that time itself may be *expected to be discontinuous*,[39] as it is in much apocalyptic literature. In such literature, a clear distinction between experienced time and imaginary time (past or future) was not made, for in that context *imaginary* time itself is *experienced* by the seer. To say that people perceived it as 'foolhardy in the extreme to make decisions for the world of experience on the basis of the imaginary and its past and/or future'[40] simply goes beyond the evidence.

---

[37] Malina, 'Christ and Time', 9.
[38] *Ibid.*, 12, quoting Bordieu, 'Attitude', 59–60.   [39] *Ibid.*, 13.
[40] *Ibid.*, 16.

Malina's application of the various models to New Testament eschatology, section 3, is relatively brief. At this point he proposes that there was a shift within the early church from the perception of Jesus as forthcoming (still within the present time frame) to the perception of his coming as beyond the temporal horizon, in the imaginary future:

> Jesus was once perceived by present-orientated people as forthcoming Messiah with power. This perception of theirs was rooted in actual, experienced time situated in an operational realm abutting on the horizon of the present. However, given the press of events, this perception had subsequently proceeded beyond that horizon into the realm of the possible, of the future, rooted in imaginary time . . . this shift from forthcoming to future occurred during the period of Christian origins.[41]

This raises many more questions than it answers. First, to which events does Malina refer in his phrase 'given the press of events'? Second, is the supposed shift which he discerns from forthcoming to future not another way of postulating a reworking of eschatological expectations, such as scholars have long sought in the literature of the early church? Third, does not the literary evidence indicate that Jesus was understood by some as forthcoming Messiah with power within his earthly ministry, but that his death and resurrection necessitated a rethinking of the nature of the expectation? And finally, does Malina's proposal not bear a striking resemblance to Dodd's notion of the early church's 're-eschatolization' of Jesus, shifting him from present to future categories, though their respective methodologies and categories differ?

Malina draws three conclusions from his study. First, there was no tension in the New Testament period between the 'now' and the 'not yet'; instead, the 'now' was understood as a broad sweep. Second, the New Testament authors and indeed Jesus himself were present-orientated; the future as the realm of the possible was held to be exclusively God's. Third, the role of the prophet, including Christian prophets, in a present-orientated society has to be rethought.

Malina's study does not, in my opinion, do away with all, or even many, of the findings of New Testament scholarship which

[41] *Ibid.*, 28.

have been reached via the more traditional methodologies. However, it does require scholars who study the thought-world of ancient societies to consider that certain fundamental categories of perception, such as time, may have been perceived quite differently from the way in which they are today. In this way, scholars can more readily recognize the cultural categories which they bring to their task.

Having considered a variety of scholarly positions on the development of eschatology in the early church, I am now in a position to outline my own approach.

3. The approach adopted in this study

As stated in the introduction, the approach of this study is not to propose a model for interpreting the development in early Christian eschatological expectation and to test its validity against a number of passages. Rather, passages that can lay claim to constituting a 'progression' of early Christian eschatological traditions have been selected, namely Mark 13, Matthew 24 and Didache 16.[42] To these I have prefixed a study of Matt. 25:1–13, which gives some access to eschatological reflection that took place well before the redaction of Matthew's Gospel. According to these texts, the widely accepted model of progressive 'de-eschatolization' due to the passing of time and disappointment at the delay of the parousia, as outlined above, fits the evidence at best only partially.

I accept, together with the exponents of consistent eschatology and other scholars including Bultmann, Thüsing, Aune and Bauckham, that the earliest years of the Christian movement were characterized by an imminent expectation of the parousia of Christ. Although, as Malina points out, the present was conceived of more broadly in the cultural context of the first century than it is today, nevertheless the challenge to the early Christian communities of the delay of the parousia was a real challenge. However, these communities found that they had certain resources to meet it. This challenge did not take place everywhere at the same time, and,

---

[42] Such a claim can be made on the basis of the two-source hypothesis, which I accept for the purposes of this study. The question of the relationship of Didache 16 to Matthew's Gospel is discussed at some length at the beginning of chapter 6, and I consider that there are sufficient grounds to postulate that the Didache knew and used Matthew's Gospel.

according to the evidence of my studies, it did not produce the sort of crisis which the proponents of consistent eschatology sought.

While one can observe a drop in imminent eschatological expectation as a characteristic development, one can also observe the opposite tendency – a heightening of imminent expectation – at work. There seems to be a correlation between the experience of persecution and the heightening of expectation, which Aune and others have noted. Perhaps more surprisingly, a heightening of expectation is evident between the writing of Mark and Matthew; there seems to be a higher expectation of an imminent End some years after the destruction of Jerusalem (i.e. in Matthew's Gospel) than during or immediately following the crisis of the Jewish War itself (i.e. in Mark's Gospel). This would seem to confirm Bauckham's observations about the Jewish apocalypses written after the destruction of Jerusalem, which show a struggle with issues of eschatological theodicy.

A third tendency is a shift in the *function* of the eschatological hope away from expectation of imminent fulfilment towards paraenesis. It cannot be said that any of the texts under scrutiny has completely abandoned the former for the latter, but in times of relative peace and security, such as is reflected in Didache 16, the paraenetic function of the eschatological hope becomes more prominent.

The passing of time will thus be shown to be a relatively minor factor in shaping the developments in early Christian eschatology. Far more prominent are the factors affecting the particular communities themselves: the death of community members, stresses from within and without, and the community's attitude to the Jewish War and the destruction of Jerusalem. The cumulative effect of the studies is to highlight the complexity of the factors involved in the development of early Christian eschatology and the diversity of Christian responses.

2

MATTHEW 25:1–13 AS A WINDOW ON ESCHATOLOGICAL CHANGE

The parable of the ten maidens[1] is of particular interest with regard to the development of eschatology because of the motif of the delay of the bridegroom. As the parable stands, it is unique to Matthew's Gospel, though verses 11–12 show affinity to the Q material of Luke 13:25–7/Matt. 7:21–3. In order to ascertain the significance of this pericope for the current study, it is necessary to examine it exegetically and determine the *Sitz im Leben* of the traditions it represents. This is particularly necessary given the history of research on the synoptic parables, which has often studied them only for the access they give to the historical Jesus. E. Linnemann is correct in saying that our task is not to 'regard what tradition has added to the parables as worthless wrapping material, which is thrown away as soon as we have unpacked the contents'.[2]

The parable presents the reader with a number of problems or surprises:[3]

   (i)   Lack of clarity as to where the ten maidens are as they wait for the bridegroom; do they fall asleep on the street?

  (ii) Lateness of the beginning of the wedding feast;

 (iii) The idea that the oil-sellers are open after midnight;

---

[1] As there is no biological significance given to the term παρθένοι in this passage, I have adopted the translation 'maiden' in preference to 'virgin'. Cf. Lambrecht, *Treasure*, 201. Gerhardsson argues in favour of a more specific term, *bröllopstärnorna* or 'wedding maidens', in 'Mashalen', 83.

[2] Linnemann, *Parables*, 46.

[3] That a parable confronts the hearer with a 'problem' or 'surprise' is not in question (cf. the work of Ricoeur who speaks of 'extravagance' and 'surprise' in relation to the parables: 'Hermeneutics', 114ff; cf. also Funk, *Language*, 158). The problematic or surprising elements to which they are referring are, however, integral to the metaphor of the plot. Ricoeur identifies the surprise of this parable with the act of 'slam[ming] the door on the frivolous maidens who do not consider the future (and who are, after all, as carefree as the lilies of the field)', 117. It is yet to be seen whether the surprising elements of this parable may be understood as integral to the plot or extraneous and therefore evidence of a complex redactional history.

(iv) The harshness of the wise maidens towards the others in sending them off when they knew that the bridegroom was about to arrive;

(v) The relevance of the motif of sleep, which has no apparent bearing on the wisdom or foolishness of the maidens, yet links with the conclusion in verse 13;

(vi) Lack of mention of a bride.[4]

Related to these odd features of the narrative is the further issue of the meaning of λαμπάδες: is it oil lamp, torch or lantern?

These difficulties or surprising elements in the parable have occasioned two main types of interpretation. The first is the attempt to explain these features by reference to the cultural setting. This approach, which goes back to A. Jülicher,[5] finds its main exponents in C. H. Dodd[6] and J. Jeremias, who himself made two quite different attempts.[7]

The second type of interpretation examines the parable as an allegorical construct. G. Bornkamm argues that the motif of the delay of the bridegroom is so much part of the substance of the parable that the origin of the parable is to be sought in the early Christian expectation of Christ's parousia and in the realization of its delay. The other 'unrealistic' features of the parable are also to be explained against this background, though the allegorization does not include every detail.[8] F. A. Strobel and J. Massingberd Ford[9] pursue this type of interpretation, but find the allegory to be continuous. However, their respective interpretations differ greatly from each other.

There is a third type of interpretation which draws upon both of the previous types and sees the parable as having been shaped by the early church, but having as its basis a genuine dominical utterance. A doctoral thesis by A. Puig i Tàrrech, published in the series Analecta Biblica, falls into this category.[10] It is the longest and most detailed study of this pericope to date, and its findings warrant some attention. By means of a redaction-critical study using lexical, syntactic and stylistic analysis, Puig i Tàrrech seeks to recover a *Vorlage* which goes back to Jesus himself. The pericope in

4 Lambrecht lists eight 'disturbing elements', in *Treasure*, 199ff.
5 Jülicher, *Gleichnisreden*.   6 Dodd, *Parables*.
7 Jeremias, *Parables*, and subsequently 'ΛΑΜΠΑΔΕΣ', 196–201.
8 Bornkamm, 'Verzögerung', 117–26.
9 Strobel, 'Verständnis', 199–227; Massingberd Ford, 'Parable', 107–23.
10 Puig i Tàrrech, *Parabole*.

Matthew's Gospel is a carefully structured 'allégorisme', a term which he adapts from H.-J. Klauck,[11] whereas the Jesuine *Vorlage* only is strictly a 'parable'.

1. A. Puig i Tàrrech's interpretation

Many scholars prior to Puig i Tàrrech had recognized the inappropriateness of verse 13 to the rest of the parable, but had nevertheless taken the pericope as a literary unity. F. A. Stobel goes so far as to speak of a type of 'common sense' that prevails among scholars in regarding the pericope (verses 1–13) as a reliable literary unity.[12]

Puig i Tàrrech, however, recognizing the striking similarity between verses 10c, 11, 12 and the Q material found in Luke 13:25, takes them to be a redactional addition constructed by Matthew from that material. Verse 13, too, could be seen to be a redactional construct on the basis of Mark 13:35 and Matt. 24:36 (par. Mark 13:32) and/or Matt. 24:50 (par. Luke 12:46). Thus the theme of waking/sleeping – which is emphasized by verse 13 and which, as was seen above (point 5), is not integral to the plot of the parable – seemed more clearly secondary. This in turn aroused the suspicion that verses 5 and 7a, which introduce this theme of waking/sleeping, could themselves be an interpolation into an earlier parable. Puig i Tàrrech pursues this line in his narrative analysis, chapter 2, and shows that the 'épisode intermédiaire', as he designates these verses, breaks the continuity of narrative on a number of levels. Puig i Tàrrech goes on to argue that they are Matthean redaction. Once these verses and verses 10c–13 (the 'épisode final') are understood as additions, the narrative recovers a coherence of dramatic line and style. The only major problem of the parable is then the late-night setting. The origin of the phrase μέσης δὲ νυκτός is therefore uncertain, and explained by Puig i Tàrrech as an addition introduced during the process of oral transmission.

These are the most significant moves which Puig i Tàrrech makes in reconstructing a *Vorlage* behind Matt. 25:1–13. He does not endeavour to present this reconstruction in Greek, on the basis that the discursive schema (*sermo*) is more significant than the actual words (*verba*).[13] The reconstruction deserves to be reiterated:

[11] Klauck, *Allegorie und Allegorese in synoptischen Gleichnistexten*.
[12] Strobel, 'Verständnis', 200.   [13] Puig i Tàrrech, *Parabole*, 214.

(i)   (The Kingdom of Heaven is like) a group of (ten) maidens who were to fulfil the task of being maids of honour of the bridegroom at a wedding banquet. Half of them (five) carried reserve oil in flasks as well as torches, while the other half (the other five) were not carrying oil in addition to the torches.

(ii) Once night had fallen, a great cry went up:
      'Here is the bridegroom! Go out to meet him!'
      Then, when the maidens set about preparing the torches, the five without reserve oil said to their companions:
      'Give us some of your oil, as our torches are going out.'
      But these ones replied:
      'Perhaps there may not be enough of it for us and for you. Go to the merchants and buy some for yourselves.'

(iii) While they had gone to buy some, the bridegroom arrived, and those who were prepared went into the wedding feast with him.

(iv) Is it not true/does it not seem to you/I tell you that the others (those who were not ready) did not enter there (will not enter there)/did not enter (will not enter) into the wedding banquet with the bridegroom (?).[14]

Puig i Tàrrech's answer to the problems posed by this parable is essentially a form-critical one, seeking to recover the history of traditions behind these verses, and having done so to examine the passage from a redaction-critical standpoint. His overall approach is more convincing than those which seek to explain the parable as a unity, a view which, until his monograph, was generally accepted, and still is by some scholars.[15]

It is the 'épisode intermédiaire' that is of particular interest for the present study, for it is here that the themes of the delay of the bridegroom and the falling asleep of all the maidens are introduced. Puig i Tàrrech has reconstructed the 'épisode' on the assumption that it is *Matthean* interpolation; the authorship of the interpolation was determined in chapter 2, and the criterion for the reconstruction of its parameters was thus evidence of the Matthean

---

[14] *Ibid.* (translation mine).
[15] Lambrecht, while speaking highly of Puig i Tàrrech's monograph as a whole in *Treasure*, finds the hypothesis of the 'épisode intermédiaire' being secondary 'highly improbable', 206, and 'radical', 207, and does not give further attention to this approach. Nevertheless, he admits that verse 5 is difficult to account for satisfactorily, 211.

28   *Eschatology in the making*

redactional hand. On this basis he sees the issues which the 'épisode' raises (delay of parousia/death of Christians) as particular concerns of Matthew's community. However, Puig i Tàrrech also recognizes that in this passage, as in other passages which touch on these subjects explicitly (Matt. 24:49; 25:19), Matthew shows a remarkable equanimity in relation to these issues:

> The First Gospel does not reflect a deception with regard to the delay, but an assimilation which does not annul the expectation of an imminent end. Moreover, in the texts which deal with the delay, it is a given which seems to function as a framework, as an exterior reference point, as a motif more than as a problem which determines or constrains . . . The theme of the delay of the parousia never gives the impression of being the problem of the evangelist or of those whom we have called the "great community" . . . [16]

Puig i Tàrrech seeks to explain this phenomenon by proposing that these issues are the problem of a small but influential group within Matthew's community. This group he postulates to be at once charismatic and apocalyptic ('un groupe charismatico-apocalyptique'). He discusses his reconstruction of this group in some detail, and draws upon the material of Matt. 7:13–27 in forming his theory.[17] However, even if one accepts that these 'charismatics' of Matt. 7 – whose deeds are described by Matthew as evil, presumably in an antinomistic or libertine sense[18] – are also at fault for their eschatology,[19] the notion that 25:5, 7a is a polemic against them is not a strong one. The 'épisode intermédiaire' does not appear to be a polemic at all, but rather an interlude which makes reference to an accepted understanding. As Matt. 7:15–23 shows, Matthew's method of confronting opposing positions is elsewhere more direct and unambiguous.

As stated above, Puig i Tàrrech assumes the interpolation to be Matthean and thus for him it must in some way reflect a problem that is current for Matthew's community. That there is no more than a passing reference to it shows, in his view, that it is not Matthew's problem nor that of the wider community, but of a

---

[16] Puig i Tàrrech, *Parabole*, 117 (translation mine).   [17] *Ibid.*, 107–10.
[18] Cf. the discussion of this issue in Luz, *Matthew*, 441ff.
[19] In my study of Matt. 24 below (chapter 5), I find reason to accept the link between the wonder-workers of Matt. 7:15–23 and the prophets of 24:24 who show great wonders to lead astray, if possible, the elect.

small group within that community, and it is this small group that has problems with accepting the death of fellow Christians and the delay of the bridegroom. However, there are some problems in the way these conclusions were reached. Puig i Tàrrech came to his conclusions about the interpolation being Matthean on the basis of a narrative analysis which defined the elements that were foreign to the dramatic action. Only later did he pursue an analysis of tradition and redaction. While I recognize the strength of such an order of procedure (first literary analysis and subsequently analysis of tradition and redaction), and in fact pursue a comparable methodology in my next chapter, I find that Puig i Tàrrech pre-empted the latter analysis by assuming that the 'épisode intermédiaire' was Matthean.[20] Had he left open the question of the source of the interpolation somewhat longer, the 'épisode intermédiaire' might not have been so readily attributed to Matthew. As it is, he has had to assume that the *Vorlage* Matthew received already had the addition of μέσης δὲ νυκτός, verse 6, which breaks the realism of the parable and moves it towards 'allégorisme', even prior to the addition of verses 5 and 7a.[21] It would be a much simpler explanation to consider the possibility that all the allegorizing material, verses 5, 6 and 7a, is a pre-Matthean interpolation. This would account for the lack of emphasis that it receives without the need to resort to an explanation that has Matthew interested in it on the one hand and playing it down on the other, or the need to postulate that general problems of the delay of the parousia and the death of Christians had become the specific problems of one faction.

2. Matt. 25:5–7a as a pre-Matthean interpolation

G. Bornkamm, in his article 'Die Verzögerung der Parusie', called attention to the allegorical motifs of the parable. These include:

  (i)   sleeping/waking, verses 5, 7;
  (ii) the middle of the night, verse 6;
  (iii) the cry, verse 6;
  (iv) ἀπάντησις (αὐτοῦ), verse 6.

The delay of the bridegroom (verse 5) provides the overall context for the 'épisode intermédiaire' and constitutes the central allegorical motif. This will be considered as the fifth motif.

---

[20] Puig i Tàrrech, *Parabole*, 51.   [21] *Ibid.*, 152–3.

These motifs, which are concentrated in verses 5–7a, belong to traditions that are attested in other New Testament writings as having belonged to early Christian imagery of eschatological expectation (cf. 1 Thess. 4:14–15; 5:10 re καθεύδειν / ἐγείρειν, 1 Thess. 5:2ff, Mark 13:35, Luke 12:38–9 re the image of night time, 1 Thess. 4:17 re ἀπάντησις). Puig i Tàrrech deals with this cluster of images which became associated with eschatological expectation by means of a number of different explanations. The first motif, that of sleeping/waking, is understood to be Matthean redaction (54–5). The second, μέσης νυκτός, was introduced during the process of oral transmission (60–1, 152–3). In the case of the third motif, ἡ κραυγή, Puig i Tàrrech disputes that there is any evidence for an eschatological cry or clamour, but nevertheless concludes that the phrase is probably pre-Matthean (157ff). The fourth motif, ἀπάντησις, is not a *terminus technicus* and presumably belonged to the original parable. The fifth motif, that of the χρονίζοντος τοῦ νυμφίου, is, as seen above, attributed to Matthew.

Before examining each of these explanations in turn, it should be noted that the eschatological imagery is densely clustered in these verses alone; only verse 13, which binds the parable thematically into its wider Matthean context, has a similarly eschatological perspective, though its interest and vocabulary are different. Puig i Tàrrech, in offering a variety of explanations for the presence of the motifs in verses 5 to 7a, has lost sight of their unity.

2.1   First motif: καθεύδειν / ἐγείρειν

The motif of sleeping/waking is seen to be redactional. The term καθεύδειν is neither obviously Matthean nor non-Matthean, but ἐγείρειν, as Puig i Tàrrech rightly observes, belongs to the preferred vocabulary of Matthew.[22] It is questionable, however, whether the presence of this word is sufficient grounds to ascribe the allegorizing insertion as a whole to Matthew, given the preponderance of non-redactional features in verses 5–7a. This question must be deferred until these non-redactional features have been examined.

There is a feature of verse 5 which speaks against Matthean redaction, namely the term ἐνύσταξαν in verse 5, which is a *hapax legomenon* within Matthew's Gospel. There is only one other

---

[22] Cf. Luz, *Matthew*, 58.

occurrence of this verb in the New Testament: 2 Peter 2:3. Although this occurrence is also found in a context of eschatological judgement, it is not strictly comparable to Matt. 25:6, for in 2 Peter it refers to the destruction 'not slumbering' (i.e. not being slow in coming), rather than to those who are to be judged. The fact that this term is not otherwise attested in a comparable context of eschatological expectation within the New Testament means that it will not be treated here as a motif in its own right, but rather in the context of the motif of sleeping/waking. Puig i Tàrrech is of the opinion that the rarity of this verb does not constitute an argument against or for Matthean authorship.[23] This would be so if it alone were made to carry the full burden of proof against Matthean redaction. However, as this discussion proceeds, the presence of other non-redactional features will be observed, and the cumulative effect of the various non-Matthean features must then be assessed.

2.2 Second motif: μέσης νυκτός

The second motif, μέσης (δὲ) νυκτός,[24] is understood as having

---

[23] Puig i Tàrrech, *Parabole*, 180.

[24] The classic usage of the genitive, which is certainly familiar to Matthew (cf. the usage of νύξ in Matt. 2:14, Matthean *Sondergut*), would denote 'time during which' rather than a point of time, such as 'midnight'. However, BDR, #186, accepts an unclassical usage which denotes a point of time. The closest parallel to the present usage is found in Acts 26:13 – ἡμέρας μέσης. The other examples given are μεσονυκτίου (Luke 11:5), ἀλεκτοροφωνίας (Matt. 26:34 variant, Mark 13:35), ὄρθρου βαθέως (Luke 24:1). However, the case for such an unclassical usage is not as strong as first appears:

(i) The Luke 11:5 and Mark 13:35 references share the term μεσονύκτιος, which is used by Mark to designate a watch of the night, i.e. a duration of time. Luke may also have understood the parable (Luke 11:5–8) as taking place during this watch of the night, hence the genitive μεσονυκτίου.

(ii) The case of the variant reading (ἀλεκτοροφωνίας) in Matt. 26:34 can be due to the preceding πρίν which sometimes governs the genitive case (cf. BAGD *ad. loc.* #2). If πρίν is indeed governing ἀλεκτοροφωνίας, it may disqualify this reference as a clear example of an unclassical use of a genitive of time.

(iii) There is no compelling reason to understand ὄρθρου βαθέως as signifying a point of time, for the action taking place in the time thus described (ἐπὶ τὸ μνῆμα ἦλθον), though in the aorist tense, allows for some duration.

(iv) It is a matter of interpretation whether the ἡμέρας μέσης of Acts 26:13 necessarily denotes a point of time, namely midday, or whether Luke understood this to be a more loose designation of middle of the day, i.e. 'towards midday' or 'around the middle of the day'. The same may be said for the reference to μέσης νυκτός in Matt. 25:6. One conclusion that can be drawn with some certainty is that this phrase is not consistent with Matthean redactional style, and should therefore be considered as pre-Matthean.

been introduced during the period of oral transmission of the parable, replacing an original reference to the early evening (hence the presence of torches). Puig i Tàrrech recognizes that the tradition of a nocturnal parousia is found elsewhere (Mark 13:33–7, Luke 12:35–40, 17:34, Matt. 24:43–4, 1 Thess. 5:1ff),[25] but sees the specific reference to midnight as an indication of a tradition which expected the Messiah on the night of Easter.[26] Although there are several proponents of this theory, the evidence for the existence of such a tradition at the time of the Matthean redaction is sparse; it rests, in fact, on the present passage.[27] The theory is, of course, attractive, as it offers an explanation of a symbol which seems almost technical in its specificity over against the more general references to night. Nevertheless, it runs directly contrary to the widely attested tradition that the day and the hour are unknown (Mark 13:32, 33, 35 *et par.*), and this constitutes the major objection to the theory that an Easter parousia was already a traditional expectation. One might argue, perhaps, that the tradition of the unknown day and hour constitutes a polemic against an Easter parousia expectation, but the more obvious intention of these sayings is to refute apathy, not certainty. Moreover, it would be most unlikely that Matthew would engage in such a polemic and yet keep an implicit positive reference to the expectation in Matt. 25:6.

One other reference to the possibility – but only possibility – of a midnight coming is found in Mark 13:35, which refers to the Roman watches as a description of the time at which Christ may

---

[25] Other texts which have been included are Rom. 13:11ff, Eph. 5:14, Rev. 3:3, 16:15. Puig i Tàrrech accepts Linnemann's reservations about the use of these passages as evidence for a tradition of a nocturnal parousia, in *Gleichnisse Jesu*, 191ff. Although the texts from Romans and Ephesians use the imagery of sleeping/waking, the constellation of ideas of night/day and darkness/light does not give evidence for the idea of a nocturnal parousia, though it does not negate it. In the passages in the book of Revelation, however, the references to the thief metaphor and to the need to keep awake do form a constellation of ideas which attests the tradition of a nocturnal parousia.

[26] Cf. Lohse, *Passafest*, and Strobel, 'Verständnis'. Strobel's overall interpretation is not accepted by Puig i Tàrrech.

[27] Le Déaut, in his book *Nuit*, 279ff, argues that there was a Jewish tradition expecting the coming of the Messiah at Passover which predates the first century CE. The primary evidence for this, according to Le Déaut, is Tg. Exod. 12:42. He recognizes that the dating of targumic material is open to question, but argues that evidence from the Palestinian Targum is admissible for New Testament exegesis. Even if one allows this, the study as a whole serves to demonstrate how scarce the evidence is for such a tradition prior to the first century CE.

return. The function of the saying is to call for Christians to be patient in waiting, and alert as sentries. This particular parabolic saying seems to have been widely known, given that Matthew and Luke had access to it not only in the form contained in Mark's Gospel, but presumably also in a more lengthy form.[28] This parabolic saying may have occasioned the specific reference to midnight that one finds in Matt. 25:6, in that whoever coined this specific time reference may have held the conviction that the first or evening watch had passed, so that, given the passing of time, the midnight watch would be the hour at which Christ would return. Such an explanation of the origin of the midnight tradition does assume that someone did coin the time reference and so was prepared to interpret an already symbolic statement allegorically.

This theory of the origin of μέσης νυκτός has the benefit of rendering unnecessary the postulate that an Easter night parousia was already part of Christian tradition well prior to the writing of Matthew's Gospel. If this had been the case, one might have expected some indication of it within the New Testament canon. That such a tradition is attested by later sources is not at issue. However, situating such a tradition in the pre-seventy years simply in order to explain the reference in this parable is a circular argument and invites a reconstruction of pre-seventy Christian eschatology that is anachronistic.

With regard to the second motif, then, Puig i Tàrrech is correct in understanding it to be pre-Matthean, but his assumption that it reflects an early tradition of an Easter night parousia is questionable.

2.3 Third motif: ἡ κραυγή

The third motif is that of ἡ κραυγή, the cry or clamour. Puig i Tàrrech claims that it is impossible to trace a tradition of this type.[29] He rejects the numerous citations which Grässer gives in support of this tradition[30] as not corresponding to ἡ κραυγή of verse 6, for he understands this specifically and exclusively as a cry or clamour announcing the coming of the Messiah.

---

[28] For a detailed study of the complexity of the interrelationship between Mark 13:34–6, Luke 12:36–8 and Matt. 24:42–25:30 see Wenham, *Rediscovery*, 15ff.

[29] Puig i Tàrrech, *Parabole*, 61.

[30] Grässer, *Problem*, 123ff, viz. Luke 1:42, Acts 7:57, 60, 23:9, Mark 3:11, 5:57, 9:26, Matt. 8:29, 27:50, Rom. 8:15, Heb. 5:7, John 11:43, Rev. 14:15, 18:2, 19:17.

Is this a cry specifically announcing the Messiah? Its function in the narrative is not simply an announcement, but also a call or summons to those who await the bridegroom's coming. If this is so, then there is indeed a parallel to such an eschatological summons in 1 Thess. 4:16–17: ὅτι αὐτὸς ὁ κύριος ἐν κελεύσματι, ἐν φωνῇ ἀρχαγγέλου καὶ ἐν σάλπιγγι θεοῦ, καταβήσεται ἀπ᾽ οὐρανοῦ καὶ ... ἡμεῖς οἱ ζῶντες ... ἁρπαγησόμεθα ἐν νεφέλαις εἰς ἀπάντησιν τοῦ κυρίου ... These verses look forward to the gathering in of the elect, and the command, the angel's voice and the trumpet are to be understood as a summons of the elect to 'come'. Matt. 25:6 is also such a summons, and it shares with the passage from 1 Thess. a common term for the meeting – ἀπάντησις.

Nevertheless, what one has here is a functional rather than a clear verbal parallel: an announcement, which is at the same time a summons to come to the Lord's/bridegroom's ἀπάντησις. Puig i Tàrrech approaches the interpretation of ἡ κραυγή in the following way. He examines its usage in the New Testament, the Septuagint and the writings of Flavius Josephus, and claims that its sense is more often collective (i.e. clamour) than individual (i.e. cry).[31] Although he is correct in claiming that Josephus uses the term exclusively in the collective sense, the weight of evidence in favour of the collective meaning is not nearly as substantial in the New Testament and the Septuagint as he implies. Of the six references to ἡ κραυγή in the New Testament (Matt. 25:6, Luke 1:42, Acts 23:9, Eph. 4:31, Heb. 5:7, Rev. 21:4), Puig i Tàrrech regards only Luke 1:42, the cry of Elizabeth, as individual.[32] It is unclear why, according to his own definition – which limits 'cry' to being the sound emitted by a person on his or her own – the cries of Jesus in the garden, Heb. 5:7, should be discounted. That the singular κραυγή may denote more than one cry has no bearing upon the fact that these cries are uttered by an individual. Moreover, the references in Ephesians and Revelation cannot be adduced as clear evidence for a collective meaning. Both the exhortation in Eph. 4:31 and the eschatological promise of Rev. 21:4 are addressed to a collective readership, but have individual behaviour and actions in view. In contrast to Puig i Tàrrech's view, one might say that only one New Testament reference unequivocally supports the collective meaning of ἡ κραυγή (Acts 23:9).

An examination of the usage of ἡ κραυγή in the Septuagint does

31 Puig i Tàrrech, Parabole, 157ff.   32 Ibid., 158.

reveal a number of examples of the individual sense: 2 Kings (2 Sam.) 22:7, Job 16:18, Pss. 5:1, 17(18):6, 101(102):1, Jonah 2:3. The collective sense is often associated with war, as also in Josephus' writings, and on several occasions with a trumpet call (2 Kings (2 Sam.) 6:15, Jer. 4:19, Zeph. 1:16, 1 Macc. 5:31). It is thus not surprising that ἡ κραυγή appears in contexts which have eschatological overtones, including the Zephaniah passage just mentioned, Isa. 29:6 (variant), 30:19, 65:19, 66:6. In three of the passages, the cry is one of distress (Isa. 30:19, 65:19, Zeph. 1:16), but in the remaining two, the cry indeed seems to be an 'eschatological cry', a 'battlecry' of the Lord bringing about judgement.[33]

A comparative study of the semantic range of ἡ κραυγή thus yields results which are not as strongly in favour of the collective meaning as Puig i Tàrrech claims. The evidence of Josephus is unequivocal, yet this gives information primarily about the stylistics of one author; the evidence of the New Testament and the Septuagint, giving a sample of a much broader range of authors and stylistic usages, indicates that the particular sense of ἡ κραυγή in any one passage must be inferred from the context.

To establish the meaning of ἡ κραυγή in Matt. 25:6, therefore, it is important to examine the unit of sense of which it is a part; it is not an unspecified cry or clamour, but one with specific content: ἰδοὺ ὁ νυμφίος, ἐξέρχεσθε εἰς ἀπάντησιν αὐτοῦ. Thus it is not a cry of distress, nor primarily a cry of joy, but a cry of announcement and summons. It is conceivable that a cry of announcement and summons could be uttered by a crowd, but it is more likely to be a cry of an individual addressed to 'a crowd'. The collective sense of κραυγή as clamour could be present if one understood verse 6a as independent of the following clauses. This would, however, leave the direct speech of the announcement and summons (verses 6b.c) without introduction, which would be most unusual. One may assume that for the evangelist, at least, the cry was that which is recorded in verse 6b.c.

---

[33] In the case of Isa. 66:6, this assumes that the subject of each clause is the same, namely the Lord; the repeated use of φωνή binds the clauses together, as does ἐκ πόλεως and ἐκ ναοῦ, verse 66aa and b. The final clause forms a climax and explication of the preceding ones – the sound is none other than the sound (or voice) of the Lord rendering recompense to his enemies. In the case of Isa. 29:6 (variant), one is dealing with an isolated attestation of κραυγή by A†. It cannot be assumed, therefore, that the reading is original, but it does show that at least one scribe or school of scribes considered it to be an appropriate designation of God's action.

Puig i Tàrrech, disputing that there is evidence for an eschatological κραυγή, favours the collective meaning, and thus is readily able to attribute this motif, and indeed the whole of verse 6, to the original parable. There is, however, a problem with the logical flow of the narrative if one accepts the proposition that verse 6 was part of the original parable; the exclamation ἰδοὺ ὁ νυμφίος, when compared with other nominal sentences formed with the demonstrative ἰδού, implies that the subject, in this case the bridegroom, is already visible.[34] Puig i Tàrrech himself recognizes this,[35] but nevertheless regards the interchange between the wise and foolish maidens as having had its place in the original parable after the bridegroom actually appeared. In my opinion, this actually heightens one of the problems that was set out at the beginning of this chapter – the unreasonableness of the wise maidens in sending the others off when the bridegroom had arrived (problem 4). This exclamation would therefore be more readily understandable as part of the allegorizing insertion.

In continuing to examine verse 6 for clues as to the history of traditions which lie behind it, one finds a feature which is uncharacteristic of Matthean style: the aorist sense of the perfect γέγονεν. Within Matthew's Gospel, one generally finds the narrative aorist ἐγένετο used in such impersonal phrases (8:24, 26, 9:10, 11:1, 19:1, 26:1, 28:2). A comparable usage of γέγονεν is to be found only at Matt. 24:21, which presumably comes from the parallel Markan passage. Puig i Tàrrech examines Matt. 19:8 as one other passage that offers a possible parallel,[36] but there is every reason to assume that an aorist rather than a perfect sense is intended by the phrase ἀπ᾽ ἀρχῆς δὲ οὐ γέγονεν οὕτως, particularly given the temporal perspective which ἀπ᾽ ἀρχῆς connotes. The usage of γέγονεν in Matt. 25:6 is not consistent with the Matthean redactional hand and is therefore a strong indication of a pre-Matthean tradition. At the very least, this pre-Matthean tradition must have included a subject in order to form a phrase (κραυγὴ γέγονεν), but one may suspect that it encompassed the following

---

[34] Cf. Matt. 12:49, Luke 22:47, John 19:5, where in each case the tangible presence of the subject gives these sentences a demonstrative sense obviating the need for a verb. Like its semitic counterpart, upon which it is presumably based, ἰδού = *hnnh*, Aram. *h'* (BDR no. 128,7), it emphasizes the immediacy of what it refers to.

[35] Puig i Tàrrech, *Parabole*, 163, n. 163.

[36] Puig i Tàrrech, *Ibid.*, 161, calls 19:8 a 'cas douteux'.

announcement and summons: ἰδοὺ ὁ νυμφίος, ἐξέρχεσθε εἰς ἀπάντησιν αὐτοῦ.

2.4　Fourth motif: ἡ ἀπάντησις.

The fourth motif under discussion is that of ἀπάντησις. The first striking feature about this term is the fact that it differs from the one used in Matt. 25:1.[37] Matthew's style, unlike Luke's, is one that prefers repetition and consistency rather than stylistic variation,[38] and so one would expect Matthew to use the same term rather than synonyms if he were formulating an addition to a received source. The presence of the synonyms may therefore be an indication that the source responsible for the term in verse 6 is distinct from the source of ὑπάντησις in verse 1.

Puig i Tàrrech argues that verse 1, which functions in the final form of the parable as a title and résumé of what is to follow rather than as part of the action, is probably a Matthean formulation.[39] This seems the obvious explanation of what would otherwise seem to constitute a structural doublet: in verse 1, the ten maidens ἐξῆλθον εἰς ὑπάντησιν, whereas in verse 6 they are summoned to ἐξέρχεσθε εἰς ἀπάντησιν αὐτοῦ. However, if verse 6 were indeed a later insertion, then verse 1 may have in fact been part of the original parable. As the parable stands, verse 1 does indeed function as a title and résumé,[40] but it is necessary to question whether either verse 1 or verse 6 is Matthean redaction.[41]

I observed above that the word ἀπάντησις belonged to the vocabulary of Christian eschatological expectation (1 Thess.

---

[37] This assumes that the reading of Nestle-Aland – which favours the text represented by Sinaiticus and Vaticanus with regard to the distinction between ὑπάντησιν in verse 1 and ἀπάντησιν in verse 6 – is correct. The Western witnesses, family 13 and the majority text read ἀπάντησιν in verse 1; this may be understood as assimilation to the more technical usage.

[38] Cf. Luz, *Matthew*, 39, in which Matthew's tendency towards repetition of words and use of formulaic language is discussed.

[39] Puig i Tàrrech, *Parabole*, 165–6.

[40] Cf. also Matt. 18:23, which has a similar introductory function.

[41] If either of the two were Matthean, it might be more likely to be ὑπάντησις in verse 1, for Matthew has introduced this term into an account taken from Mark (8:34). Nevertheless, this must be weighed against Matthew's predilection for retaining the same vocabulary, particularly if the word in question has a 'technical' usage, as ἀπάντησις seems to have acquired, given its usage in 1 Thess. 4:17.

4:17).[42] Its presence within these verses gives further evidence of conscious allegorization, but an allegorization that cannot easily be attributed to the Matthean redactor.

2.5   Fifth motif: χρονίζοντος τοῦ νυμφίου

Let us now turn to the overarching motif of the delay of the bridegroom, which will be treated as the fifth allegorical motif. The bridegroom, and indeed the context of the wedding feast, are, of course, motifs which are not limited to the 'épisode intermédiaire'. As Bornkamm rightly pointed out,[43] they are integral to the story. However, contra Bornkamm, one may pose the question whether the motif of delay, which is part of this intermediate episode, may be understood as a secondary allegorization of an earlier parable in the face of the experience of the community. It is true that both the motif of bridegroom and that of wedding feast lend themselves to an allegorical reading, given the synoptic saying which identifies Jesus as the bridegroom and the disciples as wedding guests (Mark 2:19–20 *et par.*), and the traditional imagery which associates eschatological bliss with a banquet.[44] Nevertheless, the main problem of Bornkamm's explanation of the parable as being simply an allegorical construct of the early church is that it does not account for a number of prominent features of the parable that apparently are not meant to be allegorized (the number of maidens, the vessels, possibly the oil etc.). As I stated at the beginning of this discussion, Puig i Tàrrech's approach, namely to distinguish an allegorizing insertion from an earlier *Vorlage*, accounts for all the features of the parable. The problem with his study is that he attributes the allegorizing insertion to Matthew, and reconstructs its parameters on this basis. The motifs of the bridegroom and the wedding feast necessarily belong to the *Vorlage*, as they form the framework against which the wisdom or foolishness of the maidens is enacted.

The delay of the bridegroom, however, belongs to the 'épisode

---

[42] This can be claimed independently of the theory of Peterson that εἰς ὑπάντησιν constituted a *terminus technicus* in the context of hellenistic civil ceremonies. Cf. 'Einholung', 682–702.

[43] Bornkamm, 'Verzögerung', 120.

[44] Such a banquet is described in Isa. 25:6ff. Within the New Testament, there are other parabolic descriptions of the Kingdom of God as a wedding feast, besides the logion already mentioned; cf. Matt. 22:1–14. Cf. also Isa. 62:5, in which God is depicted as the bridegroom.

intermédiaire', and should therefore be examined as part of the cluster of eschatological motifs in these verses. The verb χρονίζειν is found in the context of other passages dealing with Christian eschatological expectation. It is present in the quotation in Heb. 10:37 of Hab. 2:3 (LXX), and most notably in the Q material of Matt. 24:48/Luke 12:45. The New Testament usage of χρονίζειν is almost technical in its specificity; it is used exclusively in passages dealing (generally parabolically) with the parousia of Christ.[45] Behind each of these passages is the implicit acknowledgement that the expected χρόνος differs from the actual χρόνος, and so Bornkamm and others are correct in assuming that the *Sitz im Leben* of this verb is to be found in a community which has experienced the actual χρόνος. Puig i Tàrrech identifies this community with that of Matthew.[46] In seeing this delay as part of the insertion, however, his reconstruction speculatively replaces this narrative moment with another: 'once night had fallen' (cf. section 1 above). It remains to be seen whether such a speculative reconstruction is necessary.

To summarize the discussion to this point, there is a cluster of eschatological motifs in Matt. 25:5–7a. Puig i Tàrrech seeks to account for them by means of a number of different explanations: καθεύδειν, ἐγείρειν are Matthean redaction; μέσης δὲ νυκτός is pre-Matthean, but not part of the original parable; ἡ κραυγή belonged to the original parable, as did ἀπάντησις. The χρονίζοντος of the bridegroom is Matthean redaction, although the bridegroom belonged to the original parable. This is therefore an example of the way in which an examination of the tradition history of individual units within a text 'divides and conquers'; the disadvantage of this method is that a passage's unity (in this case verses 5–7a) may be overlooked.

I have been dealing with the history of traditions behind verses 5–7a, which has raised several interrelated questions:

(i) If these verses are understood as an interpolation into an earlier parable, to what extent does this solve the 'problems' which were set out at the beginning of this chapter?

---

[45] The broader usages, such as are found in Josephus ('to stay, remain', *J.W.*, IV.465; 'to drag on', *Ant.*, XIV.270; cf. also *Ant.*, XVI.403, which has the sense of 'hesitation') are not attested in the New Testament; cf. also 1 Clem., 23:5, which quotes Isa. 13:22.

[46] Puig i Tàrrech, *Parabole*, 53.

(ii)   If these verses were interpolated into an earlier parable, is there evidence for more than one interpolator, or is the interpolation best understood as a unity?

(iii)   How strong is the evidence for Matthean redaction in Matt. 25:1–13?

Once these questions have been treated, I will be in a position to examine the *Sitz im Leben* of the traditions which bear upon the issue of the delay of the parousia and determine more closely the nature of the development in early Christian eschatology which they reflect.

3. Does the hypothesis solve the 'problems' of Matt. 25:1–13?

There are two issues which must be addressed in order to ascertain whether it is probable that this 'épisode intermédiaire' has been interpolated into an earlier parable: first of all, whether the theory solves the 'problems' – the *aporia* – of the pericope, and secondly, whether the pericope is comprehensible without the proposed interpolation. In dealing with this latter aspect, it is useful to present a hypothetical reconstruction of the original parable.

If verses 5–7a are understood as an interpolation, the problems set out at the beginning of this chapter are dealt with in the following ways:

(i)   the maidens do not fall asleep in the street with burning λαμπάδες;

(ii)   the wedding feast does not begin after midnight, but possibly some time in the early evening;

(iii)   the oil-sellers are not expected to be open after midnight, but in the early evening;

(iv)   the wise maidens do not know how much longer it will be when they send the others off to buy oil. Their reluctance to share their oil is justified, and they do not knowingly condemn the foolish maidens to miss the coming of the bridegroom;

(v)   the motif of sleep is no longer linked with the wisdom or foolishness of the maidens. The motif of sleep in verse 13 will be discussed below.

The lack of mention of the bride (problem 6) is neither solved, nor rendered more difficult, by this proposal. The inclusion of the words καὶ τῆς νύμφης by many Western, Latin, Syriac and middle Egyptian witnesses could be understood as an addition which redresses this lack.[47] There is a difficulty associated with this explanation: the increasingly allegorical reading of parables within the early church speaks against the introduction of a figure which does not fit the symbolism. The church is symbolized in the Matthean version of the parable by the maidens (both the wise and the foolish ones – cf. the parable of the wheat and the tares, Matt. 13:24–30). Thus the attraction of another symbol – the church as the bride of Christ (cf. John 3:29) – into this context is not easily explicable.

It is relevant to mention a proposal of Jeremias, namely that the maidens are in fact at the bride's place waiting for the arrival of the bridegroom who will escort the bride, in the company of her friends, to his father's house.[48] The lack of explicit mention of the bride can be accounted for in this way. Nevertheless, the explanation is not completely satisfactory, for if this were the case, one would expect to read αἱ ἕτοιμοι εἰσῆλθον μετ᾽ αὐτῶν εἰς τοὺς γάμους. Moreover, this is not the social custom envisaged by the witnesses which include καὶ τῆς νύμφης in verse 1. It seems that no explanation on the basis of social custom is totally convincing with regard to the lack of mention of the bride.

A further question which was raised at the outset is the meaning of the term λαμπάδες. In the essay by Jeremias just cited, it is convincingly argued that λαμπάδες must be understood as 'torches', not as oil lamps, and Puig i Tàrrech confirms this finding.[49] As torches have a much shorter burning time, the problem of the sleeping maidens thus becomes even more acute. Jeremias therefore proposes that the maidens light the torches only after the cry comes, and that they do this by pouring more oil onto the oil-soaked rags wrapped around the end of the torches, and then setting them alight.[50] This, then, is understood by Jeremias as the meaning of the verb κοσμέω, namely in the sense of to 'enhance' or 'supplement' the oil which was already present. This may, however, be open to question. In Matt. 25:3–4, one reads that the foolish ones λαβοῦσαι τάς λαμπάδας αὐτῶν οὐκ ἔλαβον μεθ᾽

---

[47] Cf. Metzger, *Textual Commentary*, 62–3.
[48] Jeremias, 'ΛΑΜΠΑΔΕΣ', 199–200.
[49] Puig i Tàrrech, *Parabole*, 210ff.   [50] Jeremias, 'ΛΑΜΠΑΔΕΣ', 200.

ἑαυτῶν ἔλαιον, whereas the wise ones ἔλαβον ἔλαιον ἐν τοῖς ἀγγείοις μετὰ τῶν λαμπάδων ἑαυτῶν. Scholars commonly assume that the oil in the vessels is supplementary oil, over and above the oil already on the torches(/lamps). Puig i Tàrrech thus renders verse 4 as: 'Half of them (five) carried *reserve* oil in the flasks along with the torches . . .'[51] This understanding rests upon two factors:

(i)   Verse 3 is read in the light of verse 4, and the phrase ἐν τοῖς ἀγγείοις unconsciously appended to it;

(ii) The verb σβέννυνται, verse 8, being in the present tense, implies that the torches are already lit and about to go out.

Were it not for the second consideration, the obvious meaning of verse 3 would be that the foolish maidens had *no* oil, not simply too little. One may therefore ask whether the present passive of σβέννυνται is sufficient grounds to negate the obvious meaning of verse 3. It is possible for the verb to be interpreted as future,[52] which would then have the sense 'our torches *shall be extinguished* with no oil' and could thus imply that they are not yet lit. Somewhat more probable is the proposal that in trying to light the torches, they realized their lack, for the rags would only burn for one or two minutes. The Greek present tense would then be rendered as 'our lamps keep going out'. This returns us to the question of the meaning of κοσμέω. There is no parallel in the New Testament, LXX or Josephus for such a usage of this verb in relation to torches or lamps. Even the more general sense of κοσμέω as 'put in order' is not otherwise clearly attested in the New Testament, for the sense of 'adorn, decorate' has displaced it.[53] This may therefore be a term which betrays a Semitic *Vorlage* which, in translation, has lost the technical sense of the original term.

One Hebrew term rendered in the LXX as κοσμέω is *'rk*. Elsewhere in the LXX, this Hebrew verb is translated as the verb

---

[51] Puig i Tàrrech, *Parabole*, 214 (translation mine).   [52] Cf. BDR no. 323.
[53] With reference to Matt. 12:44/Luke 11:25, BAGD favours the meaning of 'decorated, adorned', although they recognize that 'put in order' is possible. For the Aramaic usage, cf. Klein, *Wörterbuch, sub √sbt* (the usual translation of κοσμέω). This verb appears to have the general sense 'to set in order', and a particular sense 'to trim (of wicks)'. Cf. Payne-Smith, *Dictionary, s.v.* Care must be taken in interpreting this evidence, however, because Syriac vocabulary is influenced by Greek from an early period, and because it is not justified to assume without further discussion that Syriac usage is representative of first-century Aramaic, especially since in this case the verb is apparently a denominative.

καυσόω, to burn; Lev. 24:4 reads ἐπὶ τῆς λυχνίας τῆς καθαρᾶς καύσετε τοὺς λύχνους ἔναντι κυρίου ἕως τὸ πρωΐ. The Aramaic term which has been rendered as κοσμέω in Matt. 25:7 may have therefore been more specific (and technical) than the general 'to put in order'; it may have had the sense of 'to trim' (a wick), hence 'to prepare to set alight'.

Let us turn now to the second issue which bears upon the probability of the 'épisode intermédiaire' being an interpolation into an earlier source, namely the reconstruction of the source itself.

3.1 Proposed reconstruction of the pre-Matthean parable of the wise and foolish maidens: Table 1

As I have just observed, the source may have originally been Aramaic. Nevertheless, I do not propose to offer a retroversion into Aramaic; the question at hand is whether the narrative can be understood without the 'épisode intermédiaire', and therefore the reconstruction can be presented in Greek.

> ὁμοιωθήσεται ἡ βασιλεία τῶν οὐρανῶν δέκα παρθένοις,
>
> αἵτινες λαβοῦσαι τὰς λαμπάδας ἑαυτῶν
> ἐξῆλθον εἰς ὑπάντησιν τοῦ νυμφίου.
>
> πέντε δὲ ἐξ αὐτῶν ἦσαν μωραὶ
> καὶ πέντε φρόνιμοι,
>
> αἱ γὰρ μωραὶ λαβοῦσαι τὰς λαμπάδας αὐτῶν
> οὐκ ἔλαβον μεθ' ἑαυτῶν ἔλαιον,
> αἱ δὲ φρόνιμοι ἔλαβον ἔλαιον ἐν τοῖς ἀγγείοις
> μετὰ τῶν λαμπάδων ἑαυτων.
>
> κοσμοῦσαι τὰς λαμπάδες ἑαυτῶν,
> αἱ μωραὶ ταῖς φρονίμοις εἶπαν·
> δότε ἡμῖν ἐκ τοῦ ἐλαίου ὑμῶν,
> ὅτι αἱ λαμπάδες ἡμῶν σβέννυνται.
>
> ἀπεκρίθησαν δὲ αἱ φρονίμοι λέγουσαι·
> μήποτε οὐ μὴ ἀρκέσῃ ἡμῖν καὶ ὑμῖν·
> πορεύεσθε μᾶλλον πρὸς τοὺς πωλοῦντας
> καὶ ἀγοράσατε ἑαυταῖς.
>
> ἀπερχομένων δὲ αὐτῶν ἀγοράσαι
> ἦλθεν ὁ νυμφίος,

καὶ αἱ ἕτοιμοι εἰσῆλθον μετ᾽ αὐτοῦ
εἰς τοὺς γάμους.

This reconstruction has retained virtually all of the grammar and vocabulary of the Matthean parable (on verses 10c–13, which are understood as an addendum, see below), not because they are considered necessarily authentic, but in order to demonstrate that the narrative does flow smoothly and logically without the 'épisode intermédiaire'. The reader who is accustomed to the longer version may find the reconstruction somewhat sparse in detail; nevertheless, the logic of the movement of the narrative – ἐξέρχεσθαι, κοσμεῖν, λέγειν δότε ἡμῖν, ἀποκρίνεσθαι [πορεύεσθε], ἀπέρχεσθαι – is apparent. The 'wisdom' of five of the maidens resides in the fact that they were ἕτοιμοι, in the sense of being fully prepared to meet the bridegroom, not leaving half of their preparation until it was too late. For the Matthean parable, on the other hand, the wisdom of the maidens is shown not simply in their preparedness, but in their preparedness despite the day or the hour, as is made explicit by the conclusion to the parable, verse 13.

One notable stylistic feature of Matt. 25:1–13 – the frequent use of ἑαυτῶν (verses 1, 3?, 4, 7b, 9 – ἑαυταῖς) – is peculiar to the verses from which the reconstruction has been made. Puig i Tàrrech is of the opinion that these occurrences of ἑαυτούς stem from the one hand, but suggests that they may be redactional.[54] This is, however, most unlikely. Each of the occurrences, apart from the ἑαυτοῖς in verse 9, betrays a style which prefers the reflexive pronoun to the possessive pronoun; this is not consistent with the Matthean redactional hand. Although there are several instances where Matthew introduces the term ἑαυτῶν, or its cognate forms (ἑαυτοῖς etc.), most of these are governed by the prepositions ἐν or μετά and are thus not comparable to the present usage.[55] Only two verses which are peculiar to Matthew's Gospel are comparable: 18:31 and 21:8. The former (διεσάφησαν τῷ κυρίῳ ἑαυτῶν πάντα τὰ γενόμενα) is, like Matt. 25:1–13, Matthean *Sondergut*, which suggests that such a stylistic feature may well be attributable to Matthew's special source. The latter comparable verse is 21:8, in which ἑαυτῶν is indeed redactional over against the Markan source. However, the redactor may have intended to emphasize the parallel between the

---

[54] Puig i Tàrrech, *Parabole*, 181.
[55] Cf. Matt. 9:3,21; 15:30; 16:7,8. Matthew prefers the preposition ἐν to πρός in such phrases; cf. the synoptic parallels to these verses and to Matt. 21:25, 38.

action of the disciples (ἤγαγον τὴν ὄνον καὶ τὸν πῶλον καὶ ἐπέθηκαν ἐπ' αὐτῶν τὰ ἱμάτια, verse 7) and that of the crowd (ὁ δὲ πλεῖστος ὄχλος ἔστρωσαν ἑαυτῶν τὰ ἱμάτια ἐν τῇ ὁδῷ, verse 8). The word order of verse 8 also suggests such emphasis. Thus it seems that Matthew's redactional style did not as a rule prefer the reflexive to the possessive pronoun; it is noteworthy that this usage does not occur at all in the infancy narratives. This stylistic feature is peculiar to verses 1–4 and 7b–9 of Matthew 25, and does not occur in the 'épisode intermédiaire' nor in the final verses, which gives some support to the parameters of the reconstruction.

Let us now turn our attention once again to the 'épisode intermédiaire', in order to take up the second question.

4. Verses 5–7a: more than one interpolator, or a unity?

In posing this question, I am asking primarily whether there are grounds for considering these verses as both pre-Matthean and redactional, or whether the case is stronger that the cluster of eschatological motifs is to be understood as a unity. This issue has been treated at some length in relation to each motif, and the majority of evidence points to a pre-Matthean source. Only with regard to the verb ἐγείρειν was there reason to attribute it to Matthew. Moreover, there are strong grounds for regarding verse 13, which speaks of γρηγορεῖν, as redactional, as will be seen below. This lends support to the supposition that the ἐγείρειν motif may be redactional. However, if the motifs are examined as a progression – delay, sleep, middle of the night, cry and summons, rising – it is difficult to regard the sleeping/waking as a foreign body. The function of the motifs is unequivocally allegorical, and the motifs as they stand present an allegorical portrayal which corresponds very closely in detail and chronology to early Christian eschatological expectation such as is implied by 1 Thess. 4. The church is aware of a delay; the expectation of a prompt return of the Lord has been disappointed. In the Thessalonian community there are *some* who have 'fallen asleep' (1 Thess. 4:13), but the interpolator in Matthew 25 envisages that *all* the maidens 'fall asleep'. This does not necessarily mean that all of the interpolator's community, or even all the older generation, must already have died at the time of writing, but rather that the 'falling asleep' has become one of the categories of eschatological expectation, along with the delay of the parousia.

As shown above, there is no exact parallel for μέσης νυκτός; nevertheless, the theme of night plays a significant role in the eschatological imagery of 1 Thess. 5. Then a cry is envisaged, which corresponds to 1 Thess. 4:16a; this cry constitutes a summons to the ἀπάντησιν τοῦ κυρίου and directly precedes the rising of those who have fallen asleep. Thus the 'épisode intermédiaire' is a brief allegorical portrayal of the key elements of an eschatological hope, not of the earliest church – for here the delay of the Lord and the death of community members are already accepted and incorporated elements – but of early Christian communities some years after their inception. For this reason, the motif of sleeping/rising does seem to have originated in the context of the other motifs, rather than being an additional redactional interpolation. It is also apparent that although Matthew is unquestionably interested in the theme of γρηγορεῖν, the sleeping/waking motif does not serve the evangelist's paraenetic interest well. One might have expected only the foolish maidens to sleep, had the motif come from the Matthean hand; the paraenesis of verse 13 would then have had a basis within the narrative itself. The fact that all the maidens sleep indicates that the origin of verse 13 differs from that of the sleeping/waking motif. I therefore conclude that the case in favour of the unity of verses 5–7a is considerably stronger than the case in favour of more than one interpolator.

5.   How strong is the evidence for Matthean redaction in Matt. 25:1–13?

It has just been argued that verses 5–7a are best understood as pre-Matthean. I will now examine verses 10c–13, which I have designated above as an 'addendum' to the earlier parable. It is perhaps more accurate to designate this 'addendum' as two 'addenda', for their sources differ.

Verses 10c–12 have been taken from Q material (cf. Luke 13:25) by Matthew. The precise wording of the Q passage need not detain us here; more important is the reason why Matthew has linked these traditions. There is no doubt that Matthew was vitally interested in the thought of eschatological judgement and its relevance to the community.[56] In appending this piece of Q tradition to the parable from available *Sondergut*, the evangelist

---

[56] Cf. Chapter 5.2 below for a detailed exposition of this; also Bornkamm

reinforces the need for preparedness with the thought of judgement, thus characteristically linking ecclesiological and eschatological interests. Although the idea of judgement was already implicitly present in the parable prior to the Matthean addition, the image of the closed door and the futile interchange between the foolish maidens and the bridegroom make the motif of judgement explicit and tangible. The bridegroom's rejection implies exclusion of the foolish maidens, relegating them to the darkness beyond the door. The phrase τὸ σκότος τὸ ἐξώτερον, though it may have its origins in Matthean *Sondergut*, is nevertheless a motif of which Matthew was fond (cf. 8:12, 22:13, 25:30), not in the sense that it was fascinating in its own right,[57] but as a contrast to the joy of being in the presence of the Lord at the eschatological denouement (cf. Matt. 25:21, 23). Unlike Luke (e.g. Luke 12:41–8), Matthew does not envisage gradations in eschatological punishment; for this evangelist there will simply be two groups (though which people belong to these groups cannot be determined presently), and no rationalizations or negotiations will be of any use (cf. Matt. 7:21ff, 25:31–46). Thus the presence of a Q parallel to verses 10c–12 and the Matthean interests which its inclusion at this point betrays clearly indicate Matthean redaction at work.

Verse 13 is a further addition which ties the parable to its context and makes explicit the paraenetic purpose of its inclusion. The motif of γρηγορεῖν, which is presumably taken from Mark,[58] is also introduced as an addition to Q material at Matt. 24:42–3. It is therefore a clear indication of the redactional interest of Matthew; the evangelist incorporated the parable of the ten maidens into the eschatological discourse because of its emphasis on preparedness, and because this preparedness was shown as necessary at all times. Thus the 'épisode intermédiaire', which had already been incorporated into the parable, seemed additionally appropriate to Matthew's purpose, though, as previously demonstrated, it did not serve this purpose with absolute consistency.

Verses 10c–13 are therefore to be understood as two Matthean

'Enderwartung', 222–60, in which Matthew's eschatological and ecclesiological interests are shown to be closely linked.

57 A comparison of Matthew's Gospel with the later *Apoc. Pet.*, demonstrates this most clearly.

58 Mark 13:34–7. The interrelationship of these traditions, however, is complex, as has already been observed (note 28 above).

addenda to the parable of the ten maidens, which had already been supplemented with verses 5–7a.

I am now in a position to examine the 'épisode intermédiaire', verses 5–7a of Matthew 25, in order to draw some conclusions as to the development of early Christian eschatology that they reflect.

6.   Matt. 25:5–7a and the development of early Christian eschatology

In studying Matt. 25:5–7a, one finds evidence that the delay of the parousia of Christ and the death of fellow Christians had been not only experienced, but also grappled with theologically by the author of these verses. What one is dealing with here, therefore, is the end result – the literary deposit – of a process of theological reflection. There is no direct access to the process itself. Nevertheless, the literary deposit allows certain inferences to be made as to the nature of that process. The first inference is an obvious one; the delay of the parousia and the death of Christians must have had a sufficient impact upon the community in which this formulation took shape to bring about a reworking of eschatological expectation. The literary deposit of this reworking gives us clues as to its nature.

6.1   Experienced delay (χρονίζοντος δὲ τοῦ νυμφίου)

I have already noted the specific, almost technical usage of the verb χρονίζειν in the documents of the New Testament, and the fact that its usage denotes an awareness that the actual eschatological χρόνος differed from the expected eschatological χρόνος. The options open to the community were to:

(i)   ignore the discrepancy;
(ii)   give up the expected eschatological χρόνος; or
(iii) account for the discrepancy.[59]

Option (iii) is the one adopted by the author of these verses. In order to account for the discrepancy, the author adopted the

---

[59] For a sociological study of the behaviour of a group disappointed by its eschatological expectation, cf. Festinger *et al.*, *When Prophecy Fails*. Care must be taken, however, in drawing analogous conclusions about first-century eschatological behaviour, for the central tenet of faith for the early Christians was the death, resurrection and coming of the Lord, not a specific eschatological timetable.

concept of delay. This concept recognized the actual χρόνος without detracting from the eschatological conviction that the one returning was sovereign, for the χρονίζειν was an expression of the perspective of those waiting, not an objective theological category.

How soon would this discrepancy between actual χρόνος and expected χρόνος have been felt? How soon would it have become sufficiently acute to prompt a modification in eschatological expectation? An answer to these questions must necessarily be speculative. Nevertheless, the analogous situation of the Thessalonian community is relevant. The major study by G. Lüdemann on Pauline chronology[60] has called into question the widely accepted view that the Thessalonian congregation was founded around the year 49 CE and that 1 Thessalonians was written in the early fifties, possibly with only several months between the founding and the letter.[61] In Lüdemann's opinion, the founding of the Thessalonian congregation and the writing of 1 Thessalonians must be dated significantly earlier – in the late thirties and early forties respectively. In his view there may be two, or perhaps more, intervening years between the foundation of the congregation and the issues which Paul's letter tackles; little more can be said about that interval than that it is possible for the deaths to have occurred not long after Paul's departure. Lüdemann does, however, make the point that 1 Thess. 4 reflects a stage at which these deaths were viewed as the exception. Drawing on the work of Grässer,[62] he argues that there is a progression in eschatological expectation evident in the writings of the New Testament. This progression may be traced by means of a comparison of certain texts: Matt. 10:23, which expects none or only a minority to die before the arrival of the Son of Man, Mark 13:30, in which the occurrence of more deaths is assumed, and Mark 9:1 in which not all of the first generation will have to die before the coming of the Kingdom of God with power. John 21:23 is also to be understood against the background of this latest stage, but it goes one step further and corrects the tradition that the beloved disciple would never die. On this basis, Lüdemann states:

> We have thus found a viable chronological criterion for determining the date of texts and traditions from the early period of Christianity. A text which presupposes that

---

[60] Lüdemann, *Paul, Apostle to the Gentiles.*
[61] Cf. Kümmel, *Introduction,* 256–7.   [62] Grässer, *Problem.*

Christians do not have to die before the arrival of the eschaton probably arose during the period that followed directly on the death and resurrection of Jesus, that is, not long after 27/30 CE. On the other hand, a text that limits the number of those who will not die or assumes that all will die should be considered as belonging to the end of the first generation (47–57) or to a later generation. Though chronologically exact datings cannot be expected when this criterion is employed, approximate datings can be.[63]

This is essentially a plausible argument, but there are a number of factors which advocate caution in its application as a chronological criterion.

1.   Because these are traditions that presumably arose in more than one community, one may not assume that each of the 'stages' in expectation was universally shared. It is quite possible that some communities never held the expectation of the first 'stage', while others may have held and retained it much longer, according to their own circumstances and to the factors which shaped their theology. For example, communities which experienced deaths of community members, but accounted for these deaths in a manner analogous to the case of Ananias and Sapphira (Acts 5:1–11), may have retained the first-stage expectation well into the forties and fifties.

2.   As has been suggested above, the fact that a tradition envisages the death of all does not necessarily mean that all have in fact died. Rather, such a tradition proves only that the possibility of all dying has been incorporated into the eschatological framework. Such a tradition is thus evidence of more advanced theological reflection on the deaths of community members, but it is not necessarily proof of a late date.

3.   Lüdemann's argument assumes that the Gospels in which these traditions occur have retained them despite their irrelevance and inapplicability.[64] Though this assumption is and continues to be widely accepted, it is not strictly in keeping with the tenets of form criticism nor redaction criticism. Such irrelevance is a dan-

---

[63] Lüdemann, *Paul, Apostle to the Gentiles,* 204.

[64] Lüdemann himself takes this view: 'If one considers that these texts are found in the Gospels, which were composed at a much later date and which neither could still share such a specified expectation nor maintain an interest for the tradition of such extreme eschatological statements, then the content of these texts gains in importance and the thesis propounded above seems plausible: . . . ', *Ibid.,* 204.

gerous assumption before the narrative level of the text has been considered. Even if the narrative level of the text seems to yield no adequate explanation of the redactor's understanding of a saying, it is better to work with the hypothesis that the redactor thought the saying was in some way relevant, rather than to assume the opposite.

For these reasons, any attempt at a reconstruction of the chronological order of texts must be carefully weighed; Lüdemann's criterion is attractive, but by no means watertight. In the case of the tradition represented by Matt. 25:5–7a, it states that 'all' fall asleep. According to Lüdemann's schema, this tradition should be dated to the end of the first generation (47–57) or to a later generation.[65] Given the pre-Matthean authorship of the tradition, the *terminus ad quem* is the writing of the Gospel of Matthew. I have also argued that the pre-Matthean author of these verses had access to the tradition represented by Mark 13:35 *et par.*, and if I am correct, then this tradition would constitute a *terminus post quem*. Thus it would be, in theory, possible to attribute a relatively late date to the tradition, even post 70. However, as I have argued, the tradition represents the literary deposit of a process by which the community responsible for the Matthean *Sondergut* came to terms with the delay of the parousia; this process, according to the analogy with 1 Thessalonians, may have begun as early as a few months after the founding of the community. Therefore, it seems better to date the process and the formulation of the tradition to the forties and fifties. This is essentially in keeping with Lüde- mann's proposal, though the means by which this conclusion was reached differ from those which he employed.

6.2 Drowsiness and sleep (νυστάζειν, καθεύδειν)

As stated above, the verb νυστάζειν in Matt. 25:5 is not used in a comparable way elsewhere in the New Testament. Nevertheless, as it is in this context an antonym of the verb γρηγορεῖν, which is important in both the synoptics and Pauline writings, the question arises whether this 'drowsiness' could be meant in a figurative sense. A more commonly used antonym of γρηγορεῖν is καθεύ- δειν,[66] but as this verb is required in the context to denote the sleep

---

[65] *Ibid.*, 204.
[66] Cf. the contrast between the disciples' sleep and Jesus' requirement of them to

of death, the 'ethical' meaning could have been displaced to νυστάζειν. This would then be an indication that the author of the tradition behind Matt. 25:5–7a had in view a lowered alertness among the community, a 'theological drowsiness'. However, the tradition states that *all* participated in this drowsiness.[67] The fact that there is not even a 'faithful remnant' who did not share in this drowsiness implies that the author must have included himself. Though this is not impossible, the very act of reformulating tradition implies a theological alertness. There is, moreover, an inevitability to this drowsiness which does not seem to indicate that it is intended as the counterpart to γρηγορεῖν, for no element of choice is depicted; γρηγορεῖν, by contrast, always has an element of choice and can therefore be the subject of exhortation. Thus, whilst it is possible that the verb νυστάζειν was intended figuratively, this is by no means certain.

The motif of sleep, which denotes the death of community members, raises the question as to the relationship of the problem of the delay of the parousia and the problem of the deaths. Were these two essentially distinct, though related, problems, or did the deaths cause the delay to be perceived as delay? Did the deaths serve to make an otherwise minor issue acute? The fact that the delay and the deaths are linked both here and in the analogous situation in the Thessalonian community does seem to indicate that it was in fact the deaths which brought about a crisis in eschatological expectation which made the revision of that expectation necessary. This is not to claim that the delay in the expected χρόνος could not be perceived as delay without the occurrence of such deaths; the Q reference to delay (Matt. 24:48/Luke 12:45) gives no indication that this tradition was precipitated by the experience of deaths. Nevertheless, the juxtaposition of these two problems – the delay of the parousia and the deaths of community members – both in Matt. 25:5–7a and in the Thessalonian community suggests that the deaths provided a focus against which the implications of the delay of the parousia were perceived.

'watch' (Mark 14:47ff *et par.*). 1 Thess. 5:6 also indicates this contrast: ἄρα οὖν μὴ καθεύδωμεν ὡς οἱ λοιποὶ ἀλλὰ γρηγορῶμεν καὶ νήφωμεν.

[67] It is assumed that πᾶσαι is more readily explicable as part of the pre-Matthean insertion than as a redactional addition, for it fits well with the other allegorical motifs. As has been discussed above, on the level of Matthean redaction, the πᾶσαι runs contrary to the hortatory interest of the redactional additions, which seek to emphasize the need for wakefulness.

6.3   The middle of the night (μέσης δὲ νυκτός)

This tradition expects the coming of the bridegroom in the middle of the night. The idea that this tradition is based upon an expectation of an Easter night parousia has been shown to be improbable, and an alternative theory of the origin of this phrase has been advanced above. If my theory is correct, then the pre-Matthean composer of these verses regarded the time of composition as being in the 'first watch', but was confident that the Lord was to return in the next watch, the midnight watch. Consequently, this pre-Matthean composer held an imminent expectation of the parousia, for it was at this next watch, and no later, that the Lord would come. This might, at face value, seem to be a contradiction; is it possible for a person to endorse the category of delay, as these verses do, and yet hold an imminent expectation of the return of Christ? R. J. Bauckham, whose article 'The Delay of the Parousia' I discussed at some length in the previous chapter, holds that this was quite a common phenomenon among those who maintained apocalyptic hopes. I have suggested that the concept of delay was adopted not as an objective theological category, but as a way of describing the perception of those who were waiting. If this is so, and the composer understood the delay descriptively rather than prescriptively, then it is quite conceivable that a conviction of an imminent parousia could be held simultaneously with the notion of delay. The delay was soon to be over, and yet, while it lasted, it was perceived no less as delay, for all that. The composer may have held this imminent expectation in the face of those among the community who had relinquished imminent expectation and could perceive only the delay. The passage offers hope in several ways: the delay of the parousia is a shared perception, but not cause for despair; the deaths of community members will lead to their rising again just as certainly as sleep is followed by waking; and the watch of the night is almost over, for the Lord will surely come at the next watch – at midnight.

The other elements of Matt. 25:5–7a are motifs which depict the expected parousia. They yield only one further piece of information about the community in which this piece of tradition was formulated, namely that it shared these elements of eschatological expectation with other communities which are reflected in the writings of the New Testament. This means that these elements were both widespread and early, and that they must have been disseminated as part of the teaching which formed the foundation of early Christian communities.

The tradition represented by Matt. 25:5–7a thus provides evidence of the way in which the deaths of community members confronted an early Christian community with a discrepancy between their eschatological expectation and their actual experience. This confrontation obliged the Matthean *Sondergut* community to face the issue of the delay of the parousia. The scholars who claim that this issue was a crucial one within the early church are therefore correct. However, they generally overlook the fact that by the time Matthew's Gospel was written, this was no longer a burning issue. In his assessment of the importance which Matthew gives to this issue, Puig i Tàrrech is quite right in his comment, cited above, that the delay seems to be simply a framework or motif for Matthew rather than a problem which currently constrains the evangelist or the community for which the evangelist is writing.

3

MARK 13: ESCHATOLOGICAL
EXPECTATION AND THE JEWISH WAR

In the history of New Testament interpretation in the last one hundred years, Mark 13 is one of the most carefully ploughed and reploughed fields. The farming implements have varied, the seasons have changed and the results have been correspondingly diverse. It has always seemed that if only the right methodology could be applied, the secrets of this chapter might be unlocked. There is at present an unprecedented variety of methodologies being applied to this material, ranging from the recent redaction-critical studies of J. Gnilka and R. Pesch, through the religio-historical analysis of E. Brandenburger, the socio-political analyses of H. C. Kee, W. Kelber, F. Belo, C. Myers and H. C. Waetjen, to the various literary approaches of N. R. Petersen, B. L. Mack, and M. A. Tolbert,[1] to list only a few. Given such a variety of available approaches, it is crucial for this study that the methodologies applied and the order in which they are applied are both well-suited to the purpose of the study and self-critical.

The purpose of this study is to examine the expectation of an imminent End in Mark 13; how imminent is the End, where does the evangelist consider the Markan community to be within the plotted time of Mark 13, and is this in contrast to the expectation of the community for whom the evangelist is writing? These questions are historical, but they raise the narrative-critical question of the implied reader and the wider questions of socio-political context.

1. Methodological considerations

C. Breytenbach prefaced his monograph on Markan eschatology – *Nachfolge und Zukunftserwartung nach Markus. Eine methoden-*

---

[1] Gnilka, *Markus;* Pesch, *Markusevangelium;* Brandenburger, *Markus 13;* Kee, *Community;* Kelber, *Kingdom;* Belo, *Materialist Reading;* Myers, *Strong Man;* Waetjen, *Power;* Petersen, *Criticism;* Mack, *Myth;* Tolbert, *Sowing the Gospel.*

kritische Studie – with a detailed study of the history of interpretation of Mark's Gospel. His work is a useful point of departure, because it combines both a newer literary approach upholding the unity of the text with a continued interest in the historical questions, which are indispensable to the aim of this study. I will begin by taking account of some methodological issues which Breytenbach raises, and then proceed to an examination of the text of Mark 13.

In the context of considering the contribution of W. Wrede, Breytenbach observes that in Markan research, despite Wrede's approach of dealing with the Gospel as a unified whole, literary and historical questions are still constantly mixed. Breytenbach then points out that drawing an early distinction between tradition and redaction hinders the treatment of the text as a unified whole.[2]

Breytenbach is correct in claiming that a study which moves uncritically between literary and historical questions may unduly influence its own results. To draw an example of this from the study of Mark 13, at what point does the exegete decide where the evangelist considers himself/herself to be within the chronology? Does the exegete consider the literary level as a whole, and only then move to historical questions, or does he or she make the connection between Mark and the narrative early on and proceed on that basis? Breytenbach's methodological consideration recommends the former procedure, in order to avoid losing sight of the text as a whole and, one may add, in order to avoid biasing the historical picture that results. Both methods no doubt involve some sort of hermeneutical circle, but the former leaves open the question of a historical referent longer, and is therefore likely to weigh the possibilities more even-handedly.[3] I will take up Breytenbach's

---

[2] Breytenbach, *Nachfolge*, 18.

[3] It is puzzling, in the light of this, that Breytenbach's own analysis of Mark 13 begins by taking a position on the historical locus of Mark and his community. This is not simply a summary of the conclusions that will be reached via the ensuing analysis, but actually part of the analysis itself: 'Da die Situation der markinischen Gemeinde in V. 9–13 und 33–37 besonders deutlich wird, wird man sich auf diese Teile konzentrieren müssen' (284).

When he comes to the analysis of verses 9–13, we read: 'Hier wird die Situation der Gemeinde selbst angesprochen, während sonst (5b–8.14–22) von der Zeit und den Umständen, in denen sie mit vielen anderen leben wird, die Rede ist' (292).

While it may well be true that the situation of the Markan community is reflected in Mark 13:9–13, it is dangerous to assume from the outset that the community concerns are more clearly expressed in these verses than elsewhere in the chapter. Similarly, verses 33–7 do to some extent reflect the situation of the

recommendation that the literary questions be dealt with before the historical ones.

A further aspect of Breytenbach's comments made in the context of his discussion of W. Wrede is that the separation of tradition and redaction should not precede the interpretation of the text. Not only is the unity of the text at stake, but more profoundly the theological conception of the evangelist. Breytenbach puts this issue clearly on the agenda later in his study:

> It is questionable whether only the redaction of the evangelist reflects his theological attitude. Nor is it sufficient to add the sum of redaction and tradition together. By means of his redactional-compositional approach, Mark has created a new text, made new contexts of meaning, and put the tradition in a new light. The result of this is more than the sum of redaction and tradition.[4]

This presents a challenge to grapple with both tradition and redaction as somehow 'redactional'. This is not, however, to leave the question of tradition aside altogether as irrelevant. For a study that endeavours to draw any historical conclusions from the text, the evangelist's use of tradition continues to be a critical question. This is particularly significant for Mark 13, given the prominence of the theory of the incorporation of an earlier apocalypse into this chapter.[5]

So this study of Mark 13 will begin with a literary examination of the chapter and its context within the Gospel, then move to the question of tradition and redaction. Only then will the historical questions of *Sitz im Leben* be raised. Text-critical questions have been dealt with in some detail in a recent study by K. D. Dyer,[6] and his results support the Nestle-Aland text (26/27th edns) in every respect; it is this text which will therefore be used.[7]

Markan community, but perhaps in the first instance the interests of the evangelist; this allows some reconstruction of the situation in which he was writing. If one were to base a reconstruction of the Markan community primarily on verses 33–7, one might postulate a situation in which the community was losing interest or hope in the promised parousia. Such a postulate needs to be balanced against other indications within the chapter.

[4] Breytenbach, *Nachfolge*, 32 (translation mine).
[5] A. Collins, in 'Eschatological Discourse', has critiqued the 'Little Apocalypse' theories as an endeavour to 'save' Jesus or the evangelist from eschatology, by assigning much of this material to Jewish tradition.
[6] Dyer, 'Reader', 20–33.
[7] No changes have been made to the *text* in the 27th edition.

As Norman Perrin pointed out in an article reflecting on appropriate methods for the study and interpretation of the synoptic Gospels,[8] literary criticism of the Gospels and Acts must include a concern both for their composition and structure, and for protagonists and plot. Both these concerns will be explored in relation to Mark 13, considering the text both in its narrative sequence and thematically.

2. Indispensable within the narrative framework: a literary examination of Mark 13 in context

Mark 13 opens with a scene that has strong thematic links to the preceding chapters of Mark. The first of these is a theme which has been constantly in view since chapter 11, namely the question of Jesus' relationship to the Temple and Jewish authorities. Mark's careful intercalation of Jesus' prophetic actions concerning the fig tree and Temple (11:12–25) has already prefigured the fate of the Temple and its authorities, as has the parable of the wicked tenants (12:1–12). In 13:1–2 this fate is made explicit by Mark's Jesus (hereafter to be referred to simply as Jesus). This fate is sealed both verbally and dramatically, as Jesus 'quits' the Temple. The immediate context of the chapter (12:38–44) compounds the ominous tone of Jesus' dealings with the Temple, giving a strong indictment of reliance on external appearances.[9] It is by these very appearances that the disciple is dazzled in 13:1. This points to the second thematic link: that of the misunderstanding of the disciples.

As R. C. Tannehill has pointed out, the early positive portrayal of the disciples shifts in the three boat scenes (4:35–41, 6:45–52, 8:13–21), highlighting the disciples' fear and lack of understanding.[10] From the confession at Caesarea Philippi onwards, the lack of understanding begins to take on specific dimensions: a desire for status and domination which is incompatible with the way of the cross. The three passion predictions (8:31, 9:31, 10:33–4) are the occasions for conflict between Jesus and his disciples as to the way of the cross and the way of discipleship. These conflict situations then become, in each case, the occasion for teaching

---

[8] Perrin, 'Evangelist as Author', 5–18.
[9] For a convincing reading of 12:41–4 as a critique of the Jewish authorities, cf. Geddert, *Watchwords*, 134–8.
[10] Tannehill, 'Disciples', 386–405.

which sets out to break the perceived nexus between status/domination and true greatness by means of paradox:

> 'For those who want to save their life will lose it, and those who lose their life for my sake, and for the sake of the gospel, will save it.' (8:35)

> 'Whoever wants to be first must be last of all and servant of all.' (9:35b)

> '. . . whoever wishes to become great among you must be your servant, and whoever wishes to be first among you must be slave of all'. (10:43b–44)

In the light of these teachings, the exclamation of the unnamed disciple in 13:1 about the 'stones' and 'buildings' highlights the disciples' continued incomprehension. Not only has the disciple failed to comprehend the import of Jesus' conflict with the Temple and its authorities, but he has misunderstood that true greatness lies not with externals, but with taking up one's cross and following Jesus on the way. Though the disciple addresses Jesus as 'Teacher', he has not comprehended his teaching.[11] Jesus' reply immediately picks up this lack of comprehension: βλέπεις ταύτας τὰς μεγάλας οἰκοδομάς; T. J. Geddert has convincingly argued that the verb βλέπω, as it is used in Mark's Gospel, goes beyond simply the physical act of seeing and implies discernment.[12] In Mark 13:2, then, Jesus' reply immediately highlights the incomprehension of the disciple, who 'seeing' does not 'see' (cf. 4:12).

So the opening scene of Mark 13 at once sets what is to follow in the context of the preceding Temple conflict and functions as a climax to it, making explicit what until then had been implicit in Jesus' actions and words. Moreover, it carries the motif of the disciples' misunderstanding further, showing that for all the teaching the disciples have received, it is still only external greatness that they comprehend.

There is a further aspect to this opening scene: it raises expectations within the implied reader. The buildings are undeniably great.

---

[11] This form of address in Mark's Gospel is used ironically by Jesus' opponents (12:14, 19). At other times it denotes only a partial understanding. Only in 14:14, where Jesus uses it of himself, is it possible that the title has a more positive sense, akin to the verbal form. It is of course possible that, within the context of the Gospel, this self-reference functions ironically.

[12] Geddert, *Watchwords*, 81–7.

They have provoked an exclamation of wonder, and their external greatness is not denied by Jesus. It is the contrast between this greatness, this seeming immutability, and the utterness of the destruction which Jesus predicts that raises the expectation that it could be none other than God who could effect this destruction, who could bring this great edifice to nothing. The passive constructions strengthen this impression, as does the double use of οὐ μή:

οὐ μὴ ἀφεθῇ ὧδε λίθος ἐπὶ λίθον ὃς οὐ μὴ καταλυθῇ.

It is therefore in the context of this expectation that it will be none other than God at work in this destruction that the whole of the following discourse proceeds. The disciples' questions in verse 4 strengthen the readers' expectation that further teaching about the nature of this destruction will follow. This accompanies the reader through the discourse and beyond, yet it is nowhere explicitly taken up again by Jesus, neither at verse 14, which makes no mention of destruction, nor at any other point in the Gospel narrative. In a form which the narrator stresses is distorted (cf. 14:56–7, 59), the saying forms the basis for the accusations of verse 58. Both these accusations and the taunts of 15:29 invite the readers to align themselves consciously with Jesus' perspective, that the utter destruction of the Temple will indeed take place, and that it will be God's doing.[13]

The saying of 13:2 and the subsequent dramatic positioning of the protagonists opposite the Temple (verse 3) demonstrate that the Temple is disqualified as the locus of God's presence. Though the reader's expectation of further clarification is raised, this expectation is deliberately disappointed. By disappointing the reader in this way, the evangelist underlines both the finality of this disqualification and the sovereignty of Jesus' word. In this disappointment, the readers are pushed to perceive the world as no longer temple-centred. Rather, their perspective must shift to all nations (cf. verse 10), and indeed to the whole cosmos (cf. verse 31: ὁ οὐρανὸς καὶ ἡ γῆ παρελεύσονται). The eschatological drama to be unfolded is to be much bigger than the implied readers expect. Their disappointment is to make them receptive to this fundamental shift in perspective.

---

[13] The use of the future tense here is not intended to pre-empt the historical discussion of the dating of Mark's Gospel, but rather to call attention to the literary function of the various temple sayings.

There is a subtle contrast between the readiness of the (four) disciples to ask further about matters to do with the destruction of the Temple, and their reluctance to ask Jesus about his own destruction. After the second passion prediction, the narrator explicitly tells the reader that 'they did not understand what he was saying and were afraid to ask him' (9:32). This contrast seems once again to highlight the disciples' slowness to recognize in Jesus' way of the cross the type of their own way. They are afraid to acknowledge that the way of discipleship is the way of the cross. However, they are more than ready to ask questions when the issue is vindication for Jesus' words and for themselves, because such a promise of divine intervention seems to preclude the need for the way of the cross. The ensuing discourse disappoints the disciples, and through them any readers who share their perspective. Rather than being a promise of swift vindication and glory, the discourse leads right back to the path of suffering. The whole of the discourse from verses 5–23 speaks of suffering and tribulation. There is a glimpse of vindication, but it is the darkness of the tunnel rather than the light at the end which receives most attention. The destruction of the Temple is not an alternative to the way of the cross.

There are to be beacons of light along the tunnel. The discourse itself is such a beacon, for it is to accompany them along the way, to both warn and reassure them (cf. verse 23). Moreover, there is the promise of the assistance of the Holy Spirit (verse 11), and the assurance that God has cut short the days of suffering (verse 20). The disciples, and through them the implied readers (cf. verse 37), are called to recognize that the tunnel itself is part of God's plan (δεῖ γενέσθαι verse 7). Because the persecution of the disciples is to be the occasion for mission (verses 9–11), their way of the cross is to have salvific implications, as Jesus' way does (cf. 10:45). The discourse thus shows that the disciples – those who endure (verse 13) – are to be conformed to the way of the cross that they are so consistently avoiding within the narrative.

The discourse is depicted as a private address to Peter, James, John and Andrew (verse 3), the inner core who were the first to be called (1:16–20). The order of this list draws attention to the fact that the first three of these disciples are the ones who have been shown within the narrative to be most vehemently and volubly opposed to the way of the cross. It is Peter who tries to rebuke Jesus after the first passion prediction (8:32). It is James and John

who are intent on glory after the third passion prediction (10:35ff).
The discourse of Mark 13 points back to the way of the cross, and
it is therefore peculiarly appropriate that the disciples who were
most outspoken in favouring a way other than that of the cross
become the recipients of this discourse.

However, rather than remaining a private address to these
disciples, the discourse itself breaks open the plotted time of the
narrative and interrupts the narrative fiction at verse 14 and again
at verse 37 in a way not paralleled elsewhere in the Gospel.
Though, in terms of the plot, the four disciples are the recipients of
the discourse, by means of several techniques the discourse takes on
an immediacy that addresses the implied reader directly.

The first of these techniques is the way in which the voice of the
implied author is dispensed with altogether after verse 5a. Nowhere
else in the Gospel is there a discourse which is not punctuated by
this voice which comments on the narrative and directs the reader.
In Mark 4, the implied author is always present. By contrast, Mark
13 assumes an urgency, as though there were no time for such
niceties.

The second technique is use of dialogue. If Tannehill is correct in
saying that dialogue gives emphasis,[14] then the whole discourse
from verses 5b–37 is emphatic. It would have been possible for the
evangelist to have formulated at least some of the discourse in
indirect speech, but the immediacy for the implied reader would
have been forfeited.

Third, though the viewpoint of the implied author merges with
that of Jesus in Mark's Gospel, as many scholars have argued,[15] it
is the authority of Jesus which undergirds the whole discourse. In
this way, the implied reader gains direct access to the one who is the
source of the narrator's authority, and is assured that nothing of
importance has been withheld.

The fourth device by which the discourse takes on a sense of
immediacy is the way in which the narrative fiction is broken and
the reader addressed directly: ὁ ἀναγινώσκων νοείτω (verse 14).
Whether this phrase originated in the tradition or on the level of
redaction is not at issue at this point; its presence heightens the
immediacy of the discourse in an unprecedented way. It is a phrase
best suited to the implied author/narrator, for within the narrative
fiction, Jesus is unaware of the implied reader. And yet the

---

[14] Tannehill, 'Disciples', 138.   [15] E.g. *Ibid.*, 138.

authority and prescience of Jesus is shown in this discourse to be such that the implied readers are not able to exclude the possibility that this Jesus can turn to them and speak through the window of text. At the close of the discourse, verse 37, this impression is strengthened: ὃ δὲ ὑμῖν λέγω πᾶσιν λέγω, γρηγορεῖτε. On the level of the narrative, this could simply be understood as a way of instructing the disciples to convey the warning to be alert to others, and in this sense it does not break the narrative fiction. However, given the immediacy of the discourse and the fact that already at verse 14 the readers find themselves glimpsed through the window of the narrative, the effect of this final exhortation is as though Jesus turns his head and looks the reader straight in the eye.

There is a fifth technique whereby the immediacy of the discourse is heightened. This discourse goes beyond the plotted time of the narrative, which runs from the ministry of John the Baptizer to shortly after the resurrection of Jesus.[16] Only at the end of the Gospel, 16:7–8, does another such break with the plotted time occur. The events of 16:7–8, which are portrayed as future within the narrative fiction, are nevertheless past for the implied reader. They are, in fact, foundational past, for without the fulfilment of them, the narrative itself would not have come into being. In contrast, the discourse of Mark 13 breaks the plotted time in quite a different way. Here, the plotted time of the narrative is left behind, and the perspective travels 'through time' to the immediate temporal context of the implied reader, whether future, present or immediate past. This in itself would be sufficient to imbue the discourse with a sense of immediacy, but when combined with the other techniques, the result is so striking as to have prompted some scholars to view it as a foreign body within the Gospel.[17]

It is no foreign body, though, as I have argued with reference to the Markan theme of discipleship as the way of the cross. The Markan theme of the conflict between Jesus and the Temple which opened the chapter also firmly anchors the discourse within the Gospel framework. Although no further *explicit* mention is made of the destruction of the Temple, verses 14ff implicitly touch upon the nature of its end by means of the Danielic allusion to the βδέλυγμα τῆς ἐρημώσεως. The destruction will involve desecra-

---

[16] Cf. Mack, *Myth*, 329, fig. 24.
[17] Pesch, *Naherwartungen*, 65, 67. However, he took a different position in *Das Markusevangelium II*, 3 (n.3) and 264.

tion, and it is to be in keeping with scripture. The appropriate action will not be to stand in its defence, but to flee. Such action will confirm their allegiance to Jesus, whose prophetic actions and words indicated that the Temple was a place disqualified by God. So although on one level, the oracle in verses 14ff is a seeming misfit within the Gospel, in terms of the broader Markan theme of the disqualification of the Temple, it is firmly anchored in its context.

The fig tree similitude of verses 28–9 gives another reminder of the fate of the Temple, because of its association with Jesus' prophetic action with the fig tree in chapter 11. If the Gospel is read as literature, it is not possible to interpret this similitude other than as further interpretative words about the action of chapter 11. The word order of verse 28, which gives emphasis to the fig tree, strengthens the impression that the reference is not simply to any tree: ἀπὸ δὲ τῆς συκῆς μάθετε τὴν παραβολήν. In chapter 11, using the technique of intercalation, the evangelist symbolized the Temple and Jewish authorities by means of the fig tree and its fate. There was no doubt that the tree was in leaf (this is mentioned twice in 11:13), but the sought-for fruit was not there. The Temple and its authorities were fulfilling their duties in outward appearance, but the fruit (ὁ καρπός) was lacking (cf. the theme of the bearing of fruit in chapter 4:8, etc.). The branches had become tender and put forth leaves, but no fruit was born. In the terms of the Markan parables of chapter 4, it is not the shoots, but only the fruit that is significant. Though once the fruit may have been produced, the reader is told that it was not the time (ὁ καιρός) for expecting fruit from this source. The cursing of the fig tree took place between Bethany and Jerusalem, Mark notes. If one interprets the cursing and withering of the fig tree according to 13:28–9, then Jesus was portrayed as near, at the very gates, and yet the Temple and its authorities bore no fruit. Summer was indeed near, the messianic time of fruitfulness foreshadowed in such passages as Ezek. 47:12, but the fig tree, the Jewish authorities, bore no fruit. Understood in this way, 13:29 is a call to readiness, lest the disciples (and the implied reader!) be found, like the fig tree, bearing no fruit. When the disciples see these things, the various aspects of the discourse, taking place, they are to be in readiness, so as not to be caught unawares. Such readiness therefore consists more in appropriate action and less in accurate knowledge or prediction of the future. This interpretation of the fig tree similitude is similar in import to the following parable of the householder who goes on a journey (13:34ff). It does not provide externally verifiable signs, but calls for watchfulness and readiness to discern the one who is near. Elsewhere within the Gospel, Mark has a negative view of sign-seeking (cf. Mark 8:11–13, 13:22), and even here one does not find the sort of sign that the disciples are requesting in 13:4.[18] Read in this way, this similitude further anchors the discourse within the Markan framework, by rejecting sign-seeking as elsewhere in the Gospel, and by alluding to the cursing of the fig tree in chapter 11.

A further Markan theme which demonstrates that this discourse is an integral part of the Gospel is that of mission. The central concern of Mark's Gospel is the εὐαγγελίον Ἰησοῦ Χριστοῦ (Mark 1:1). The calling of the first disciples, Simon and Andrew, makes explicit that the purpose of their call is to follow Jesus along the way of the cross, not only for their own sake but also for the sake of others: δεῦτε ὀπίσω μου, καὶ ποιήσω ὑμᾶς γενέσθαι ἁλιεῖς ἀνθρώπων (Mark 1:17). When Jesus appoints the twelve, once again it is to be with him and to be sent out to proclaim the message, this time with authority to cast out demons (3:14–15). In chapter 6, the twelve are sent out. Both here (6:11) and in chapter 13:9, there is the phrase εἰς μαρτύριον αὐτοῖς. The fact that some translations render the first instance as 'as a testimony against them' and the second as 'as a testimony to them' should not obscure the links between the mission discourse of 6:6b–13 and what might be called the 'mission discourse' of 13:9–13. The purpose of both is to fulfil the initial calling which was described metaphorically as 'becoming fishers of people'. In the first mission, they go out in strength, for they are given (δίδωμι) authority over unclean spirits. In the second mission discourse, they are to go out in weakness, armed only with what will be given to them (δίδωμι) to speak in that hour. Nevertheless, in this way they are to have unprecedented access to both Jews and Gentiles, for this latter 'fishing net' is cast wide, with all nations as its quarry (verse 10). So the Markan theme of mission also anchors this discourse within the framework of the Gospel.

Even the references to false messiahs and false prophets who would lead the disciples astray (verses 21–2, verse 6) are not foreign bodies within the Markan framework. The narrative constantly

---

[18] I accept Geddert's thesis that sign-seeking is rejected altogether by the evangelist. Cf. *Watchwords*, 32ff.

raises the question of Jesus' identity and the source of his authority, and with it the question of who is a true prophet, who is the true Messiah? After the confession at Caesarea Philippi, the disciples are shown as people who have an inkling about Jesus' identity as the Christ, but are dangerously vague on the import of it. While the disciples continue in their failure to grasp the nature of Jesus' messiahship as one that leads to the cross, they are vulnerable to impostors who would lead them along the path of signs and wonders. In Mark 13, this is shown to be not simply an issue for the disciples before the crucifixion and resurrection, but in fact an ongoing challenge; only by grasping the true nature of Jesus' messiahship can the disciples, and the implied reader, be assured that they will not be led astray.

The discourse is connected not only to the preceding Markan narrative in the ways outlined above, but also to the passion narrative which is to follow. The passion and the resurrection are never explicitly mentioned in this discourse, but they are known to the implied reader as a *sine qua non*, without which the narrative would not have been written. Certain features of the discourse correspond to elements of the passion narrative, as was pointed out by R. H. Lightfoot.[19] The first of these are the references to παραδίδομαι, which occur in Mark 13 at verses 9, 11 and 12. This verb occurs ten times in chapters 14 and 15 with reference to Jesus' being handed over; Mark 13:9–13 show that Jesus' followers are to share his path of suffering.

The second element in the discourse which has links with the passion narrative is the exhortation to watch, and not to fall asleep (13:33–7). This is clearly connected with 14:32–42, where the disciples receive the same exhortation (γρηγορεῖτε), and fail miserably. The parable of the householder who goes on a journey is the final element of the discourse which, I have argued, has a heightened sense of immediacy for the implied reader. The repeated warning to watch accompanies the reader through the narrative of the disciples' failure in the garden of Gethsemane, and thus the narrative of the garden reiterates that warning and calls the implied reader not to repeat that failure.

A third correspondence between Mark 13 and the passion narrative is found in the references to ὥρα, which occurs in 13:32

---

[19] Lightfoot, *Mark*, 48–59.

and then twice in the narrative of the garden of Gethsemane (14:35, 41).

A further more subtle correspondence which can be discerned is the 'four watch schema' (13:35), which is reflected in the events of the passion night: ὀψίας γενομένης, 14:17a; the midnight watch, though not named, is signified in 14:32–42 by the three times one hour schema, ἀλέκτωρ ἐφώνησεν, 14:72; πρωΐ, 15:1.

In addition to these correspondences, there are other motifs which link Mark 13 to the passion narrative. The first of these is the reference to the darkening of the sun, verse 24. Such a darkening takes place during the hours of the crucifixion (15:33). This is not to say that the evangelist sees the fulfilment of 13:24 in 15:33, though this has been argued,[20] for, as has been shown, the rest of the discourse projects beyond the plotted time of the narrative, and there is no indication that the evangelist means this section (verses 24ff) to be understood otherwise. Rather, on the level of the narrative, 13:24 prepares the reader to recognize the cosmic significance of 15:33 and to see it as a prefigurement pointing beyond the plotted time of the narrative.

Another motif of Mark 13 that occurs in the passion narrative is the destruction of the Temple, which has already been discussed with reference to chapters 11 and 12. The accusation that Jesus has said he will destroy the Temple is a central element in the trial narrative (14:55–59), and again in the crucifixion narrative (15:29–30). Although the evangelist makes clear that the testimony is false, the implied readers are invited to 'see' the irony. Their expectations have been raised that it is God who will destroy the Temple, and they have some insight into the relationship between God and Jesus, the Son of God. Mark 13 is crucial to the question, in what sense are the accusations of 14:58 and 15:29 false, and in what sense true? Only in the light of Mark 13 are the implied readers equipped to see the irony of the accusations against Jesus and to align themselves with the perspective of the implied author rather than that of the accusers and taunters. For these numerous reasons, Mark 13 is by no means a foreign body to the narrative plot of the Gospel, but in fact indispensable to the functioning of the narrative.

Mark 14:61bf is also a passage of the passion narrative with strong links to Mark 13:

[20] Myers, *Strong Man*, 390ff.

πάλιν ὁ ἀρχιερεὺς ἐπηρώτα αὐτόν· καὶ λέγει αὐτῷ· σὺ εἶ
χριστὸς ὁ υἱὸς τοῦ εὐλογητοῦ; ὁ δὲ Ἰησοῦς εἶπεν· ἐγώ
εἰμι, καὶ ὄψεσθε τὸν υἱὸν τοῦ ἀνθρώπου ἐκ δεξιῶν
καθήμενον τῆς δυνάμεως καὶ ἐρχόμενον μετὰ τῶν
νεφελῶν τοῦ οὐρανοῦ.

In 13:6, Jesus warns the disciples of many who will come in his
name and say ἐγώ εἰμι. In 14:62 these words are spoken by Jesus
himself.[21] The words ἐγώ εἰμι at 14:62 refer to ὁ χριστὸς ὁ υἱὸς τοῦ
εὐλογητοῦ. By means of the verbal association with 13:6, the false
leaders' ἐγώ εἰμι is confirmed as a messianic claim, a claim to be
the anointed one of God. This gives the impression, which will be
discussed in more detail below, that the false leaders of 13:5–6
represent the same danger as the false christs and false prophets of
13:21–2.

Within the narrative framework of the Gospel, 14:62, though it
echoes both Ps. 110:1 and Dan. 7:13, is most closely associated with
13:26. Both 13:26 and 14:62 speak of seeing the coming of the Son
of Man with the clouds of heaven, and both refer to the coming as
being 'with power' (μετὰ δυνάμεως). Only the reference in 14:62 to
being seated at the right hand (of the Power) has no parallel at
13:26, but the messianic background to this has already been given
in the debate about the interpretation of Ps. 110:1 at 12:35ff.
Chapter 14:62 therefore speaks of Jesus' vindication as Messiah.
Though it has been argued that this vindication refers only to Jesus'
exaltation,[22] the strong links between this verse and 13:26 imply
that both refer to a parousia beyond the plotted time of the
narrative.

Through the discourse of Mark 13, the implied reader is privy to
much more information than are the various chief priests, elders
and scribes depicted at the trial. Only the information of 14:62 and
an inkling of the Temple's destruction are depicted as being
vouchsafed to those at the trial. Because of the implied readers'
access to the information of Mark 13, their reaction is to be in stark

---

[21] The variant reading of θ f¹³ 565. 700 *pc* and Origen, σὺ εἶπας ὅτι ἐγώ εἰμι, is
presumably an assimilation to Matthew 26:64, despite Cranfield's reservations
(*Mark*, 443–4).
[22] Cf. Glasson, *Advent*, 63–8, who makes reference in this respect to the commen-
taries of Lagrange and V. Taylor. Myers, *Strong Man*, 343ff argues a similar case,
as does Dyer, 'Reader', 233ff. Cf. also France, *Jesus*, 227ff, who argues that
verses 24–7 should be understood as referring to the fall of Jerusalem, not the
parousia.

contrast at this point to that of the high priest who tears his clothes and calls for a verdict on the charge of blasphemy. In this way, it may be seen once again that Mark 13 is no afterthought, but carefully structured and situated to give the implied reader the perspective from which the passion narrative may be grasped and interpreted.

Therefore, in these ways, the discourse of Mark 13 is shown to be an integral part of the Gospel of Mark, not only in the way in which Markan themes are further explored, but also by the chapter's notable links to the passion narrative. Nevertheless, despite all these ways in which the chapter is firmly anchored in its context, it does present the reader with a break in the thread of the narrative, and the *function* of this break requires interpretation. As I have already observed, Mark 13 gives the reader privileged insights into the cosmic implications of Jesus' person and ministry, and thus the passion narrative, and even the enigmatic ending of 16:8, read not as a story of failure, but rather as one of hope. To those who are not given the perspective of Mark 13, Jesus' passion and the decimation of his group of followers remain what they seem on the surface to be – a story of dashed hopes and possibilities. Those who are given 'understanding', however, have access to the reality beyond the apparent failure. Thus the positioning of Mark 13 within the structure of the narrative both illustrates and effects the polarity between those who 'see' and those who do not.

Mark 13 breaks the breathless onward movement of the narrative prior to the climactic events of the passion. This gives readers the opportunity to orientate themselves in relation to the central narrative of their faith, by recognizing themselves as addressed, and thus in a sense as part of what is to follow. One could perhaps compare this to the function of the chorales in Bach's passion oratorios. The audience is drawn by them into the passion story and itself becomes a protagonist. The story is thus no longer experienced as 'objective' history to be observed from the outside, but rather as a reality into which one enters. Such an interpretation of course implies that the structure of the Gospel has much closer links to oral narrative than to a structure based upon individual pericopes. I will have cause to take up the question of orality and the Gospel below. However, at this point I will make some observations about the genre and form of the discourse.

3. Questions of genre

This chapter has been known as the 'Markan apocalypse', because
of certain features that it shared with apocalyptic writings.[23] More
recently, considerable progress has been made in the study and
classification of this diverse group of writings, and this has raised
questions as to the appropriateness of the use of the name
apocalypse in relation to Mark 13.[24] If an apocalypse is characterized by the following features, Mark 13 fits the description only
partially: against a background of persecution and spiritual
turmoil, a series of visions is granted to a seer; these visions are
generally mediated by an angelic being, and call those who are still
faithful among the people of God to endurance, because the
present age of darkness will soon be at an end; there is an urgent
expectation of the impending overthrow of all earthly conditions in
a vast cosmic catastrophe; the language is veiled in secrecy and is
rich in symbolism and mythical imagery. In Mark 13 there is no
vision, no angelic mediator or interpreter. So instead, it seems
better to make use of J. J. Collins' distinction between 'apocalypse'
and 'apocalyptic eschatology':[25] 'apocalypse' refers to the literary
genre, whereas 'apocalyptic eschatology' refers to a religious perspective and looks for the cataclysmic End of the age. According to
this distinction, though Mark 13 is not strictly an apocalypse, it
certainly demonstrates apocalyptic eschatology. Given its adoption
of apocalyptic motifs and concerns, the discourse cannot be understood as 'anti-apocalyptic', as E. Brandenburger has rightly
pointed out.[26]

The discourse of Mark 13 shares certain features with the 'farewell discourses' of the Old Testament (e.g. Gen. 49, where Jacob
predicts what will happen to his descendants, Deut. 32–3 where
Moses addresses the people before his death, and 1 Chr. 28–9,
where David hands over his kingdom to Solomon), the intertestamental period (e.g. the Testaments of the Twelve Patriarchs) and
also the farewell discourse in the Gospel of John, which is attributed to Jesus at the same point in the narrative – between the final
scene of Jesus teaching in the Temple and the beginning of the
passion narrative.

---

[23] Cf. Hooker's evaluation of this classification in 'Trial', 78–99.
[24] A. Y. Collins, 'Apocalypses', 96–7.   [25] Cf. J. J. Collins, 'Genre', 2– 20.
[26] Brandenburger, *Markus 13*, 11.

Some of the features of Mark 13 are in keeping with characteristics of other farewell discourses. The first characteristic is imminence of death; the discourse directly precedes the opening of the passion narrative. The evangelist makes clear that Jesus is aware of this imminence, though the disciples are not (cf. passion predictions). The second characteristic is that farewell discourses speak of the future, and offer reassurance in the face of sorrow. Mark 13 contains a number of sayings which offer reassurance: verse 13: the one who endures to the End will be saved; verse 23: I have already told you everything; verse 31: Heaven and earth will pass away, but my words will not pass away. The third is that farewell discourses often speak of those who persecute the just, and this characteristic is present in verses 9–13. A fourth similarity between other farewell discourses and Mark 13 is the theme of the endurance of one's name; this is reflected in verse 13: καὶ ἔσεσθε μισούμενοι ὑπὸ πάντων διὰ τὸ ὄνομά μου. ὁ δὲ ὑπομείνας εἰς τέλος οὗτος σωθήσεται.

On the other hand, there are features often found in farewell discourses which are not present here: recollection of what God has done in the past or of the speaker's past life; the theme of unity and loving one another; a closing prayer for the followers. Nevertheless, given that this material is presented not as a vision but as a discourse delivered before Jesus' death, Mark 13 is closer to the genre of the farewell discourse than to an apocalypse. Of course, many farewell discourses from the intertestamental period have apocalyptic features,[27] so the farewell discourse model is by no means at odds with the apocalyptic eschatology of Mark 13. Therefore, Mark 13 is a type of farewell discourse, much of which is expressed in the language and imagery of apocalyptic eschatology.[28]

V. K. Robbins introduces a further literary model, this time from the Graeco-Roman tradition, that may have influenced Mark 13, namely the Temple dialogue.[29] Robbins' work is instructive, as it

---

[27] The Testaments often share interests in eschatological events, as well as in angels, cosmology and ethics, with apocalyptic writings. One example among many is noted by Priest in his introduction to the Testament of Moses (in Charlesworth, ed., *The Old Testament Pseudepigrapha*, I), 922: '. . . the Testament of Moses . . . reflects the general outlook of the later Hasidic movement with a stress on apocalyptic motifs. Whether this was an individual or sectarian view cannot be ascertained.'

[28] A. Y. Collins adopts 'scholastic dialogue' as the basic form, in 'Discourse', 1129, in agreement with Brandenburger, *Markus 13*, 15, 17.

[29] Robbins, *Jesus the Teacher*, 171ff.

shows the intertwining of various literary forms which has created a hybrid suited to a writing which is itself a new form.[30]

4. Structure of Mark 13:5b–37

Let us now move to the question of the structure of the discourse, 13:5b–37. One of the most prominent features is the repeated use of the imperative βλέπετε. It occurs in verse 5, at the very beginning of the discourse, then at verses 9, 23 and 33. There seems to be some correlation between these occurrences and the thematic divisions of the chapter, which could be set out as follows:

> Verses 5–8 speak of the beginning of the birth pangs, which is an apocalyptic image of the tribulations which are expected to precede the End. Here is the first mention of false prophets.
>
> Verses 9–13 speak of the integral link between persecution and testimony; the disciples' testimony to Jesus will result in persecution, but the persecution will also be the occasion for testimony.
>
> Verses 14–20 contain a prophecy addressed to those in Judea concerning a mysterious figure – the desolating sacrilege – and resume the theme of suffering.
>
> Verses 21–3 give the second warning against false prophets, and reassurance that the disciples have been equipped to deal with the danger.
>
> Verses 24–7 form the climax of the chapter. They speak of the cosmic disasters which herald the arrival of the Son of Man, and of the gathering in of the elect.

There follow two sections, each containing a parable and associated sayings. The exact division of these will be discussed below.

The imperative βλέπετε begins the discourse and also the following section, verses 9–13, where its object is specified by the reflexive pronoun: βλέπετε δὲ ὑμεῖς ἑαυτούς. At verse 23 it concludes the section verses 21–3, and its final occurrence is at verse 33. Given the apparent correlation between this imperative and the thematic divisions – it either begins them or concludes

---

[30] Cf. Kelber's discussion of attempts to classify the Gospel of Mark according to genre, *Oral and Written Gospel*, 117ff.

them – it is probable that one should read verse 33 as the beginning of the final section, with verse 32 as the conclusion to verses 28ff. The layout of many modern texts favours a division before verse 32,[31] probably in part to relieve the perceived tension between verses 30 and 32. However, it is too atomistic a view of the text to think that linking verse 32 with verse 33ff deals with the problem. It is better to see these verses as intended to hold in tension the known and the unknown, mediated by the double assurance of verse 31 that the End will take place and that the reliability of Jesus' words can be trusted.

I have argued that this chapter has a heightened sense of immediacy for the implied reader. The repeated occurrence of βλέπετε contributes to that sense, for it seems to earmark the most pressing issues: false prophets (verses 5bf, 21ff), persecutions (verses 9ff), and that the time of the End is unknown (verses 33ff). I will not as yet seek to draw any historical conclusions from this, but simply note that the imperative βλέπετε is *not* appended to the oracle of the desolating sacrilege (verses 14ff) nor to the description of the cosmic disturbances and the coming of the Son of Man (verses 24–7).

This repeated use of βλέπετε, though it does give some indication of the implied author's concerns, does not primarily warn the disciples and the implied reader of external pressures, but rather calls on them to take heed of, or 'discern', their own position *vis-à-vis* these pressures. This is most apparent in verse 9 (βλέπετε δὲ ὑμεῖς ἑαυτούς), but is also true for the other references, which call for 'self-awareness': βλέπετε μή τις ὑμᾶς πλανήσῃ (verse 5), ὑμεῖς δὲ βλέπετε (verse 23), βλέπετε, ἀγρυπνεῖτε· οὐκ οἴδατε γὰρ πότε ὁ καιρός ἐστιν (verse 33). The evangelist could conceivably have formulated these phrases to warn directly against the specific external pressures, as is found in Phil. 3:2: βλέπετε τοὺς κύνας, βλέπετε τοὺς κακοὺς ἐργάτας, βλέπετε τὴν κατατομήν. In contrast to these formulations, the evangelist keeps the focus squarely on the disciples/implied reader, and not on the pressures or threats themselves. This is in keeping with the theme of the misunderstanding of the disciples which has been discussed above; the implied reader is called upon to perceive the misunderstanding and move towards discernment.

---

[31] Nestle-Aland is agnostic on this point, allowing verse 32 to stand alone, but the *UBSGNT*, and most translations, link verse 32 to what follows, on the basis of the theme that the day and hour is unknown.

So the repeated use of βλέπετε functions in a number of ways: it adds to the immediacy of the discourse, it gives some sense of its structure and most pressing concerns, and it calls upon the implied reader to manifest greater discernment than the disciples manage to do within the whole of the Gospel narrative. Another feature that has a bearing on the structure of this discourse is that there are two references to false prophets. The first is in verses 5–6, at the very beginning of the discourse:

> βλέπετε μή τις ὑμᾶς πλανήσῃ· πολλοὶ ἐλεύσονται ἐπὶ τῷ ὀνόματί μου λέγοντες ὅτι ἐγώ εἰμι, καὶ πολλοὺς πλανήσουσιν.

The second is in verses 21–3, which directly precedes the description of the coming of the Son of Man (verses 24ff):

> καὶ τότε ἐάν τις ὑμῖν εἴπῃ· ἴδε ὧδε ὁ χριστός, ἴδε ἐκεῖ, μὴ πιστεύετε· ἐγερθήσονται γὰρ ψευδόχριστοι καὶ ψευδο-προφῆται καὶ δώσουσιν σημεῖα καὶ τέρατα πρὸς τὸ ἀποπλανᾶν, εἰ δυνατόν, τοὺς ἐκλεκτούς. ὑμεῖς δὲ βλέπετε· προείρηκα ὑμῖν πάντα.

The exact nature of these false prophets' claims and whether they are to be understood as the same ones or different ones are not my concern at this point. On the literary level, they constitute an important theme which provides a frame around all the material prior to the final events of verses 24ff. The material of verses 5b–23 is concerned with inner-wordly disturbances, whereas the verses which follow (verses 24ff) deal with cosmic disturbances and the 'End' proper. The framing of the inner-worldly disturbances by the references to false prophets and by the warning βλέπετε serves to distinguish verses 24ff from the preceding section. Within the narrative fiction, the whole of the discourse deals with the future, but for the implied reader, verses 5b–23 are in some sense present (either immediate future, present or immediate past). By bracketing together verses 5b–23, and distinguishing them from the final events of verses 24–7, the evangelist gives some indication of his or her own chronological perspective. It seems that for the implied reader, and also for the implied author, the various disturbances of verses 5b–23 belong to the same time frame, which is seen to be distinct from the 'End' proper. Another strong indication that a break is intended between verses 5b–23 and verses 24–27 is the use of ἀλλά at the beginning of verse 24. It is striking that the text does *not* read καὶ ἐν ἐκείναις ταῖς ἡμέραις μετὰ τὴν θλῖψιν ἐκείνην ..., but instead uses the adversative conjunction ἀλλά. The two nearest parallels to such a usage of ἀλλά in Mark's Gospel, where this conjunction begins a sentence, are 14:28 and 16:7:

> 14:27–8 καὶ λέγει αὐτοῖς ὁ Ἰησοῦς ὅτι πάντες σκανδαλ-ισθήσεσθε, ὅτι γέγραπται·
> πατάξω τὸν ποιμένα, καὶ τὰ πρόβατα διασκορπισθή-σονται.
> ἀλλὰ μετὰ τὸ ἐγερθῆναί με προάξω ὑμᾶς εἰς τὴν Γαλι-λαίαν.

> 16:6–7 ὁ δὲ λέγει αὐταῖς· μὴ ἐκθαμβεῖσθε· Ἰησοῦν ζητεῖτε τὸν Ναζαρηνὸν τὸν ἐσταυρωμένον· ἠγέρθη, οὐκ ἔστιν ὧδε· ἴδε ὁ τόπος ὅπου ἔθηκαν αὐτόν.
> ἀλλὰ ὑπάγετε εἴπατε τοῖς μαθηταῖς αὐτοῦ καὶ τῷ Πέτρῳ ὅτι προάγει ὑμᾶς εἰς τὴν Γαλιλαίαν· ἐκεῖ αὐτὸν ὄψεσθε, καθὼς εἶπεν ὑμῖν.

In both these instances, the conjunction denotes a break or shift in perspective from that which precedes it. There is therefore good reason to allow the ἀλλά in 13:24 its full adversative sense. A comparison of the synoptic parallels to Mark 13:24 confirms this, for Luke has the conjunction καί instead of ἀλλά (Luke 21:25), while Matthew introduces εὐθέως δέ (Matt. 24:29). Both these evangelists choose not to adopt the adversative conjunction; Matthew in fact counters it by making the connection between this verse and the preceding material closer.[32]

So both the use of ἀλλά in verse 24 and the thematic frame around verses 5b–23 give the impression that verses 24ff are being distinguished from the preceding material. This brings me to the question of the chronology of the discourse.

5. Chronology of the discourse

It seems clear that the events of verses 24ff are to follow the events depicted in verses 5b–23. Does this mean that the discourse as a whole is to be understood chronologically, with the false prophets, wars, earthquakes and famines (verses 5b–8) preceding the persecu-

---

[32] For a full discussion of this, see Chapter 5.5 below.

tions (verses 9–13), then the appearance of the desolating sacrilege (verse 14a), the flight (verses 14b–16), more suffering, and finally further, perhaps different, false prophets and messiahs (verses 21–2)? Some scholars have certainly read the discourse this way.[33] However, there are several considerations which speak against such a strict chronological reading. The first is the 'frame' which I have already discussed. It is as though the first reference to those who will seek to lead many astray has been inserted for reasons of emphasis rather than chronology. The two instances of βλέπετε in verse 5b and verse 23 – which, as shown above, have a sense of urgency for the implied reader – do not support an interpretation which suggests the former danger has past and the latter still threatens; the imperative suggests that they are both warning of a present danger.

The second consideration is that verses 7–8 seem to form the introduction to the discourse. They are ominous but somewhat distant omens which form a prelude to what is to come: δεῖ γενέσθαι, ἀλλ᾽ οὔπω τὸ τέλος (verse 7); ἀρχὴ ὠδίνων ταῦτα (verse 8). Both these phrases link these distant omens to the events to follow, but only as a beginning. These phrases would seem to lend support to the interpretation that the discourse is to be understood strictly chronologically, but the fact that the evangelist precedes these introductory verses with the reference to the leaders who will lead many astray already relativizes the chronology of the discourse.

The third consideration is that it is very difficult to interpret verses 9–13 and verses 14–20 as being chronologically sequential. Verses 9–13 depict a situation of increasing isolation and ostracism, as well as displacement from the familiar environment and imprisonment. Verses 14–20, on the other hand, envisage a situation in which the specifically Judean addressees are at liberty to see the βδέλυγμα τῆς ἐρημώσεως and to flee. Although I will not enter into the question of tradition history at this point, the two scenarios do not seem to be related primarily chronologically, but rather as two concurrent glimpses of persecution, possibly with two distinct groups of implied readers. The reference to οἱ ἐν τῇ Ἰουδαίᾳ implies an awareness of those who are not in Judea, for it would be superfluous to include this qualifying phrase if all implied readers were in Judea. It might be argued that the two sections could be

---

[33] E.g. Hooker, 'Trial', 78–99.

understood chronologically if verses 9–13 referred only to a certain small group, perhaps the leaders of the community, who were scattered, while the majority remained settled in Judea. However, this would be to harmonize rather than to exegete, as verses 9–13 are in no way earmarked for a distinct group only. If anything, verses 14ff are earmarked for a distinct group by the phrase 'those in Judea'. For these reasons, it is preferable to view these two sections (verses 9–13 and verses 14–20) not as chronologically sequential, but as two distinct glimpses of this period of persecution.

A fourth consideration, which will be dealt with more fully in the chapter on the eschatology of Matthew 24 (chapter 5), is the fact that apocalyptic writings are not strictly chronological from beginning to end. There may be sequences, but they often double up and present the same events in a different guise, or from a different perspective.[34]

For these reasons, verses 5b–23 are not to be understood as a strict chronological sequence; in fact, to insist on such a sequence is to misunderstand these verses. Rather, this material is best understood as a number of oracles which speak of the tribulations the followers of Jesus must expect, given from various angles.

To summarize the discussion of Mark 13 from a literary perspective, I began by taking particular account of the Markan themes and motifs which bind the chapter to its context and which are further developed by the discourse. I then examined the form and structure of the discourse. I will now proceed to the issue of tradition and redaction, and will then draw the various threads together by discussing the *Sitz im Leben* for the evangelist and community, so that their respective expectations of the imminence of the End may become apparent.

6. Tradition and redaction

Although many recent scholars, particularly those influenced by the newer literary approaches, have not deemed the question of source to be a major concern, the question of pre-Markan sources cannot be ignored if one hopes to draw any historical conclusions from the text. Given that Mark 13 is indeed the text on the basis of which assumptions about the date and provenance of the Gospel are

[34] Cf. Chapter 5.5, 5.7, 5.8 below.

made, this, of all texts, must be examined from a source-critical perspective.

It is not my purpose to undertake a full review of the various conclusions scholars have reached on the question of tradition in Mark 13; this has, to a large extent, been done already.[35] The history of the interpretation of this chapter may be characterized as one in which the majority of scholars discerned some sort of apocalyptic source, but the extent and nature of the source remained disputed. The verses most often attributed to the source were 14–20 and 24–7, with 7, 8 and 12 often included.[36] Form-critical scholars such as Bultmann followed T. Colani's hypothesis of an underlying Jewish apocalypse which, despite some Christian additions in verses 5–6, 9–11, 13a and 23, remained largely unchanged.[37] However, on the basis of the preceding literary analysis, which has shown how strong the Markan themes and motifs are at each point in the discourse, it is not possible to postulate that the evangelist simply adopted an existing Jewish discourse and inserted some minor additions. Moreover, it is not necessarily the case that the source(s) behind Mark 13 were continuous or all written. Factors which caution against too simple a reconstruction of the tradition history behind Mark 13 include first of all the way in which verses 9–13 and verses 14–20, according to the literary analysis, seem to envisage two differing social settings and groups. Secondly, the discourse contains some possible Q parallels (13:9–13, 21, 31), which raise the question of how this material reached the evangelist, and suggest that the history of traditions behind Mark 13 is probably more complex than Bultmann's hypothesis. Thirdly, verses 28ff retain a number of features which, according to W. J. Ong's study of the psychodynamics of orality, suggest that they were already linked prior to their incorporation into their present Markan context.[38] Fourthly,

---

[35] For a review of earlier scholarship, see Beasley-Murray, *Jesus and the Future* and *Jesus and the Last Days*. Subsequent scholars have invariably spoken highly of Beasley-Murray's literature review, without necessarily accepting his theses. See also Verheyden, 'Persecution'.

[36] This summary statement includes the views of Wendt, *Teaching*, Loisy, *Evangiles*, Wellhausen, *Marci*, Bultmann, *Geschichte*, Hölscher, 'Ursprung', Hahn, 'Parusie', Pesch, *Naherwartungen*, and Brandenburger, *Markus 13*. Many of these scholars also include verses 6–8 and 12, as does Gnilka, *Markus*, though he omits verses 15–16. There are on the other hand scholars who explicitly reject a continuous source, such as Harder, 'Geschichtsbild', and many more recent scholars who do not attempt any sort of reconstruction.

[37] Bultmann, *Geschichte*, 129.   [38] Ong, *Orality*, 37ff.

K. D. Dyer has presented some new syntactical evidence that verses 14–20 and verses 24–7 were not part of a continuous source.[39] The second, third and fourth points require further elaboration.

6.1 Possible Q parallels

(i) Mark 13:9–13. There are two possible Q parallels to parts of this section:
(a) Matt. 10:19/Luke 12:11–12 (cf. S.39, Kloppenborg *Q Parallels*, 126–7).

Although the majority of scholars accept that this tradition was found in Q, I am not convinced of this supposed Q parallel. Only πῶς ἤ and the lack of prefix to the verb μεριμνάω (both textually disputed in Luke) support this parallel. Luke 12:12 has closer links to John 14:26 than to Matthew. This material may have been known to Matthew and Luke apart from Mark (cf. Johannine parallels), but they used Mark's Gospel as their primary source.

(b) Matt. 5:11/Luke 6:22 (cf. S.8, Kloppenborg, 24ff).

This tradition was presumably found in Q. The Q beatitude envisages a situation of insults and (inter-synagogue) conflict, whereas Mark's version expands to beating at the hands of sanhedrins and synagogues and betrayal to Gentile officials. The traditions behind Q and Mark were probably linked at an early oral stage, but have been embellished and adapted according to the experience of the respective communities.

(ii) Mark 13:15/Luke 17:31 (cf. S.66, Kloppenborg, 192).

Luke has positioned this saying in a context in which Q material is prominent, and there is a minor agreement: Matthew/Luke read καὶ ὁ ἐν τῷ ἀγρῷ against Mark's ὁ εἰς τὸν ἀγρόν. However, the agreement is readily explicable as a grammatical improvement to Mark, and the agreement between Mark and Matthew is otherwise so close as to make a Q *Vorlage* improbable, and certainly not demonstrable. I have cause to discuss Luke's use of the eschatological traditions of Mark and Q in chapter 4 (4.4).

---

[39] Dyer, 'Reader', esp. chapter 3.

(iii) Mark 13:21. The Q parallel is Matt. 24:26/Luke 17:23 (cf. S.66, Kloppenborg, 190ff).

At this point, Mark and Q are seen to have made use of the same tradition. This material raises the question, did Mark know the whole Q tradition of Matt. 24:26–8/Luke 17:23–4, 32b, or only the first section (which is used in Mark 13:21)?

The following arguments support the hypothesis that Mark knew the latter Q sayings (Matt. 24:27–8/Luke 17:24, 32b) and omitted them.

(α) The verses on the lightning flash and the corpse seem closely linked in oral tradition to Mark 13:21, for they function as an explanation of why one ought not to follow such prophets – the parousia of Christ will be apparent to all. If these verses were closely linked to Mark 13:21, could Mark have known the one without the others?

(β) Mark may have known them and omitted them. One can see that the evangelist abbreviated heavily in verses 33–7 according to a specific interest in paraenesis (βλέπετε, γρηγορεῖτε).

(γ) These verses contradict the need for careful vigilance which Mark stresses in verses 33–7.

(δ) By using verse 21 without the rest, Mark is able to focus on the issue of false prophets, which seems to be a particular concern of the community.

However, arguments in favour of the hypothesis that Mark did not know the latter Q sayings are:

(α) Mark does not include them.

(β) They would suit the general theme of the material.

(γ) The verses would be in general agreement with Mark 13:26–7.

(δ) If Mark knew these verses, and false prophets were an issue for the community, it would have been logical to include them.

In summary, Mark did indeed have access to a tradition which is also found in Q. The extent of the tradition to which Mark had access is debatable, but it is possible that the evangelist omitted some of the tradition, so as not to contradict the stress on the need for careful vigilance.

(iv) Mark 13:31. The possible Q parallel is Matt. 5:18/ Luke 16:17 (cf. S.61, Kloppenborg, 180–1).

There is no necessary connection between Mark and Q at this point. Given the parallels of this motif of heaven and/or earth passing away outside the synoptic Gospels as well, this saying seems to have been attached in various contexts to indicate the importance and enduring significance of what followed:

Q – the Law;
Mark *et par.* – Jesus' words;
1 John 2:17 – those who do the will of God;
Gospel of Thomas 11 – the living ones.

(v) Mark 13:34–6. The presumed Q parallels are Matt. 25:13–15/Luke 19:12–13 and Matt. 24:45–51/Luke 12: 41–6 (cf. Ss.67, 44, Kloppenborg, 196ff, 138–9).

The divergence of opinion on the sources of these traditions is set out by Kloppenborg in *Q Parallels*, 200. The relative paucity of verbal agreement requires a theory that one or both evangelists redacted the parable substantially. D. Wenham, in *The Rediscovery of Jesus' Eschatological Discourse*, begins his study with this material. He offers insightful and balanced observations about the interrelatedness of the traditions. However, his study is conducted according to the form-critical assumption that there was a single version of the tradition that is recoverable, and I will have cause to question this below. It is quite probable that Q, or two different recensions of Q, formed a source at this point. However, the diverse forms of this parable suggest that various versions may have been passed on independently.

The most significant result of this brief analysis is that verse 21 is seen to have a close parallel in another Christian tradition (Q), so that Bultmann's theory that it belonged to a continuous Jewish source, though not impossible, is most unlikely. More recent scholars such as E. Brandenburger have convincingly attributed verses 9–13 (with the exception of verse 10), verses 21–2 and verse 31 to an oral source or sources.[40]

---

[40] Brandenburger, *Markus 13*, 166. Verheyden largely supports Brandenburger's interpretation, but remains sceptical about the need to postulate a source or sources, 'Persecution', esp.1158–9.

6.2   Oral characteristics of verses 28–32

Many scholars, including M. Hooker in her commentary on Mark's Gospel,[41] have attributed the compilation of verses 28ff to the evangelist. It has often been noted that there are verbal associations which serve to link verses 28 and 29 (ἐγγύς) and verses 30 and 31 (παρέρχομαι). In the light of heightened awareness of the sophistication and skill of the evangelist's compositional technique which the newer literary studies have awakened, there are good grounds for postulating that this material had already been linked at an oral stage prior to its incorporation into Mark's Gospel. The study of oral modes of expression has progressed greatly, to the extent that it is now possible to define characteristics of orally based thought and expression. Let us now consider some of these characteristics as set out by W. Ong in his book *Orality and Literacy: The Technologizing of the Word,* in order to see how they are reflected in Mark 13:28ff.

(a)   Aggregative rather than analytic

Ong states that 'the elements of orally based thought and expression tend to be not so much simple integers as clusters of integers, such as parallel terms or phrases or clauses, antithetical terms or phrases or clauses, epithets'.[42] According to this, the problem which has always vexed scholars, namely the apparent contradiction between verses 30 and 32, would be accounted for as due to the orally based linking of antithetical epithets. Ong explains that in an oral culture, information that could not be readily recalled was lost. The linking of epithets was made on the basis of ease of recall, not strictly linear argument as our contemporary literary-based culture understands it:

> In a primary culture, to solve effectively the problem of retaining and retrieving carefully articulated thought, you have to do your thinking in mnemonic patterns, shaped for ready oral recurrence. Your thought must come into being in heavily rhythmic, balanced patterns, in repetitions or antitheses, in alliterations and assonances, in epithetic and other formulary expressions, in standard thematic settings

[41] Hooker, *Mark*, 320ff.   [42] Ong, *Orality*, 38.

. . . in proverbs which are constantly heard by everyone so that they come to mind readily and which themselves are patterned for retention and ready recall, or in other mnemonic form. Serious thought is intertwined with memory systems.[43]

(b) Rhythmic balanced patterns, alliteration and assonance

Verses 28 and 29 display a balanced pattern, each with a ὅταν clause followed by an apodosis introduced by the imperative γινώσκετε. Moreover, in addition to the repetition of ἐγγύς, the terms θέρος and θύραις form an alliterative link between verses 28 and 29.

Verses 30 and 31 are linked by the repetition of οὐ μή and παρέρχομαι. A more subtle link is the repeated reference to the reliability of Jesus' words:

ἀμὴν λέγω ὑμῖν (verse 30);
οἱ δὲ λόγοι μου οὐ μὴ παρελεύσονται (verse 31).

Verses 32 and 33 may also have been part of this unit of oral tradition, for they are associated by the verb οἶδα and by the synonymous phrases ἡ ἡμέρα ἐκείνη and ὁ καιρός. However, by means of the redactional addition of βλέπετε, verse 33 now forms the introduction to the final section of the discourse. Verse 34 was presumably an originally independent piece of oral tradition, given the Q parallels discussed above.

These features indicate that verses 28–33 were a pre-Markan unit of oral tradition, with the structure of three balanced pairs (verses 28–9, 30–1, 32–3). Verse 33 has been modified by the redactor, through the addition of βλέπετε, and possibly by the omission of the conjunction οὖν, which however appears in verse 35, a verse which functions as a reprise: γρηγορεῖτε οὖν οὐκ οἴδατε γὰρ πότε ὁ κύριος τῆς οἰκίας ἔρχεται.

(c) Agonistically toned

Ong states that 'proverbs and riddles are not used simply to store knowledge but to engage others in verbal and intellectual combat: utterance of one proverb or riddle challenges hearers to top it with

---

43 *Ibid.*, 34.

a more apposite or a contradictory one'.[44] Something of this linking of opposites may be behind the linking of the imperative γινώσκετε, verse 29, to the impossibility of knowing, verse 32, and also the solemn claim of verse 30, backed up by verse 31, to the same impossibility even of the Son knowing, verse 32.

By their juxtaposition, these sayings function not so much as a piece of formal deductive logic, but rather as a riddle: 'The riddle belongs in the oral world. To solve a riddle, canniness is needed: one draws on knowledge, often deeply subconscious, beyond the words themselves in the riddle.'[45] This is one reason why the parable, itself a type of riddle, belongs to oral culture, and why one can be called upon to 'learn a lesson' from a fig tree.

The approach taken here differs from that of W. Kelber in his pioneering work *The Oral and the Written Gospel*. Though he distances himself from his form-critical predecessors in their notion of continuity between oral tradition and written Gospel, Kelber nevertheless chooses to examine Mark's oral legacy in stories exhibiting particular forms (heroic stories, polarization stories, didactic stories and parabolic stories). The sayings material is primarily significant to Kelber for its relative paucity, for this supposedly shows Mark's rejection of the oral medium. Kelber does not endeavour to distinguish between Mark and oral tradition, but rather seeks to show the strong oral legacy which underlies the Gospel. However, lest this imply continuity, he stresses that in writing the Gospel, Mark brought about 'a veritable upheaval of hermeneutical, cognitive realities'.[46] Kelber is convinced that the essential difference lies in the fact that 'performer and audience no longer jointly participate in the making of the message. The writer works in a state of separation from audiences, and hearers or readers are excluded from the process of composition.'[47] This, however, goes beyond what the specialists in orality would accept:

> A text does certainly separate an utterance from its author who, once he has written down his text, may as well be dead. In this sense, writing creates autonomous discourse. But removing an utterance from its author is not removing it from discourse. No utterance can exist outside discourse, outside a transactional setting.[48]

---

[44] *Ibid.*, 44.   [45] *Ibid.*, 3.   [46] Kelber, *Oral and Written Gospel*, 91.
[47] *Ibid.*, 92.   [48] Ong, 'Text', 9.

Although the transactional setting of a written text differs from that of an oral discourse, the written text is nevertheless written for an audience, and an author does not write altogether independently of his or her hearers. It is therefore my opinion that Kelber has drawn the distinction between oral and written discourse, particularly that which is intended to be read aloud, too sharply. Kelber's thesis itself must be understood in its transactional setting over against the excesses of form-criticism.

In view of Mark's strong oral legacy, Kelber does not seek to reconstruct a pre-Markan oral tradition; such an endeavour might be associated with the form-critical notion of a single, continuous oral tradition or with the futile search for the *ipsissima verba* of Jesus. Although there is much to be said in favour of his approach, it is worth considering whether Markan compositional activity can nevertheless be distinguished from pre-Markan oral traditions in their 'frozen' or 'fossilized profiles'.[49] Is it possible to distinguish Markan composition, with its strong oral legacy, from pre-Markan tradition? Some of Kelber's own observations shed light upon this question and enable an affirmative answer. Kelber argues that the Gospel itself is a product of literacy.[50] The shaping of oral traditions into a continuous narrative which is unified and given sequence by the device of the journey is a product of writing, not oral transmission. It follows that in the very act of writing the Gospel, Mark was introducing causal connections and a logical progression, the very features that distinguish written from oral discourse. Kelber states that: 'Devices that foster narrative competence – such as the construction of causal connections, logical relations, close followability, and a tight temporal framework – all thrive under textuality.'[51] Consequently, redactional activity is more likely to be found in connections that display causal or logical relations and which foster 'close followability'. It is less likely to be found where the connections are made more obviously according to sound patterns (rhythmic balance, alliteration, assonance), memory aids such as repetition, or the linking of antithetical epithets. For this reason, I conclude, contra Hooker *et al.*, that Mark did not forge the links in verses 28–33, but rather incorporated an already connected tradition into the eschatological discourse at this point. Such a conclusion does not mean a return to form-criticism as it was prior to Kelber, for it in no way implies

---

[49] Kelber, *Oral and Written Gospel*, 44.   [50] *Ibid.*, 207ff.   [51] *Ibid.*, 188.

that this pre-Markan tradition must have been passed on exactly in this form with no oral variations permitted. On the contrary, the abbreviated 'parable' of verse 28 illustrates Kelber's point about the 'inevitability of change, flexibility and degrees of improvisation in oral transmission',[52] for its synoptic parallels have retained longer, and presumably more complete versions of the parable of the sentry, the thief, the steward and the talents, as discussed above.

6.3   Syntactical evidence for sources behind Mark 13?
K. D. Dyer's syntactical analysis

Let us now turn to the much debated issue of an apocalyptic *Flugblatt* or written source. I do not intend to give a full review of the debate on this issue, as stated above, but rather to give attention to a recent contribution which produces some interesting results, namely K. D. Dyer's syntactical analysis of Mark 13.[53] Dyer argues on the basis of a computer-assisted analysis of Markan syntax that verses 14–20 and verses 24–7 are not from the same source.

According to Dyer, syntax is a more reliable indicator than vocabulary of whether certain material is redactional or belongs to an underlying source. Vocabulary necessarily varies according to the subject matter at hand, but the style of an author can be traced with greater accuracy by his or her use of syntax. Dyer analyses all three word sequences in Mark 13 according to their grammatical categories and makes a comparison of these grammatical sequences with the sequences found in the rest of the Gospel narrative. Where these grammatical sequences differ significantly from those found elsewhere in the Gospel, the likelihood of an underlying source must be reckoned with.

One surprising result of this analysis is that of all the sections in Mark 13 (which he divides as follows: 1–2; 3–6; 7–8; 9–13; 14–20; 21–3; 24–7; 28–31; 32–7), verses 24–7 is the section in which the syntax is most in keeping with that of the Gospel as a whole. By contrast, verses 14–20 have the highest percentage of *unique* syntax of any section in the Gospel of Mark. This means that given the unusual concentration of characteristic, *recurrent* syntax – as Dyer puts it – in verses 24–7 (71.8% according to his analysis) and the

[52] *Ibid.*, 27.   [53] Dyer, 'Reader', 172.

unusual concentration of *unique* syntax in verses 14–20 (12.9%), they can hardly have been part of the same source originally.

Dyer puts forward the hypothesis that there was indeed a written source originally addressed to Jewish Christians in Judea, and that this came to be incorporated in verses 14–20. Verses 24–27, however, were not originally a part of it, for they are, in Dyer's view, a Markan compilation of septuagintal allusions. Scholars have generally reconstructed a pre-Markan source which includes both sections, but Dyer's findings speak strongly against the reconstruction of one unified source for verses 14–20 and 24–7.

There are certain methodological criticisms which one can level at Dyer's method of syntactical analysis. The first is his choice of triple-word syntactical sequences.[54] The problem with such a choice is that it does not take specific account of syntactical units of meaning, which are not necessarily sequential in terms of word order. An analysis of all triple-word sequences, whether or not they are syntactically related, gives equal weighting to both meaningful syntactical units, and to triads composed of fragments from two or more of those units. Although word order is an aspect of syntax, its significance must be analysed relative to the syntax of the sentence or phrase as a whole. For example, in verse 16, a three-word *syntactical* unit would be μὴ ἐπιστρεψάτω . . . ἆραι, not μὴ ἐπιστρεψάτω εἰς, or τὰ ὀπίσω ἆραι or ὀπίσω ἆραι τό which are the 'syntactical units' upon which Dyer's statistics are based and which are listed by him as features unique to Mark 13.[55] The actual syntactical units (such as μὴ ἐπιστρεψάτω . . . ἆραι) are not reflected in his statistics, except when they coincide with word order. Therefore, his statistics are, strictly speaking, an analysis of word order, not syntax, and cannot be given the full weight which might be given to a Markan 'syntacticon'. Dyer himself recognizes that 'the focus of [his] analysis is syntactical word order, rather than a complete analysis of grammar',[56] but he is nevertheless confident (more so than I am!) that this methodology can and does produce suitably representative results.

A second problem of Dyer's method is his grammatical categories or 'tags'. These tags are an abbreviated form of the code developed by B. and T. Friberg in *The Analytical Greek New Testament*, by which they label every Greek part of speech with a

[54] Dyer justifies this choice on 95, n.183.
[55] Dyer, 'Reader', 97.   [56] *Ibid.*, 345.

single letter, and parse each word with a string of these letters. These tags may be useful as a parsing guide, but they do not give a wider picture of syntactical relations. To continue with the example of verse 16, the grammatical tag Dyer gives to ὀπίσω is 'adverb used as an adjective', while the more complex Friberg tag is 'adverbial adjective used as a pronominal adjective'. Either way, these tags virtually guarantee that ὀπίσω will be considered unique, for the emphasis is on grammatical rubrics rather than function. It would have been better to regard the three-word grouping εἰς τὰ ὀπίσω not as an example of unique syntax, but as a necessary part of an idiomatic phrase. A further and perhaps even more obvious example is the tag given to ἴδε, verse 21. Dyer defines it as a 'particle'; if it had been given the tag 'imperative', the results for this verse, in which two occurrences of ἴδε yield five instances of unique syntax, would presumably have fallen out differently.

A third problem, not exclusively of Dyer's analysis, but rather of all such analyses, is the difficulty in attributing particular features to Markan redaction. Recurrent syntax may indicate the recurrent use of a source, as Dyer himself acknowledges.[57] The fact that Mark's syntax appears to be heavily influenced by the Septuagint complicates matters even further, for a passage which contains a number of septuagintal allusions, as verses 24–7 do, will necessarily appear redactional.

Nevertheless, despite these reservations as to the ability of Dyer's method of syntactical analysis to quantify and interpret unique and recurrent syntax with quite the precision that he claims, his results are sufficiently striking as to make it quite unlikely that verses 14–20 and 24–7 were originally part of the same source. For my purposes, it is worth considering whether the hypothesis that verses 14–20 and 24–7 were originally independent can be supported in other ways.

7.   A Judean oracle behind Mark 13:14ff?

One striking difference between verses 14–18 and the other material in Mark 13 that has been frequently attributed to an apocalyptic source (verses 7, 8, 12, 24–7) is the lack of parallels to its key words and ideas in other New Testament writings.

(i)   τὸ βδέλυγμα τῆς ἐρημώσεως does not appear elsewhere in

---

the New Testament except in the Matthean parallel to this passage.[58]

(ii) τὸ βδέλυγμα appears in Luke 16:15, Rev. 17:4–5, 21:27, but without the specific Danielic reference and connotation.

(iii) Such urgent flight is nowhere else enjoined in the New Testament. The closest parallel is Rev. 12:6,[59] which has been understood by some scholars as a reference to the flight of the Jerusalem church to Pella.[60] Flight to the mountains and great urgency has a parallel in Gen. 19:12ff, and also in 1 Macc. 2:28, but these are not in contexts which are concerned primarily with future eschatological events. Where the motif of flight to the mountains appears in an eschatological context, it is not enjoined upon the reader. Rather, it is used as a description of the fear that will overcome the enemies of God's people, and as a warning that the mountains are not a safe haven in the face of God's wrath (cf. Isa. 2:9–21, 34:3, Ezek. 32:5–6, Hos. 10:8, which is echoed in Rev. 6:15–16, 4 Ezra 15:42, 58, 62). This suggests strongly that Mark 13:14ff has a tradition history more closely aligned with this-worldly conflict, such as is found in 1 and 2 Maccabees, and not with the eschatological passages of the Hebrew scriptures and the intertestamental writings. If this is so, this sets Mark 13:14ff in sharp contrast to the other traditions behind the eschatological discourse in Mark 13.

(iv) Prayer that events may not happen in winter/a storm (verse 18) is nowhere enjoined. On the contrary, the various writings of the New Testament reflect an expectation that 'that day' will bring such cataclysmic changes that the weather will be rendered irrelevant. This also suggests that the tradition originated not as a prophecy of the final eschatological summation, but as an oracle intended to have a specific and localized application.

For these reasons, it seems likely that Mark 13:14ff does indeed

---

[58] The background of the phrase τὸ βδέλυγμα τῆς ἐρημώσεως in Daniel and 1 Maccabees is discussed below.

[59] I assume that Luke 17:31 is dependent on Mark 13:15.

[60] Cf. Sowers, 'Circumstances'. The question of the historicity of this tradition will be dealt with in chapter 4 below.

have a tradition history that differs from the other material that has often been attributed to the one source, namely verses 7, 8, 12 and 24–7. This supports Dyer's results at least partially.[61] It is therefore possible to examine verses 14ff further, in order to ascertain the probable parameters of this pre-Markan tradition. Rather than calling this tradition a *Flugblatt* or flier, with all the associations that this has, I will call it a 'Judean oracle'.

One of the criteria for isolating this Judean oracle is its lack of New Testament parallels, and also its closer association with passages from the Hebrew scriptures and intertestamental writings which reflect contemporary political concerns rather than those which deal with future eschatological visions. Verses 14–18, with the possible exception of verse 17, fit this criterion, whereas verses 19–20 have parallels (cf. Joel 2:2, Dan. 12:1, Rev. 1:9, 7:14). I will therefore proceed on the assumption that verses 14–18, possibly with the exception of verse 17, contain an adapted version of this oracle. If this was a specific Judean oracle which has been subsequently incorporated into the Gospel, it is quite likely that the phrase which qualifies the addressees – οἱ ἐν τῇ Ἰουδαίᾳ – is redactional, as has often been observed. This phrase implies an awareness of the concerns of those who are not in Judea, which is more readily attributable to the redactor of the tradition than to the original tradition itself. The original tradition most probably would have read not τότε οἱ ἐν τῇ Ἰουδαίᾳ φευγέτωσαν εἰς τὰ ὄρη, but rather τότε φεύγετε εἰς τὰ ὄρη, in keeping with the second person plural imperative in verse 14a.

The phrase ὁ ἀναγινώσκων νοείτω could be attributed either to the pre-Markan oracle, in which case the oracle would have been passed on in written form, or to the hand of the redactor. It is impossible to be absolutely certain either way, but the balance of probabilities favours a pre-Markan origin, as such a direct address to the reader occurs nowhere else in the Gospel. It would be overstating the case, however, to call the phrase 'unmarkan', as the evangelist chose to retain, if not to formulate, the phrase.

The attribution of verse 17 to this Judean oracle is uncertain on several grounds. In form, it is more readily connected to the other material in this chapter, particularly verse 24, where the phrase ἐν

---

[61] I made these observations independently in 1988, prior to the appearance of Dyer's thesis, and presented them at a *Doktorandenkolloquium* in Basle, Switzerland, on 4 February 1989.

ἐκείναις ταῖς ἡμέραις also appears. Moreover the 'woe' formula is more characteristic of apocalyptic writings (e.g. 4 Ezra 15:24, 47, 16:63, 77) than of specific urgent instructions. In verse 17, unlike in the rest of the Judean oracle (verses 14–18), no specific action is urged. In terms of thematic parallels to this verse, 4 Ezra 16:37ff and also 1 Cor. 7:28–9 may be mentioned; in both these texts, the impending disaster cautions against bearing and rearing children. The 4 Ezra passage is of particular interest, because a description of the apocalyptic birth pangs is followed by warnings against childbearing; this is similar to the reference to the apocalyptic birth pangs in Mark 13:8 and to the 'woe formula' addressed to pregnant women and nursing mothers, Mark 13:17. For these reasons, verse 17 may be tentatively assigned to the other material in Mark 13. Consequently, the following reconstruction of the Judean oracle may be attempted.

7.1 Proposed reconstruction of the Judean Oracle.
Table 2

> ὅταν ἴδητε τὸ βδέλυγμα τῆς ἐρημώσεως ἑστηκότα ὅπου
> οὐ δεῖ
>   ὁ ἀναγινώσκων νοείτω
> τότε φεύγετε εἰς τὰ ὄρη,
> ὁ ἐπὶ τοῦ δώματος μὴ καταβάτω
> μηδὲ εἰσελθάτω ἆραι τι ἐκ τῆς οἰκίας αὐτοῦ,
> καὶ ὁ εἰς τὸν ἀγρὸν μὴ ἐπιστρεψάτω
> εἰς τὰ ὀπίσω ἆραι τὸ ἱμάτιον αὐτοῦ.
> προσεύχεσθε δὲ ἵνα μὴ γένηται χειμῶνος.

Certain characteristics of this oracle can now be discerned:

(i) It consists of specific urgent instructions for a localized group, namely those who can see a particular localized sign (τὸ βδέλυγμα τῆς ἐρημώσεως).

(ii) It features direct address, both in the second person plural imperative (ἴδητε, φεύγ[ετε], προσεύχετε) calling to positive action, and in the third person singular imperatives (μὴ καταβάτω, μηδὲ εἰσελθάτω ἆραι, μὴ ἐπιστρεψάτω ἆραι) urging avoidance of certain actions.

(iii) It presupposes in its readers a prior knowledge of, or readiness for the sign (i.e. at least some idea of what τὸ βδέλυγμα τῆς ἐρημώσεως is).

(iv)   The masculine participle ἑστηκότα does not agree with its
        neuter antecedent – τὸ βδέλυγμα – and indicates that the
        oracle envisages a man standing where he should not be.

(v)   It possibly indicates that the writer wishes the reference to
        remain cryptic to outsiders.

Any interpretation of Mark 13 has to account for these verses. The
explanation that they refer to the 'antichrist' is difficult for two
reasons. The first is that the supposed parallel in 2 Thess. 2 is
probably much later than was once thought[62] and, therefore,
cannot serve as an interpretative key. Moreover the differences
between Mark 13:14ff and 2 Thess. 2 are more striking than the
similarities.

The second reason that Mark 13:14 cannot easily be explained as
a reference to an antichrist figure is the warning in Mark 13:22
against false christs and false prophets, which does not sit easily
with the notion of a single antichrist figure. For these reasons, it
seems better to explain Mark 13:14ff as an oracle which arose in the
face of a particular historical situation in Judea, rather than one
which originated as a vision of an antichrist as is found in 2 Thess.
2.[63] The simplest, and in my opinion most convincing, explanation
of these verses is that there was indeed an oracle incorporated by
Mark into the eschatological discourse at this point. The historical
implications of this will be dealt with at the end of this Chapter.

8.   An apocalyptic source?

Let us now turn our attention to the other material in this discourse
which has often been attributed to an apocalyptic source, namely
verses 7, 8, [17], 19, 20, 24–7. J. Wellhausen and F. Hahn have also
included verses 21 and 22, but in view of the Q parallel discussed
above, most scholars have not included these verses in their
reconstructions of the source. Verses 9–13 are widely regarded, I
think correctly, as distinct from the source. They are often attributed, with the possible exception of verse 10, to a distinct oral

---

[62] Cf. Trilling, *Thessalonicher*, 22ff.

[63] This is not to deny that the oracle, once incorporated into Mark's Gospel,
contributed to the development of the concept of an antichrist figure. Hengel
convincingly traces the origin of the single antichrist figure to the fear of *Nero
redivivus*, in his essay 'Origin and Situation'. However, I do not accept his
interpretation of the relationship between Mark 13 and 2 Thess. 2, nor his
explanation of the origin of Mark 13:14ff.

tradition which was transmitted in various forms and is reflected both in Q (cf. Kloppenborg, S39) and John 16:2, 15:21, 14:26.

Once one has excluded the material of the Judean oracle, it is not immediately apparent whether the remaining material, often attributed to an apocalyptic source (7–8, 17, 19–20, 24–7), came to Mark in an already unified form, or whether the evangelist was responsible for bringing these traditions together. However, the material shares certain characteristics which suggest the former:

(i) With the exception of verse 7, the material is descriptive rather than paraenetic. One result of this is that, with the exception of verse 7, there is no direct address. This is striking, given the frequency of and emphasis in the discourse on paraenesis and the preference given in all the other major sections of the discourse (9–13, 14–18, 21–3, 28–32, 33–7) to direct address.

(ii) There are recurrent words and phrases in the material that are not obviously redactional and which suggest that the material was already unified prior to Markan redaction. These include ἐν ἐκείναις ταῖς ἡμέραις, verses 17 and 24, as well as the related phrases αἱ ἡμέραι ἐκεῖναι, verse 19 and ἐκολόβωσεν τὰς ἡμέρας, twice in verse 20; the reference to θλῖψις, verses 19 and 24, the concern for τοὺς ἐκλεκτούς, verses 20 and 27. The material also contains examples of genuine redundancy: ἀπ᾽ ἀρχῆς κτίσεως ἣν ἔκτισεν ὁ θεός, verse 19, and διὰ τοὺς ἐκλεκτοὺς οὓς ἐξελέξατο, verse 20. As such redundancy has been shown to be rare within Mark's Gospel as a whole,[64] these examples and the other repetitions indicate a pre-Markan formulation.

(iii) The sequence of the material, logically and chronologically, suggests that the material may well have been unified prior to the Markan redaction. In fact, the chronology of the material is clearer than that of the Markan discourse as it stands, for, as argued above, the two references to false prophets break down any strict chronological sequence. Moreover, it is not clear on the redactional level that the events of verses 14ff are expected to follow directly the persecution described in the preceding

---

[64] Neirynck, *Duality*, 46.

8.1 Proposed reconstruction of apocalyptic source for Mark 13: Table 3

	Some OT and extra-canonical parallels	NT thematic parallels.*
A: National disturbances		
v.8 Ἐγερθήσεται ἔθνος ἐπ' ἔθνος καὶ βασιλεία ἐπὶ βασιλείαν, ἔσονται σεισμοὶ κατὰ τόπους,	4 Ezra 13:30–2; 2 Chr. 15:6 4 Ezra 13:30–2; Isa. 19:2 Isa. 13:13	Rev. 16:14 (Matt. 27:54; 28:2?) Rev. 6:12; 8:5; 11:13, 19; 16:18
ἔσονται λιμοί ἀρχὴ ὠδίνων ταῦτα.	Isa. 8:21 Ps. 48:6; Jer. 4:31	John 16:20–2; 1 Thess. 5:3
B: Fate of the elect		
v.17 οὐαὶ δὲ ταῖς ἐν γαστρὶ ἐχούσαις καὶ ταῖς θηλαζούσαις ἐν ἐκείναις ταῖς ἡμέραις.	(1 Enoch 99:5)	cf. 1 Cor. 7:28–9
v.19 ἔσονται γὰρ αἱ ἡμέραι ἐκεῖναι θλῖψις οἵα οὐ γέγονεν τοιαύτη ἀπ' ἀρχῆς κτίσεως ἣν ἔκτισεν ὁ θεὸς ἕως τοῦ νῦν καὶ οὐ μὴ γένηται.	Joel 2:2; Dan. 12:1; Exod. 9:18	2 Cor. 4:17–18; Rev. 1:9; 7:14
v.20 καὶ εἰ μὴ ἐκολόβωσεν κύριος τὰς ἡμέρας, οὐκ ἂν ἐσώθη πᾶσα σάρξ·	4 Ezra 2:13; 1 Enoch 5:5, 9	cf. 1 Cor. 7:29 Rom. 8:33 (links elect with suffering)
ἀλλὰ διὰ τοὺς ἐκλεκτοὺς οὓς ἐξελέξατο ἐκολόβωσεν τὰς ἡμέρας.	4 Ezra 2:13; 1 Enoch 5:5, 9	Rev. 17:14

C: Cosmic disturbances

v.24 [καὶ] ἐν ἐκείναις ταῖς ἡμέραις		
μετὰ τὴν θλίψιν ἐκείνην	Joel 2:10b; 3:4; 4:15; Isa. 13:10	e.g. Rev. 9:6
ὁ ἥλιος σκοτισθήσεται		Rev. 6:12ff; 8:12; (21:23)
καὶ ἡ σελήνη οὐ δώσει τὸ φέγγος αὐτῆς	Isa. 13:10; Joel 2:10	
v.25 καὶ οἱ ἀστέρες ἔσονται ἐκ τοῦ οὐρανοῦ πίπτοντες	Isa. 34:4;	Rev. 6:12ff; 8:12; (21:23)
καὶ αἱ δυνάμεις αἱ ἐν τοῖς οὐρανοῖς σαλευθήσονται.	cf. Isa. 13:10a	

D: Future of the elect

v.26 καὶ τότε ὄψονται		
τὸν υἱὸν τοῦ ἀνθρώπου ἐρχόμενον ἐν νεφέλαις	Dan. 7:13	1 Thess. 4:16; Mark 14:62?
μετὰ δυνάμεως πολλῆς καὶ δόξης	Zech. 14:5	2 Thess. 1:7
v.27 καὶ τότε ἀποστελεῖ τοὺς ἀγγέλους	Deut. 30:4	
καὶ ἐπισυνάξει τοὺς ἐκλεκτοὺς αὐτοῦ	Zech. 2:10	1 Thess. 4:17
ἐκ τῶν τεσσάρων ἀνέμων		
ἀπ᾽ ἄκρου γῆς ἕως ἄκρου οὐρανοῦ.	Deut. 30:4	

---

* Only those are listed which are not directly dependent on Mark 13.

verses, because the conjunction τότε does not connect verse 14 to what precedes it; rather, the more open-ended ὅταν is used. The specific time references of the discourse (other than τότε) such as ἀρχὴ ὠδίνων ταῦτα, verse 8, and μετὰ τὴν θλῖψιν ἐκείνην, verse 24, belong to this material.

For all of the above reasons, one may postulate that there is a pre-Markan, presumably oral tradition discernible in the discourse which is distinct from the Judean oracle. I offer the preceding reconstruction, which omits verse 7 for the reasons set out below.

This reconstruction (pp. 94–5) indicates a suggested emendation to the Markan text with square brackets. At the beginning of section C (verse 24), the Markan ἀλλά is replaced by καί, for, as argued above, the adversative conjunction reflects Markan rather than pre-Markan interests. Verse 17 has been included because of its thematic links to what precedes it (ἀρχὴ ὠδίνων ταῦτα), and because the verb in the third person is in keeping with the rest of the reconstructed source.

The omission of verse 7 is the most controversial aspect of this reconstruction. Although verse 7 shows similar apocalyptic interests and *topoi* to the subsequent material, two of the three verbs (ἀκούσητε, μὴ θροεῖσθε) are in the second person and show the paraenetic interest of the rest of the discourse, which of course reflects the interests of the evangelist. Secondly, the divine δεῖ, although also an apocalyptic *topos*, appears elsewhere in the chapter only at verse 10, which is widely regarded as a redactional addition to the traditional material in verses 9–13. Moreover, the retarding aspect of verse 7 (οὔπω τὸ τέλος) is also a feature of verse 10: καὶ εἰς πάντα τὰ ἔθνη πρῶτον δεῖ κηρυχθῆναι τὸ εὐαγγέλιον. This suggests that both these verses may be Markan insertions. Thirdly, the assurance of οὔπω τὸ τέλος does not sit well with the chronological indicator in verse 8: ἀρχὴ ὠδίνων ταῦτα, which itself indicates that the End has not yet arrived. For these reasons, I attribute verse 7, despite its apocalyptic flavour, to the evangelist.

There are several structural features of the reconstruction that add weight to its plausibility:

(i)   A and C focus on disturbances in the 'natural order', first national (A) and then cosmic (C).

(ii) B and D focus on the fate of the elect. Both refer to οἱ ἐκλεκτοί in their final phrase.

(iii)   B and C share the key phrase ἐν ἐκείναις ταῖς ἡμέραις and the key word θλῖψις.
(iv)   B and D both have the construction ἀπ᾽ . . . ἕως.
(v)   A commences and D ends with parallelism.

The reconstructed source has a great range of parallels from the Hebrew scriptures and intertestamental writings, as well as many New Testament thematic parallels. These are set out in the columns in Table 3. Given these parallels, it is no surprise that the language is strongly septuagintal, as Dyer observed. There is, however, no reason to postulate that verses 24ff originated with Mark, as Dyer does, for the indications are that Mark has utilized a pre-existing tradition and incorporated it into the discourse in order to provide, not a series of objective and observable signs (as the pre-Markan tradition seems to have done), but rather a re-presentation of early Christian eschatological hope shaped according to the interests of paraenesis.

This reconstruction therefore supports the view of many scholars that the primary interest of the Markan discourse is paraenesis. However, this is not because Mark was in any sense anti-apocalyptic, as Brandenburger has rightly argued. If this were the case, the eschatological discourse of Mark 13 would presumably not have included the apocalyptic source reconstructed above. Rather, the evangelist has incorporated and shaped an early Christian tradition which was shared by many other streams of early Christianity (though not necessarily in this form), and has focussed the discourse in order to address perceived issues within the community. Now it remains to ascertain what these were, and what can be said of the historical circumstances which are revealed in Mark 13.

9.   The *Sitz im Leben* of Mark 13

The evangelist and the Markan community are in no sense to be located chronologically in a 'gap' between verses 23 and 24, but rather in the main body of the discourse, verses 5b–23, with verses 7–8 as implied past. This means that verses 14ff, in which I have discerned a Judean oracle, are regarded as pertaining to the present, though the flight itself has presumably taken place, bringing the oracle, with the result that it became available to Mark. This implies that there may well have been an influx of

Judean Christians into the Markan community, a theory which Dyer supports as well. That the flight has already taken place is supported by the *lack* of the Markan βλέπετε at verse 14, for this imperative signals the most pressing issues for the community. In what sense, then, could the flight be viewed as present? Does this reflect a differing view among this ancient society of what constitutes the present, such as Malina claimed (cf. the discussion in chapter 1, 2.3 above)? This may be so, but I would suggest that even in our modern society, in times of war, events that have taken place are not viewed as past or over and done with until such time as the war is finally over and its effects have been put behind the people affected. In this sense, the flight belonged to wartime and the effects of wartime were still present reality. This does not necessitate a pre-seventy dating. On the contrary, the disturbing repercussions of the first Jewish War and the fall of Jerusalem were to continue to resound for many years to come. However, the location of Mark's community was outside Judea, presumably Syria, and so the community itself was relatively isolated from the most severe effects of the war. If there was indeed an influx of Judean Christians, which is the most straightforward explanation for the presence of the Judean oracle in Mark's discourse, then this must have had a destabilizing effect upon the community. As the effects of persecution and war throughout history have led to a heightening of apocalyptic expectation, one may postulate that the influx of Christians from war-torn Judea, bearing an oracle which had led to their escape, led to a heightened expectation among the Markan community. Such a heightened expectation would make the community particularly vulnerable to prophets who spoke with the authority of Christ himself, and it is these prophets that Mark particularly warns against, using the authority that the prophets themselves claim – that of Jesus' own words. It is likely that the false prophets in question were not 'home-grown', but rather came in with the influx of Judean Christians, which heightened their aura of authority in the eyes of the primarily Gentile Markan community. It has been pointed out by W. Kelber, among others, that Mark does not afford great respect to Jerusalem and the Christian authorities that were based there, and perhaps it was for this reason.

A central motif in Mark's Gospel which is also implicit in the eschatological discourse is the disqualification of the Temple in Jerusalem. The Judean oracle is relevant, not simply to humour the

Judean Christians and their supporters, but as a model for *leaving* the Temple. The emphasis that Mark gives to the disqualification of the Temple is a strong indication that for at least some of Mark's community, the Jerusalem Temple was of great concern. This could be interpreted as evidence for a pre-seventy dating, but the extent of Mark's concern with its disqualification is more comprehensible as a theological response to its destruction. In my view, this is an indication of the Gospel's date of composition, perhaps the strongest indication in the Gospel (though by no means incontrovertible). The destruction of the Temple is foreshadowed in verse 2, but the discourse as a whole directs the disciples' and the readers' attention away from the destruction of the Temple as a factor of any significance. Moreover, the Judean oracle, which most nearly has a bearing on the fate of the Temple, is in no way linked chronologically with the eschatological denouement in verses 24ff. In order to make the absence of such a link absolutely clear, the evangelist includes the warnings about false christs and false prophets as well as some traditions from the reconstructed apocalyptic source between the Judean oracle and verses 24ff. Mark's approach pushes the community to perceive the world as no longer Temple-centred. The destruction of the Temple is foreshadowed by Jesus and is a direct result of its failure to receive the Son (cf. the parable of the wicked tenants, Mark 12:1–12). Conversely, though, its destruction does not offer an alternative to the way of the cross. Mark perceives that the destruction of the Temple is not an occasion for exultation or apocalyptic fervour. Rather, Mark interprets the war and its effects as calling Jesus' followers to a deeper commitment to the way of the cross. It is this theology of the cross that enables the evangelist to step back from the enthusiasm within the community and to write a remarkably balanced discourse which neither rejects future hope nor succumbs to apocalyptic fervour.

There are several features which I have attributed to Mark which retard, though do not negate, the expectation of an imminent End: verses 7, 10, and the adversative conjunction ἀλλά in verse 24. The final sections of the discourse, which emphasize the fact that the time of the End is unknown, lend further weight to this. The eschatological drama, in which they are all players, is to be much bigger than the community thinks. All nations, and in fact the whole cosmos, are God's concern, and Christ's followers are to make this concern their own (verse 10). The persecutions of which verses 9–13 speak are to be understood as a sharing in Christ's mission and in the way of the cross.

I claimed earlier that the discourse was interested in paraenesis rather than in objective signs. The issues facing the community which require exhortation are clearly signposted by the redactional βλέπετε: false prophets, persecutions, and the fact that the time of the End is unknown. These concerns can be accounted for as the evangelist's call to the way of the cross in the face of apocalyptic expectation. The warnings are not about the pressures themselves so much as about the readers' position *vis-à-vis* these pressures.

My purpose has been to examine the expectation of an imminent End in Mark 13. I have argued that there was a heightened expectation of the End within Mark's community, fuelled by the destruction of the Temple, and the influx of Judean Christians and their prophets who spoke in the name of Jesus. The evangelist is critical not of the expectation itself but of the power the heightened expectation has to distract the community from the way of the cross. The evangelist considers the 'present' to be the time represented within verses 5b–23, with the time of the eschatological culmination unknown.

4

THE JUDEAN FLIGHT ORACLE (MARK 13:14FF) AND THE PELLA FLIGHT TRADITION

In the discussion of Mark 13:14ff I discerned a Judean oracle which was incorporated into the Markan eschatological discourse, and I undertook to explore the historical implications of this further. The discernment of such an oracle re-opens the much-debated question of the relationship between this synoptic material and the tradition of a flight by Jerusalem Christians to Pella prior to the Jewish War. I will outline the state of the question with regard to the origin of this tradition and offer some criticisms of the debate as it stands. Having done this, I will weigh the evidence which speaks for and against an association between the flight tradition of Mark 13:14ff and the Pella flight traditions of Eusebius and Epiphanius. In conclusion, I will present some historical reflections on the circumstances during which the Judean oracle may have been composed, as well as the circumstances which led to its transmission to the Markan community. The aim of the discussion is to see whether further evidence can be adduced which supports this present historical reconstruction of the factors shaping the eschatology of Mark and the Markan community.

1. The debate about the historicity of the Pella flight tradition

There has been renewed interest recently in the question of the historicity of a tradition recorded by Eusebius and Epiphanius of a flight of Jerusalem Christians to Pella just prior to the Jewish War of 70 CE. This interest was sparked by an essay by G. Lüdemann which appeared in 1980,[1] in a revised and extended form in *Paulus, der Heidenapostel* II in 1983, and in English translation in 1989 in *Opposition to Paul in Jewish Christianity*. Lüdemann's thesis is that

---

[1] Lüdemann, 'Successors'.

the Pella tradition arose in the second century among Jewish Christians in Pella who sought to legitimize their form of Christianity by linking it to the original Jerusalem congregation. He discusses first of all the texts which explicitly refer to this flight and those which have been seen to refer to it implicitly. He then examines indications which point to a continual Christian presence in Jerusalem, and concludes that the Pella tradition has no value for the question of the fate of the Jerusalem church during the Jewish War.[2]

An American scholar, C. Koester, examined Lüdemann's arguments in an article entitled 'The Origin and Significance of the Flight to Pella Tradition'. He takes issue with Lüdemann's position, arguing that 'the ancient sources do not suggest that the Pella tradition was created or ever used to legitimate the Pella congregation's form of Jewish Christianity'.[3] Rather, 'the Pella tradition was used to strengthen Christian claims by showing how God spared Christians from the destruction experienced by Jews in A.D. 70'.[4] Koester takes what might be called the more traditional position, namely that the most plausible explanation for the origin of the tradition is that it recalls actual events of the first century.

J. Verheyden takes up the debate in his article 'The Flight of the Christians to Pella', and argues against the historicity of the flight. He gives an extended evaluation of Koester's arguments, and seeks to show that the Pella flight tradition is to be attributed to Eusebius himself, whose account is theologically motivated and who mentioned Pella in order to give the account credibility. Verheyden's understanding of the *function* of the Pella tradition in Eusebius is not unlike Koester's, who, as quoted above, sees the tradition strengthening Christian claims by showing how God spared Christians from the destruction of Jerusalem. It is with regard to the *origin* of the tradition that Verheyden and Koester disagree; in Verheyden's view, Eusebius himself is the inventor of the tradition, whereas for Koester, 'Eusebius almost certainly did not contrive the story.'[5]

Most recently, F. Blanchetière and R. Pritz defend the historicity of a flight, citing a Roman policy of the resettlement of refugees which they discern from Josephus.[6] Their article does not, however, contribute substantially to the debate.

---

[2] Lüdemann, *Opposition*, 211.   [3] Koester, 'Origin', 106.
[4] *Ibid.*, 106.   [5] *Ibid.*, 91.   [6] Blanchetière and Pritz, 'Migration'.

The present discussion must begin with some reflections on the appropriateness of linking Mark 13 with a discussion of the Pella flight tradition at all. In order to avoid unduly biasing the discussion, I will examine the synoptic material as it is found in the Gospels, rather than in the form of the reconstructed Judean oracle.

The enigmatic oracle of Mark 13:14 makes reference to flight to the mountains: ὅταν δὲ ἴδητε τὸ βδέλυγμα τῆς ἐρημώσεως ἑστη-κότα ὅπου οὐ δεῖ, ὁ ἀναγινώσκων νοείτω, τότε οἱ ἐν τῇ Ἰουδαίᾳ φευγέτωσαν εἰς τὰ ὄρη . . . This reference to flight, with its Judean provenance and its presumed links with the Jewish War of 66–70 CE, has long encouraged scholars to associate it with the tradition that an oracle given prior to the Jewish War led Jerusalem Christians to flee the city and settle in the Transjordanian city of Pella and the surrounding region of Perea (viz. Eusebius' *Historia ecclesiastica* 3.5.3, and Epiphanius' *Panarion* or *Refutation of all Heresies* (*Pan.*) 29.7.7–8, 30.2.7 and *De mensuris et ponderibus* or *Treatise on Weights and Measures* (*W&M*)15). However, in recent years, this association has been called into question.

Lüdemann includes some brief remarks on Mark 13:14ff in his discussion of the Pella flight tradition, but rejects the material as an implicit witness to a Pella flight tradition for two reasons. The first is that Mark 13:14ff speaks only generally of a flight and that the reference to mountains cannot be equated with the mountains east of the Jordan. The second is that Mark 13:14ff presupposes a different chronology from that of Eusebius; Eusebius records that the prophecy was given before the war, whereas Mark 13:14ff calls for a flight during the war.[7] On examination, neither of these reasons for rejecting an association between the traditions is compelling. The first claims that Mark 13:14ff is to be rejected as an implicit witness because it is not *explicit*: Pella itself is not mentioned, nor are the mountains specified. Pella and the specific mountain range are not mentioned in the relevant Pseudo-Clementine passages either, yet these are to be accepted as implicit witnesses, according to Lüdemann, because they originated in the Pella region and are therefore in keeping with Lüdemann's theory of the origin of the flight. This argument is narrowly circular, and presupposes certain theories of the place and date of the origin of

---

[7] Lüdemann, *Opposition*, 207.

Mark's Gospel which preclude the possibility that Mark could have been aware of such a tradition. Such a case could perhaps be made, but Lüdemann does not make it.

Lüdemann's second reason for rejecting Mark 13:14ff as an implicit witness is a supposed incompatibility of chronology between Eusebius and Mark 13:14ff. The text of Eusebius to which Lüdemann refers reads as follows:

> ... καὶ τοῦ λαοῦ τῆς ἐν Ἱεροσολύμοις ἐκκλησίας κατά τινα χρησμὸν τοῖς αὐτόθι δοκίμοις δι᾽ ἀποκαλύψεως ἐκδοθέντα πρὸ τοῦ πολέμου μεταναστῆναι τῆς πόλεως καί τινα τῆς Περαίας πόλιν οἰκεῖν κεκελευσμένου, Πέλλαν αὐτὴν ὀνομάζουσιν, ἐν ᾗ τῶν εἰς Χριστὸν πεπιστευκότων ἀπὸ τῆς Ἱερουσαλὴμ μετῳκισμένων, ὡς ἂν παντελῶς ἐπιλελοιπότων ἁγίων ἀνδρῶν αὐτήν τε τὴν Ἰουδαίων βασιλικὴν μητρόπολιν καὶ σύμπασαν τὴν Ἰουδαίαν γῆν, ἡ ἐκ θεοῦ δίκη λοιπὸν αὐτοὺς ἅτε τοσαῦτα εἰς τε τὸν Χριστὸν καὶ τοὺς ἀποστόλους αὐτοῦ παρηνομηκότας μετῄει, τῶν ἀσεβῶν ἄρδην τὴν γενεὰν αὐτὴν ἐκείνην ἐξ ἀνθρώπων ἀφανίζουσα. (*Hist. eccl.* 3.5.3)

> ... the people of the church in Jerusalem were commanded by an oracle given by revelation before the war to those in the city who were worthy of it to depart and dwell in one of the cities of Perea which they called Pella. To it those who believed on Christ migrated from Jerusalem, that when holy men had altogether deserted the royal capital of the Jews and the whole land of Judea, the judgement of God might at last overtake them for all their crimes against the Christ and his Apostles, and all that generation of the wicked be utterly blotted out from among humanity.[8]

Lüdemann assumes without discussion that the prepositional phrase πρὸ τοῦ πολέμου (before the war) qualifies the infinitive which follows it (μεταναστῆναι τῆς πόλεως – to depart the city) and not the participial phrase which precedes it (δι᾽ ἀποκαλύψεως ἐκδοθέντα – given by revelation). It has been read both ways (cf.

---

[8] The edition cited is Loeb with some minor modifications by the present author in the interests of accurately reflecting the Greek distinction between men specifically and humanity in general.

K. Lake's and C. Koester's translations),[9] and is therefore not a strong basis upon which to claim an incompatibility between the chronology of Mark 13:14ff and Eusebius' account. On these grounds alone, it would seem that Lüdemann has been too ready to dismiss Mark 13:14ff as a text which may have some connection with the Pella flight tradition.

The second issue which Lüdemann has raised – the relationship between the flight tradition of the synoptic Gospels (Mark 13:14ff *et par.*) and Eusebius' account – requires more attention. In contrast to Lüdemann's position, Verheyden argues that Eusebius draws the inspiration for his presentation of a flight from Jerusalem to Pella from the New Testament passages, and that Eusebius' passage on Pella seems to be a 'historicising way of presenting the same kind of ideas'.[10] To Lüdemann, the accounts are incompatible; to Verheyden, they are conceptually closely associated. How can such diametrically opposing positions be drawn from the same data?

2. The evidence of Eusebius

If Eusebius does indeed draw the inspiration for his presentation of a flight from Jerusalem to Pella from New Testament passages, as Verheyden claims, one passage that would be central is Luke 21:20ff, which speaks explicitly of the siege of Jerusalem and flight from the city. However, when one examines Eusebius' *Historia ecclesiastica* 3.7, one finds that despite the quite extensive quotations which Eusebius makes from Luke 21, direct reference to verse 21 is absent. Verheyden observes that the motif of ἡμέραι ἐκδικήσεως in Luke 21:22 is central to Eusebius' presentation, and therefore assumes that Eusebius has also drawn on Luke 21:21 in order to devise a Pella flight tradition. However, if we look more carefully at the beginning of *Historia ecclesiastica* 3.7, we find that Eusebius applies the flight tradition (in the Matthean form) *not to the Jerusalem church*, but to the *Jewish population of Judea* as a whole.

---

[9] Compare the cited translation by Lake, especially the phrase '*given by revelation before the war*', with Koester's translation, in 'Origin', 91: 'The people of the church in Jerusalem, in accordance with a certain oracle that was given through revelation to those who were worthy in the place, were commanded *to migrate from the city before the war* and to settle in a certain city of Perea – Pella it was called . . .' (emphasis mine).

[10] Verheyden, 'Flight', 381–2.

By applying Matt. 24:19–21 to the Jews (rather than to the Jerusalem church), the oracle is made to serve as a further instance of Jewish impiety; instead of regarding the Saviour's prophecy to flee, they turned to the city for protection:

> Τοιαῦτα τῆς Ἰουδαίων εἰς τὸν Χριστὸν τοῦ θεοῦ παρα-
> νομίας τε καὶ δυσσεβείας τἀπίχειρα, παραθεῖναι δ᾽ αὐτοῖς
> ἄξιον καὶ τὴν ἀψευδῆ τοῦ σωτῆρος ἡμῶν πρόρρησιν, δι᾽
> ἧς αὐτὰ ταῦτα δηλοῖ ὧδέ πως προφητεύων οὐαὶ δὲ ταῖς ἐν
> γαστρὶ ἐχούσαις καὶ ταῖς θηλαζούσαις ἐν ἐκείναις ταῖς
> ἡμέραις· προσεύχεσθε δὲ ἵνα μὴ γένηται ὑμῶν ἡ φυγὴ
> χειμῶνος μηδὲ σαββάτῳ. ἔσται γὰρ τότε θλῖψις μεγάλη,
> οἵα οὐκ ἐγένετο ἀπ᾽ ἀρχῆς κόσμου ἕως τοῦ νῦν, οὐδὲ μὴ
> γένηται.   (*Hist. eccl.* 3.7.1)

Such was the reward of the iniquity of the Jews and of their impiety against the Christ of God, but it is worth appending to it the infallible forecast of our Saviour in which he prophetically expounded these very things, – 'Woe unto them that are with child and give suck in those days, but pray that your flight be not in the winter nor on a Sabbath day, for there shall then be great affliction such as was not from the beginning of the world until now, nor shall be.'

To Eusebius, the synoptic flight oracle and the Pella flight oracle are quite distinct. The synoptic flight oracle prophesied the general plight of Jews in Judea at the time of the Jewish War, whereas the Pella flight oracle was given later 'by revelation' specifically to the church in Jerusalem. In Eusebius' view, then, the synoptic flight oracle and the Pella oracle did indeed have a different chronology, the former being a prophecy of the earthly Jesus concerning the course of the war, and the latter being given and heeded directly before the war.

At face value, this might seem to favour Lüdemann's position: the chronology of the synoptic flight oracle and Eusebius' Pella oracle are different, and so the origins of these traditions are not linked. However, it is one thing to say that Eusebius saw the traditions as distinct, and another to say that Eusebius' view settles the matter. One important consideration is that if Eusebius learned that the Pella flight was enjoined upon the Jerusalem church by an oracle given to certain worthy people, it could not, in Eusebius' view, be the same oracle as that recorded in the Gospels, as this was spoken by Jesus himself. Contemporary scholarship does not share the same compulsion to see these as necessarily distinct, for it is recognized that the evangelist(s) incorporated later oracles of the 'Risen Lord' as part of the Gospel accounts of the earthly Jesus' teaching.

When this difference in perspective between ourselves and Eusebius is taken into account, an interesting implication emerges. There is little doubt that Eusebius historicizes biblical accounts when at all possible, as Verheyden argues. *The fact that he keeps these flight traditions quite separate speaks against the idea that the Pella flight tradition is his own invention.* Had he invented it, he could have associated the Pella flight with the synoptic oracle, and understood the synoptic passage as addressed to Christians (as it is in the Markan and Matthean accounts).[11] Instead, *it seems that the Pella flight tradition which came to him included the detail that it was an oracle given by revelation.*

Thus it may be said that both Lüdemann's and Verheyden's arguments have some truth to them; the chronologies of the synoptic flight oracle and the Pella flight oracle do differ in Eusebius' *Historia ecclesiastica* and Eusebius does tend to historicize biblical accounts. Nevertheless, neither position goes far enough in examining the relationship of the flight oracles. Eusebius keeps these oracles separate, and this implies that he did not invent the Pella tradition, but in fact learned of it in a form that included some reference to its having been given by revelation to certain worthy people. This neither proves nor disproves the historicity of the Pella tradition, nor does it prove or disprove that the synoptic flight oracle and the Pella flight oracle were originally linked. What

---

[11] The flight oracle is not part of the public ministry of Jesus in the Gospels of Mark and Matthew. Peter, James and John receive the eschatological discourse in Mark, while in Matthew the disciples receive it. In both cases, the evangelists note that it took place κατ᾽ ἰδίαν, with the implication that those outside the circle of Jesus' followers were not privy to the information. Luke does not specify who the audience was, but indicates by the summary verses which conclude the discourse (Luke 21:37–8) that the teaching was public. Eusebius' understanding of the eschatological discourse relies most heavily on the Lukan version, and it may be that his notion that the Jews culpably disregarded Jesus' prophecy concerning them stems from Luke's presentation of the eschatological discourse as public teaching. It is, however, equally possible that Eusebius was not concerned about whether the teaching was public or private; in his view, had the Jews not rejected their saviour, they would not have been subjected to the fearful events of the Jewish War.

it does indicate is that the Pella tradition was not invented by
Eusebius, as Verheyden proposes, but that it came to Eusebius with
certain details which he retained in his own account.

If the Pella tradition predates Eusebius, why does he not
acknowledge his source? Often, Eusebius does indicate his sources,
but he is also quite capable of acknowledging the fact that he does
not know a particular source (e.g. *Hist. eccl.* 3.36.11) or indicating
the suspicious nature of a piece of information (e.g. *Hist. eccl.*
5.16.13–15). In general, though, it seems that the orthodoxy of a
source was the guarantee of its reliability (cf. *Hist. eccl.* 3.23.2), and
thus M. Gödecke writes of Eusebius: 'If he considers a source of
information to be reliable, even if that is only on the basis of its
"authority", then Eusebius tests its assertions much less thoroughly.'[12] One may assume, then, that Eusebius considered his
source at this point to be orthodox and reliable. Just prior to this
passage, Eusebius summarizes some information from Hegesippus'
Hypomnemata, without acknowledging his source, so Hegesippus
has long been held to be the likely source of the Pella tradition as
well. Lüdemann, however, takes up a proposal of A. Harnack and
A. Schlatter that Ariston of Pella was Eusebius' source for the
tradition of the flight to Pella. While this is possible, the balance of
likelihood still rests with Hegesippus, given that there is no way of
showing whether Ariston described the first Jewish War at all.
What can be said is that Eusebius' account indicates that the
apostles were not part of the fleeing church (*Hist. eccl.* 3.5.2). It is
therefore unlikely that Eusebius' source implied otherwise, as we
might expect if the source arose amongst a group seeking to
legitimize their apostolic origins (Lüdemann's theory). Moreover,
the source cannot have been explicitly Ebionite, given Eusebius'
opinion of them (cf. *Hist. eccl.* 3.27).[13]

The fact that Eusebius does not name his source at this point
need not and presumably does not mean that he had no source;

---

[12] Gödecke, *Geschichte*, 32–3 (translation mine).
[13] On the question of Ariston's relationship to Jewish Christianity, cf. Lüdemann,
Opposition, 205 and n.30 on 311–12. If Ariston did have Jewish-Christian
connections, then these cannot have been very explicit in the *Dialogues* available
to Eusebius. Given that any reconstruction of Ariston depends upon Eusebius,
the question of Ariston's Jewish-Christian links remains open. However, one
cannot have it both ways; either Ariston shared the supposed tendency to
legitimize the apostolic origins of Jewish Christianity in and around Pella, or he
was accepted and used by Eusebius as an orthodox source.

rather, it more probably indicates that he thought of his source as sufficiently reliable to obviate the need for such acknowledgement.

3. The evidence of Epiphanius

The question of the source of Epiphanius' three references to a Pella flight (*Pan.* 29.7.7–8, 30.2.7, *W&M* 15) is also much debated. The traditions are as follows:[14]

Pan. 29.7.7–8

7. ἔστιν δὲ αὕτη ἡ αἵρεσις ἡ Ναζωραίων ἐν τῇ Βεροιαίων περὶ τὴν Κοίλην Συρίαν καὶ ἐν τῇ Δεκαπόλει περὶ τὰ τῆς Πέλλης μέρη καὶ ἐν τῇ Βασανίτιδι ἐν τῇ λεγομένῃ Κωκάβῃ, Χωχάβῃ δὲ Ἑβραϊστὶ λεγομένῃ. 8. ἐκεῖθεν γὰρ ἡ ἀρχὴ γέγονε, μετὰ τὴν ἀπὸ τῶν Ἰεροσολύμων μετά-στασιν πάντων τῶν μαθητῶν ἐν Πέλλῃ ᾠκηκότων, Χριστοῦ φήσαντος καταλεῖψαι τὰ Ἰεροσόλυμα καὶ ἀναχωρῆσαι δι᾽ ἣν ἤμελλε πάσχειν πολιορκίαν. καὶ ἐκ τῆς τοιαύτης ὑποθέσεως τὴν Περαίαν οἰκήσαντες ἐκεῖσε, ὡς ἔφην, διέτριβον. ἐντεῦθεν ἡ κατὰ τοὺς Ναζωραίους αἵρεσις ἔσχεν τὴν ἀρχήν.

7. This heresy of the Nazoraeans exists in Beroea in the neighbourhood of Coele Syria and the Decapolis in the region of Pella and in Basanitis in the so-called Kokaba, Chochabe in Hebrew. 8. For from there it took its beginning after the exodus from Jerusalem when all the disciples went to live in Pella because Christ had told them to leave Jerusalem and to go away since it would undergo a siege. Because of this advice they lived in Perea after having moved to that place, as I said. There the Nazoraean heresy had its beginning.

Pan. 30.2.7

γέγονε δὲ ἡ ἀρχὴ τούτων μετὰ τὴν τῶν Ἰεροσολύμων ἅλωσιν. ἐπειδὴ γὰρ πάντες οἱ εἰς Χριστὸν πεπιστευκότες τὴν Περαίαν κατ᾽ ἐκεῖνο καιροῦ κατῴκησαν τὸ πλεῖστον, ἐν Πέλλῃ τινὶ πόλει καλουμένῃ τῆς Δεκαπόλεως τῆς ἐν τῷ εὐαγγελίῳ γεγραμμένης πλησίον τῆς Βαταναίας καὶ Βασανίτιδος χώρας, τὸ τηνικαῦτα ἐκεῖ μεταναστάντων

---

[14] Texts and translations of *Panarion* are from Klijn and Reinink, *Patristic Evidence*.

καὶ ἐκεῖσε διατριβόντων αὐτῶν, γέγονεν ἐκ τούτου πρόφασις τῷ Ἐβίωνι.

Their [i.e. the Ebionites'] origin goes back to the time after
the capture of Jerusalem. For after all those who believed
in Christ had generally come to live in Perea, in a city
called Pella of the Decapolis of which it is written in the
Gospel that it is situated in the neighbourhood of the
region of Batanaea and Basanitis, Ebion's preaching originated here after they had moved to this place and had lived
there.

W & M. 15[15]

ἡνίκα γὰρ ἔμελλεν ἡ πόλις ἁλίσκεσθαι ὑπὸ τῶν Ῥωμαίων,
προεχρηματίσθησαν ὑπὸ ἀγγέλου πάντες οἱ μαθηταὶ
μεταστῆναι ἀπὸ τῆς πόλεως, μελλούσης ἄρδην ἀπόλλυ-
σθαι. οἵτινες καὶ μετανάσται γενόμενοι ᾤκησαν ἐν
Πέλλῃ ... πέραν τοῦ Ἰορδάνου, ἥτις ἐκ Δεκαπόλεως
λέγεται εἶναι.

For when the city [i.e. Jerusalem] was about to be taken by
the Romans, it was revealed in advance to all the disciples
by an angel that they should flee from the city, as it was
going to be completely destroyed. After they had fled,[16]
they settled in Pella ... across the Jordan, which is said to
be of the Decapolis.

C. Koester argues in favour of Epiphanius' independent use of the
Pella tradition, whereas Lüdemann and Verheyden seek to show
that Epiphanius' references are all dependent upon Eusebius. While
it is instructive to weigh the occurrence of similar and identical
words in Eusebius' and Epiphanius' accounts, as Koester does, it is
possible to make a case either way. If one is of the opinion that
Eusebius himself was the source of the tradition, as Verheyden is,
then Epiphanius must necessarily be dependent upon Eusebius at
this point. However, if it is accepted that Eusebius did not invent
the Pella tradition, but used a source, then the similarities between
Eusebius' and Epiphanius' Pella references may not be due to
Epiphanius' direct use of Eusebius (or memory of Eusebius), but
rather to a common source.

[15] Text from *PG* 43, cols. 260–1, translation mine.
[16] Cf. 4.1.iii below.

While the interrelationship between Eusebius' and Epiphanius' Pella references may be open to various interpretations, one may glean some clues from the contexts of these references. The two references in *Panarion* to the Pella flight both occur in the context of the origin of a Jewish-Christian sect, which Epiphanius calls ἡ αἵρεσις ἡ Ναζωραίων and ἡ κατὰ τοὺς Ναζωραίους αἵρεσις in 29.7.7–8, and πρόφασις τῷ ᾿Εβίωνι in 30.2.7. It seems clear that Epiphanius is seeking to emphasize the connection between the Nazoraeans and the Ebionites.[17] Epiphanius links the flight to Pella and the rise of the Ebionite heresy by means of locality – Perea, and Pella in particular. This is in contrast to Eusebius, who makes no mention of Perea or Pella in relation to the Ebionites (*Hist. eccl.* 3.27). Epiphanius also informs his readers that the heresy stemmed from 'Ebion's pretence', making it clear that, according to his sources, Ebion was a person. Eusebius, on the other hand, derives the name ᾿Εβιωναίους not from a person, but from the Hebrew word meaning 'poor'. These two dissimilarities between Epiphanius and Eusebius indicate that Epiphanius must have had access to a source other than Eusebius, which linked the Ebionites with Perea/ Pella, and this source was presumably not at the disposal of Eusebius, who is completely positive with regard to the flight and completely negative with regard to the Ebionites. Epiphanius may have conflated this source either with the Pella account from Eusebius or perhaps with Eusebius' source (presumably Hegesippus), or this source may itself have contained reference to the Pella flight tradition. Thus, though I cannot show that Epiphanius did not know Eusebius at this point, there is evidence that Epiphanius used at least one source other than Eusebius which referred to Pella.[18] One could perhaps postulate that Epiphanius recalled Eusebius' flight reference and invented the Perea/Pella connection to the Ebionite heresy himself. However, it does not seem as though we are dealing with an invention by Epiphanius at

---

[17] Cf. Pritz, *Nazarene Jewish Christianity*, 21–2, whose thesis is that the Nazoraeans and the Ebionites differed in their christology, the former being more 'orthodox'. On the divergent orthography of Nazoraean, Nazarean etc., see Blanchetière, 'Secte des Nazaréens'.

[18] Pritz, *Nazarene Jewish Christianity*, 26, proposes Tertullian (*De praescriptione haereticorum* X 8; XXXIII 5: 11; *De virginibus velandis*. 6,1; *De carne Christi* 14; 18; 24) or Pseudo-Tertullian (*Ref. omnes haereses* VII 35, 1; *Adversus omnes haereses* as the source.

this point, given the other indications that the Ebionites were indeed based in that region.[19]

To summarize the discussion to this point, then, I have shown that there is good reason to assume that Eusebius made use of a source in his mention of a flight to Pella. Epiphanius, for his part, had access to a different source which linked the Ebionites and Pella: one which was, therefore, neither Eusebius, nor Eusebius' source. Eusebius' source included the detail that the flight oracle was given by revelation to certain members of the Jerusalem church before the war.[20]

4. Is there a link between the Pella flight tradition and the Judean flight oracle?

Let us now move to the question of whether the Pella flight tradition and the synoptic flight oracle may have been originally linked. The scholars who maintain the likelihood of a historical flight to Pella, such as C. Koester and M. Hengel, are prepared to postulate a link between the Lukan form of the synoptic flight oracle (Luke 21:21) and the flight to Pella,[21] but reject either explicitly (M. Hengel) or implicitly (C. Koester) any link with the Markan form of the oracle. It is necessary to examine the Lukan material in order to see whether a Pella flight can be more readily associated with Luke than with Mark.

It is clear that Luke has adapted the Markan *Vorlage* to reflect the events of the Jewish War. Luke replaces the enigmatic βδέλυγμα τῆς ἐρημώσεως with an explicit reference to the military siege of Jerusalem (Luke 21:20), omits the reference to winter (the destruction of Jerusalem took place in late August/early September), and makes explicit what fate the Jewish people will suffer at the hands of the Gentiles (Luke 21:23–4). Luke fundamentally reworks Mark 13:14–20 in order to make clearer what refers to Jerusalem and what to the world, what refers to the tribulation of the Jewish War and what is still to come, and also what is a message for the Jewish nation and what is primarily for those who

---

[19] Cf. Strecker, *Judenchristentum*, 253. See also Pritz, *Nazarene Jewish Christianity*, Appendix II: Geography, 120–1.

[20] Whether one reads πρὸ τοῦ πολέμου as qualifying what precedes or what follows it, both have the implication that the oracle was given in time for the Jerusalem church to flee.

[21] Koester, 'Origin', 103ff; Hengel, 'Origin and Situation', 18, n.111.

follow Christ.[22] Luke takes what was in Mark a piece of esoteric teaching only to Peter, James, John and Andrew and transforms it into an oracle to the Jewish nation spoken publicly within the Temple (Luke 21:37). The injunction to flight and the words against returning to retrieve any goods are split, not simply by placing the latter in a different location (Luke 17:31), but by radically altering their application. Flight from the city is enjoined upon all Jews and clearly refers to the events of the Jewish War. The latter words against retrieving goods, however, are addressed to the disciples, and refer exclusively to the final events of the eschatological drama, at which time the only appropriate action is to stand up and raise one's head to receive the approaching redemption (Luke 21:28). Luke thus makes the distinction between past and future events clearer, and shifts the narrative audience, so that the flight oracle addresses the Jewish nation prior to the War.

Given that this is so, the idea that Luke had access to a Pella flight oracle, which was addressed to Jewish Christians, enabling them to escape the destruction of the city, is rendered highly unlikely. The Lukan version of the saying is in no way seen to be addressing an audience comparable with that addressed by the Pella flight oracle. Thus Luke does not seem to have been aware of any such flight, and it is unconvincing to postulate a greater knowledge in Luke than in Mark of a flight to Pella. The scholars that do so are assuming that the greater detail which Luke gives about the Jewish War may also include a greater knowledge about a flight to Pella, but they do not take into account the Lukan shift in the narrative audience from Jewish-Christian to the Jewish nation, and thus they are mistaken in seeking to link the Pella flight oracle to the Lukan form of the synoptic flight oracle.

Therefore, if there is any link between the Pella flight oracle and the synoptic flight oracle, this link must be sought with the Markan version. As Lüdemann points out in his discussion of the Pella tradition, it is methodologically unsound to introduce the question of historicity too early or to move too quickly to the historical circumstances surrounding a possible flight.[23] If this question is introduced early, the discussion of the Markan passage is made to hinge on whether such a flight seems plausible to a scholar. It seems implausible to Hengel, who claims that this instruction does not

---

[22] Cf. Fitzmyer, *Luke (X-XXIV)*, 1329.   [23] Lüdemann, *Opposition*, 202.

tally with any historical situation known to us,[24] and therefore concludes that it cannot date from the time of the Jewish War. One problem with such an argument is that it assumes that our knowledge of the Jewish War is so thorough and reliable as to imply that Josephus was omnipresent; his account is taken to be lacking only when he is being obviously tendentious. This is perhaps something of a caricature of such a position, but my intention is to point out the danger which exists when one has such an apparently comprehensive external source as Josephus, namely that one assumes too readily the ability to judge what is historically possible and what is not. It is no simple matter to judge what actually took place on the basis of Josephus' writings, and it is just as difficult, or even more so, to judge what did not take place. Any extrapolation from Josephus' writings as to what *cannot* have taken place needs to be viewed very circumspectly.

Another problem of such an argument is that while the text may not slot readily into what is known about the Jewish War, it does not slot readily into any other historical context either, as Hengel's statement admits. Hengel therefore takes Mark 13:14 as a reference to the antichrist, specifically *Nero redivivus*, and takes the flight reference as allegorically addressed to Mark's own community in Rome.[25] Such a hypothesis requires (a) the conviction that Mark's community was in fact located in Rome, (b) that one takes the reference to Judea allegorically, (c) that there is a surprising and by no means obvious shift in verses 14ff from a *Nero redivivus* in the *Jerusalem* sanctuary to the flight of Christians from *Rome,* and (d) a certainty that the primary meaning can in no way be compatible with Josephus' portrayal of the Jewish War. Whether this hypothesis is more plausible than one which locates the origin of the flight oracle in Judea will be addressed presently.[26] Before this takes place, it is necessary to suspend our presuppositions as to what was or was not historically possible during the Jewish War, and undertake a comparison of the synoptic flight oracle and the Pella flight oracle, so as to weigh the likelihood of a link between them.

---

[24] Hengel, 'Origin and Situation', 17.
[25] *Ibid.*, 20. Note that the allusion to the Jerusalem Temple (verse 14) is not interpreted allegorically by Hengel (27–8).
[26] It is, however, worth noting at this point the criticisms which Theissen has of Hengel's 'fascinating interpretation': the sequence in Mark 13 is first wars and then persecutions, whereas the historical situation of Rome in the 60s was that the persecutions (*c.* 64 CE) preceded the wars (66–70). Secondly, the governors and kings of Mark 13:9 point to the East rather than to Rome. See *Gospels*, 126, n. 3.

C. Koester isolates three main elements in the Pella tradition of Eusebius: (a) the miraculous escape of Christians from Jerusalem, (b) their relocation in Pella, (c) the subsequent destruction of Jerusalem.[27] While this is correct, it is important for my purposes to emphasize certain aspects of the tradition which have long made its association with the synoptic flight oracle attractive. The following comparison is made on the basis of Eusebius' version of the Pella flight tradition (printed above, page 104) and Mark 13:14.

4.1   Factors which speak in favour of an association between Mark 13:14 and *Hist. eccl.* 3.5.3

4.1.i. Provenance

Eusebius' Pella flight oracle is specifically located in Jerusalem. The Jerusalem provenance of the synoptic oracle is indicated by:

(a)   the allusion to the Temple implicit in the phrase τὸ βδέλυγμα τῆς ἐρημώσεως ἑστηκότα ὅπου οὐ δεῖ, appropriating the imagery and vocabulary of the Book of Daniel (Dan. 9:27, 11:31. 12:11), which refer to the desecration of the Jerusalem Temple under Antiochus IV Epiphanes;
(b)   the mention of Judea;
(c)   the narrative setting within the Gospel of Mark, though this cannot bear the same weight as the previous indications.

Given these factors, it is highly likely that these oracles are of the same provenance.

4.1.ii. Date

Eusebius' Pella flight oracle is dated prior to the Jewish War. The original date of the synoptic flight oracle is more difficult to ascertain. I have been working on the assumption that we are dealing with a pre-Markan oracle; even Mark 13:14b (ὁ ἀναγινώσκων νοείτω), which is the phrase most likely to betray the evangelist's hand, may well be pre-Markan, given that nowhere else does the evangelist directly address the reader in such a

---

[27] Koester, 'Origin', 91.

way.[28] The oracle presumably originated prior to the events which it foreshadows; this is the most straightforward explanation of the exhortation to flight that it contains. One of Mark's earliest interpreters, Luke, understood the enigmatic warning as a description of Jerusalem being surrounded by camps (or armies),[29] and had no apparent problem with the question of whether or not it had still been possible to escape (Luke 21:21). It is most probable that the synoptic flight oracle was understood by Mark as pertaining to the Jewish War.

Nevertheless, it has been argued that the oracle originated at the time of Caligula when he gave orders to raise a statue of himself in the Temple, 40 CE.[30] The basis of this theory is, once again, that the oracle does not seem to fit well enough with what is known of the first Jewish War, particularly of the events in 70 CE, but this assumes that the βδέλυγμα τῆς ἐρημώσεως must necessarily be identified with the Roman general Titus, which is open to question, as I shall argue below. A further disadvantage of this early dating of the oracle is that one must postulate a further stage in which the earlier oracle was perceived as becoming relevant once again. E. Schweizer assumes that in the turmoil of the years prior to 70, it was feared that the events that had been prevented at the last moment back in the year 40 would now come about.[31] If this (old) oracle could be perceived as relevant, then such an oracle could just as well have originated at the time. Schweizer cites the Maccabean flight as a model (cf. 1 Macc. 2:28), but there is no reason why the Maccabean model should more clearly pertain to 40 CE than to 66 CE. It is therefore most logical to assume that the oracle originated prior to the events it was understood to address, namely the Jewish War.

There is therefore reason to conclude that the two flight oracles originated prior to the Jewish War of 70 CE.

4.1.iii. Content

I have, for the sake of clarity, been calling the oracle to which Eusebius refers in *Hist. eccl.* 3.5.3 a 'flight' oracle. However, the

---

[28] Cf. the discussion of this question in Lührmann, *Markusevangelium*, 222.

[29] Cf. Fitzmyer, *Luke (X–XXIV)*, 1344.

[30] E.g. Schweizer, *Mark*, 272. The most recent edition of the commentary, *Markus*, 17th newly revised edition, 144, continues to maintain this position.

[31] Schweizer, *Markus*, 144.

noun φυγή and the verb φεύγω are not used in Eusebius' text; the relevant verbs in this text are μεταναστεύω and μετοικίζω, the former meaning 'remove, depart, flee', and the latter 'go to another country, emigrate'. The latter has the connotation of an orderly migration or resettlement, while the former gives the sense that those departing are doing so as fugitives.[32] Eusebius gives no specific indication of the extent of the oracle itself, but if any of Eusebius' text reflects the wording that he received from his source, it would be the verb μεταναστεύω rather than μετοικίζω, which seems to belong to Eusebius' own commentary, the extent of which I will discuss below. If this is so, then the term 'flight oracle' is not inappropriate, given that μεταναστεύω also has the connotation of fleeing.

I have observed that some of the material seems to be Eusebius' own commentary. When Eusebius moves on from the material dealing with the flight to describe how this enabled the destruction of Jerusalem, one is almost certainly dealing with Eusebius' own interpretation of and commentary on his source, for this theme is a hallmark of *Historia ecclesiastica*. On this basis, it seems likely that the material which follows the mention of Perea and Pella is Eusebius' commentary, but the reference to Perea and Pella belonged to his source. Eusebius gives no indication that he had the actual words of the oracle at his disposal; rather, it seems that his source was already in the form of a report on the oracle which led to the flight from Jerusalem and resettlement in Pella.

If it is the case that Eusebius, and presumably his source before him, had access to a *report* on the flight oracle rather than to the oracle itself, there is little point in endeavouring to make direct comparisons between the wording of Eusebius' material and the wording of the synoptic flight oracle. Dissimilarity between the wording could not, on this basis, disprove a link between them. It is content, then, rather than wording, that must form the basis of any comparison between *Hist. eccl.* 3.5.3. and Mark 13:14.

The content of Eusebius' flight tradition has two main elements, apart from provenance and date: the command to flee or depart, and the reference to Perea/Pella. The former has a synoptic counterpart, whereas the latter does not.

Before moving on to the issue of the reference to Perea/Pella, I will summarize the elements which are comparable and which have

---

[32] LSJ, 1114.

long made the association between the synoptic flight oracle and Eusebius' oracle attractive: the provenance, the date and the command to flee all speak in favour of an association between the oracles. The dissimilarity of wording speaks neither for nor against such an association, if it is accepted that Eusebius had access to a report of the oracle rather than the oracle itself.

4.2   Factors which speak against an association between Mark 13:14 and *Hist. eccl.* 3.5.3

The primary factor which speaks against an association between the oracles is the reference to Perea/Pella in *Hist. eccl.* 3.5.3. The task at hand is to evaluate the weight which should be given to this factor and whether it renders an association between the oracles unlikely or impossible.

I have postulated that Eusebius had access to a *report* concerning an oracle commanding flight from Jerusalem to Pella, and not to the original oracle itself. If this is accepted, then we are dealing with material which looks back on the flight, including its outcome. It is conceivable that one or more elements of the outcome may have been incorporated into the report in such a way as to imply that they were part of the original oracle. The reference to Perea and Pella may be one such element, indicating what came to be the destination of the flight.

It is possible, then, that Pella became the destination of the flight because of its location on the northward trade route along the edge of the East Jordan plateau which ran from Arabia to Damascus. The Jordan valley is the most likely direction for a flight from Jerusalem, and all the more so if the flight were to take place during the winter months, given its much more temperate conditions.[33]

---

[33] Archeological excavations of Pella (Tabaqat Fahl) in a joint project of Wooster College and Sydney University have led R.H. Smith to publish what he takes to be evidence of Christian presence in Pella in the latter part of the first century, *viz. Pella of the Decapolis 1*, 143–9. The evidence hinges on the interpretation of the presence of a first-century Roman sarcophagus in the floor of the northern apse of a sixth-century Byzantine church. This part of a Byzantine church sometimes served as a martyr's chapel and repository for relics of saints. The church seems to have been built in such a way that the grave would rest just below the paving, suggesting that the positioning was intended to venerate the remains of a very important person. When excavated, the sarcophagus was found to contain the remains of a second interment from the mid-seventh century, when a small cross seems to have been added to the edge of the receptacle. Smith postulates that Persian looting which devastated many Christian sites in the period may have led

However, Pella has seemed to scholars an unlikely destination
for a band of fleeing Jewish Christians, not simply because of the
strongly hellenistic nature of this Decapolis city, but also because
of Josephus' reference to a pillaging of certain Decapolis cities
including Pella in 66 CE by bands of Jews enraged at the pogrom at
Caesarea (*J.W.*, II.457–65). R. A. Pritz points out that this
pillaging should not be overrated, though, for in Gerasa, another
Decapolis city which came under attack, whatever happened was
not serious enough to damage the previous good relations between
the Gentile and Jewish inhabitants; in this city at least, the Gentile
inhabitants subsequently protected and aided their Jewish fellow
citizens (*J.W.*, II.480).[34] Nevertheless, whatever the nature of the
pillaging, it is not easy to postulate that a group of Jewish
Christians chanced upon Pella and found themselves welcome
there. Rather, a more reasonable assumption would be that they
had some connections in Pella, familial or religious, which made
Pella a suitable destination. It is reasonable to assume that there
could have been a Jewish or Jewish-Christian population in Pella,
given that there were Jewish populations in Pella's sister cities
Scythopolis and Gerasa (*J.W.*, II.466–80).[35]

If there were familial or religious connections between the
Jerusalem congregation and certain people within Pella, this would
mean that the leaders of the Jerusalem church may have thought of
Pella as a destination before they left Jerusalem, bringing the
command to flee and the destination of Pella into close connection.
Whether this is so or not, it is possible to view the reference to
Perea/Pella as a later accretion.

The synoptic flight oracle records no destination, but only
direction: εἰς τὰ ὄρη. Given the allusion to the Jerusalem Temple
implicit in the reference τὸ βδέλυγμα τῆς ἐρημώσεως, the function
of the oracle is to enjoin flight in the opposite direction to that
which would normally have presented itself – into the city. Rather
than referring to a destination, the words εἰς τὰ ὄρη are the

---

to the disturbance of the grave and to the second interment. The original grave he
links with the flight of Jewish Christians to Pella. His interpretation is most
recently supported by Weber in *Pella Decapolitana*, 18, 76–7.

[34] Pritz, *Nazarene Jewish Christianity*, 125.

[35] Pritz postulates that the connection would have been a Gentile Christian church.
While this is possible, the harmony which this implies between Jewish and Gentile
Christian congregations may be somewhat idealistic, given what is known of
Paul's struggle to bring Jewish and Gentile Christians into fellowship.

functional equivalent of 'away'. They echo the flight of the Maccabees to the hills (ἔφυγον εἰς τὰ ὄρη 1 Macc. 2:28), and in doing so
maintain the cryptic nature of the oracle.

J. Murphy-O'Connor, in a recent article entitled 'The Cenacle–
Topographical Setting for Acts 2:44–45', has given some attention
to this aspect of my argument as it stood prior to the present
revision. He expresses reservation with regard to the inclusion of
the phrase 'to the mountains' in my reconstructed flight oracle, as
'it is lowland language and inappropriate for Jerusalemites living
on the mountain of the Lord'.[36] While his point is well made, he
does not give sufficient weight, in my opinion, to the Maccabean
parallel (1 Macc. 2:28), where flight to the hills marked the
beginning of their organized resistance. The hills referred to in 1
Maccabees were those in the vicinity of Modein, not those of
Transjordan, but this indicates in my opinion how certain phrases
could become *topoi*, which could be reused and reapplied at will. A
Jerusalemite could make use of this phrase as much as a 'lowlander'
in order to spread an injunction to flee from the city while
maintaining the anonymity afforded by a known *topos*.

Thus, while this direction – to the mountains – is the functional
equivalent of 'away' and therefore certainly not incompatible with
a flight to Pella, as C. Koester has pointed out, it is not directly
comparable with the destination recorded by Eusebius' report.

To conclude this discussion of the reference to Perea/Pella, one
may say that it represents a dissimilarity, though not incompatibility, between the oracles in question. It introduces an element of
destination that is not present in the synoptic oracle. It is possible
that the reference to Perea/Pella is a later accretion, either as a
remembrance of the outcome of the flight, or a remembrance of the
chosen destination for the flight. Alternatively, if one considers a
scenario in which some of the fleeing Jerusalem Christians did not
remain in Pella, but continued northwards towards Syria and came
into contact with the Markan community, then the lack of any
reference to Pella in the synoptic version is not at all surprising.
Whether this lack is due to the suppression of the Pella reference or
due to the fact that the Pella reference was a later accretion is
impossible to say. Epiphanius' second reference to the flight, in
Pan. 30.2.7, lends some support to the hypothesis that not all the

---

[36] Murphy-O'Connor, 'Cenacle', 317 n.66

refugees settled in Pella, in that he notes that τὸ πλεῖστον settled in Perea: ἐπειδὴ γὰρ πάντες οἱ εἰς Χριστὸν πεπιστευκότες τὴν Περαίαν κατ᾿ ἐκεῖνο καιροῦ κατῴκησαν τὸ πλεῖστον . . . ('for after all those who believed in Christ had generally come to live in Perea' . . .). One of this discussion's most significant contributions to the debate is the observation that Eusebius' source seems to have been a report of the oracle rather than the oracle itself. In the light of this, one must reckon with the possibility or even probability that such an accretion to or adaptation of the original form took place.

In addition to the dissimilarity between the oracles which the reference to Pella represents, there have been other factors which have discouraged an association of the oracles. In some cases, these have less to do with any incompatibility between Mark 13:14 and Eusebius' account than with the specifics of the particular *Flugblatt* theory being put forward and its reconstruction of a written source – a 'flier' – behind the traditions recorded in Mark 13. Not only have there been almost as many reconstructions as there are scholars attempting it, but the reconstructions are for the most part too broad to be in any way comparable to Eusebius' material. Moreover, the *Flugblatt* was often seen as having a Jewish rather than Jewish-Christian readership, which further obstructed any comparison. For these reasons, the preceding comparison has been conducted on the basis of Mark 13:14 only, and not on the basis of the reconstruction of the written oracle. Even so, the observations which have been made so far in this chapter support the reconstructed Judean oracle.

To summarize, then, I have shown that there are various factors which speak in favour of an association between Mark 13:14 and *Hist. eccl.* 3.5.3: the provenance of both oracles is Jerusalem, the date of both oracles is prior to the Jewish War, and the content of both oracles includes a command to flee the city. The difference in wording between the oracles has been seen to be neutral, speaking neither for nor against an association. The main factor which speaks against an association of the oracles is the reference to the destination of Perea/Pella, but there is, as has been shown, good reason to expect such a dissimilarity due to the distinctive transmission history of each oracle. The evidence therefore favours an original association between the oracles, with a quite distinct history of transmission.

5. **Circumstances under which a flight to Pella may have been possible**

The question of the circumstances under which a flight from Jerusalem may have taken place has been dealt with on numerous occasions.[37] Those who raise questions about the possibility of a flight do so primarily on two fronts: first, the difficulty of identifying τὸ βδέλυγμα τῆς ἐρημώσεως with Titus, and second, Josephus' depiction of the impossibility of escape from Jerusalem during the Jewish War. The following discussion will re-examine these considerations and propose a possible historical scenario.

To what, then, did τὸ βδέλυγμα τῆς ἐρημώσεως refer in Mark's source, namely the Judean oracle? I have already noted that this phrase alludes to the desecration of the Jerusalem Temple. This is done by echoing a number of passages from Daniel and I Maccabees, which were themselves ambiguous as to their referent.[38] This

---

[37] Some scholars who write in favour of the historicity of the flight are: Schoeps, 'Ebionitische Apokalyptik'; Sowers, 'Circumstances'; Simon, 'Migration'; Günther, 'Fate of the Jerusalem Church '; Pesch, *Markusevangelium II*, 295–6; Breytenbach, *Nachfolge*, 312; Pritz, *Nazarene Jewish Christianity*, 122–7; Theissen, *Gospels*, 127.

[38] The passages in Daniel and 1 Maccabees to which the Judean oracle may have been alluding by using the phrase τὸ βδέλυγμα τῆς ἐρημώσεως may be set out as follows:

(i)   In Dan. 8:11ff, the full term τὸ βδέλυγμα τῆς ἐρημώσεως does not appear; the reference is to ἡ ἁμαρτία ἐρημώσεως (*hppšʿ šmm*) in verse 13. Nevertheless, the reference is clearly linked thematically to the later ones (9:27, 11:31, 12:11). If it is correct that the Hebrew phrase *šqqûṣ šmm* was originally coined as a derogatory parody of the name of the Syrian god Belshamim (Rowley, *Relevance*, 52; Lacocque, *Daniel*, 164) then the constitutive element in the phrase was *šmm*, not *šqqûṣ*. The Dan. 8:11ff passage is formulated in the Hebrew in such a way as to allow the cessation of the continual burnt offering to be linked to the transgression (*pšʿ*) of the 'host' (*ṣbʾ*), referring to the Jewish people in general or the priesthood in particular, which is viewed as of heavenly significance because of their relationship with the God of heaven (Goldingay, *Daniel*, 209–10). This passage does not seem to envisage an altar, nor a person, but an action in its usage of *hppšʿ šmm*.

(ii) In Dan. 9:27, the one who makes desolate seems to be a person. Notably, this passage once again links the abomination to the compliance of the Jewish people.

(iii) Dan. 11:29ff gives the most explicit reference to Antiochus IV Epiphanes. However, the abomination does not refer to Antiochus IV himself, but to a pagan altar. Verse 32 closely links the setting up of the abomination with those who violate the covenant (i.e. the hellenizing Jews). These violators of the covenant are contrasted with the 'people who know their God', who are prepared to suffer (verses 33ff).

(iv) Dan. 12:11ff shares the perspective of 11:29ff, whereby the abomination

means that an interpreter of these passages had an open field when applying these passages to his or her own time. It is clear that the author of the source behind Mark 13:14ff *did not* identify the βδέλυγμα with an altar.[39] Moreover the interpreter did not necessarily have to see the desolating sacrilege as the conquering general. One feature that is striking about the Danielic passages is the recurrent theme of the Jewish people violating their own covenant. The author of the source behind Mark 13:14ff could have applied these prophecies of the 'End times' (cf. Dan. 8:17) to whomever or whatever was seen as disrupting the sacrifice and thus desolating the Temple.

The reference to τὸ βδέλυγμα τῆς ἐρημώσεως is intended to be cryptic. Nevertheless, a particular person and event is in view. If the author of this source had someone specific in mind, who could it have been?

There are two reasons why it is implausible to identify τὸ βδέλυγμα τῆς ἐρημώσεως with Titus and his proclamation of victory in the forecourt of the Temple. The first is the fact that this would have been too late a point in the chronology of the first Jewish War to explain adequately the call to flight which the oracle contains. The second is that the perfect participle ἑστηκότα indicates the beginning of a *process which is bound to a specific person.* Titus' acclamation as victor would rather be understood as a *single* event.

It is therefore better to look for someone other than Titus who could have been considered as disrupting the Temple sacrifice. Although one cannot assume that the author of the oracle necessarily shared Josephus' views, there are nevertheless some

follows the cessation of the continual burnt offering and seems to refer to an altar.
One may summarize this review of the Danielic passages as follows. It is not correct to say that the βδέλυγμα τῆς ἐρημώσεως refers to the entrance of Antiochus IV Epiphanes into the Temple. Dan. 11:31 and 12:11 indicate that an altar is meant by the final redactor. Dan. 9:27 seems to imply a person, and Dan. 8:11–13 an action. By contrast, I Macc. 1:53 and 6:7 make it clear that the desolating sacrilege is something built on the altar of the Temple, which could be pulled down (a pagan altar or statue).
39 The Markan allusion refers to τὸ βδέλυγμα τῆς ἐρημώσεως ἑστηκότα. As mentioned in chapter 3, 7.1, the striking lack of agreement between the neuter noun, τὸ βδέλυγμα, and the masculine perfect participle ἑστηκότα indicates that the reference is to a *person*, not an altar or statue. Furthermore, the fact that it is a *perfect* participle indicates that the event envisaged is not a single event, but the beginning of a process attached to this specific person (See Hengel, 'Origin and Situation', 18–19).

important clues in Josephus' writings as to the possible identification of τὸ βδέλυγμα τῆς ἐρημώσεως in the Judean oracle.

The first is that a pollution of the house of God need not be an act of a Gentile, but could just as well be effected by a Jew. There is a clear indication of this in *J.W.*, IV.388: 'For there was an age-old saying of inspired men that the City would be taken and the most Holy Temple burnt to the ground by right of war, if ever the citizens strove with each other and *Jewish hands were the first to pollute the house of God*'[40] (emphasis mine). The notion that the sacrilege could be due to Jewish rather than Gentile actions could also find some support in the passages in Daniel discussed in note 38, for Dan. 8:11ff, 9:27 and 11:32 either link or at least permit the linking of the cultic transgression to Jews who violate the covenant.

The second clue that one can glean from Josephus as to the identity of τὸ βδέλυγμα τῆς ἐρημώσεως is his conviction that the prophecy about the pollution of the house of God was fulfilled by the Zealots: 'the Zealots caused the prophecies against their country to be fulfilled.' (*J.W.*, IV.387)

If one examines the vocabulary that Josephus uses to describe the actions of the Zealots, it is striking how prominent the language of cultic transgression is. The verb μιαίνω (to stain, sully), with its cultic overtones, occurs frequently in books IV, V and VI of *Bellum Judaicum*, and various other terms also express Josephus' conviction that the action of the Zealots' express contempt against God.[41] These, and other less-specifically cultic terms for evil actions

---

[40] The translation used here is by Williamson. Its more modern and vivid rendering of the Greek commends it in this context over the older Thackeray translation of the Loeb edition.

[41] These include:
  (i) τὸ μίασμα (pollution, sacrilege), VI.110;
  (ii) ἡ ὕβρις (insolence, contempt), cf. esp. IV.150, where it occurs in conjunction with μιαίνω and refers to the Zealots' insolence against God;
  (iii) ὑβρίζω (to behave arrogantly, including to commit sacrilege), cf. esp. IV.190, again against God;
  (iv) ἀνόσιος (unholy, wicked), which refers to the Zealots explicitly in Books IV and VI, where it occurs four times, and also implicitly in VII.379;
  (v) ἀσέβεια (ungodliness, sacrilege), which refers to the Zealots eight times in Books IV–VII, with only one reference (IV.484) in these Books to other ungodliness, namely that of Sodom;
  (vi) ἀσεβέω (to act in an ungodly manner, commit sacrilege), which refers exclusively in Books V–VII to the Zealots and occurs five times in those Books (the one reference in Book IV – IV.100 – is also an ironic reflection on John of Gischala, who parades his piety before Titus and calls upon him not to act impiously; the tables are turned in VI.95 and 127, where Titus calls upon John to stop polluting the Holy Place);

are used by Josephus with such frequency to refer to the Zealots
that they leave the reader in no doubt as to Josephus' conviction
that it was the impious actions of the Zealots, rather than the
Romans, that led to Jerusalem's downfall.

It is evident from *J.W.*, V.394 (and also from the reference in
Ant., XII.320) that Josephus was familiar with the Danielic formulation τὸ βδέλυγμα τῆς ἐρημώσεως, for he alludes to the phrase
in book 5, where he reports his own impassioned speech to the
Zealots:

> Again, when Antiochus Epiphanes was blockading the
> City and had committed gross sacrilege (πρὸς τὸ θεῖον
> ἐξυβρικότος), and our ancestors advanced in arms against
> him, what happened? They were cut to pieces in the battle,
> the town was plundered by the enemy, and the Sanctuary
> was desolated for three years and a half (ἠρημώθη δ᾽ ἔτη
> τρία καὶ μῆνας ἓξ τὸ ἅγιον). Need I go on with the story?
> But who enlisted the Romans against our country? Wasn't
> the impiety (ἀσέβεια) of the inhabitants responsible?
> (*J.W.*, V.394–5)

Josephus shows himself to be fully aware that the language of
sacrilege was applied in his sources to Antiochus Epiphanes.
However, when he refers to the desolation of the Sanctuary, he
renders the verb ἐρημόω in the passive (ἠρημώθη), in keeping with
his intention to shift the blame from Antiochus Epiphanes or, by
analogy, Titus, to the inhabitants of Jerusalem. It is therefore not
at all surprising that the Danielic phrase τὸ βδέλυγμα τῆς ἐρημώσεως itself is not used by Josephus. Rather, the weight of cultic
transgression is laid at the feet of the various Zealot groups.

Is it legitimate to regard Josephus' obviously biased viewpoint
with regard to the Zealots as a possible clue to the reference in the
Judean oracle? Could the Jewish Christian who formulated the
Judean oracle have shared the view that the Zealots' actions
constituted impiety towards God?

In order to answer these questions, it is worth noting W. C. van
Unnik's insight that there is more profit to be gained from Josephus
than has hitherto been recognized, though that profit may not

(vii) τὸ ἀσέβημα (ungodly act, sacrilege) which is used exclusively of the
Zealots and occurs five times;
(viii) ἀσεβής (impious, sacrilegious), which refers exclusively to the Zealots
occurs four times in Books IV–VI.

always be accessed in a direct way, but rather via *Lebens- und Gedankenkomplexe*.[42] It is clear that one cannot postulate a direct link between Josephus and the Jewish Christian who formulated the Judean oracle. Nevertheless, both Josephus and the unknown Jewish Christian made use of Daniel, and saw themselves in some sense as prophetic. Van Unnik has cogently argued that Josephus regarded himself as a prophet who stood in the tradition of the prophets of doom and was therefore rejected by his countrymen, just as they had been.[43] For Josephus, his political shift away from the Zealot movement with which he had once been allied had to be expressed not simply in political but in theological terms, and terms which laid claim to his own legitimacy as the heir of Jewish tradition.

If one compares this *Gedankenkomplex* with that of the Jewish Christian who formulated the Judean oracle, certain similarities become apparent. The Jewish-Christian formulator had also parted ways with the Zealot interpretation of theology and the world; if this were not the case, the oracle calling for flight would be incomprehensible. However, the parting of ways reflected in the Judean oracle is not identical with Josephus' parting. Hitherto there had been a sufficiently stable balance to allow the co-existence of the Jewish Christians with other Jewish groups within the pre-war diversity of Jerusalem. The oracle marks a crisis point at which this co-existence becomes no longer viable. The nature of that crisis will be explored below. Thus both Josephus and the Jewish Christian parted ways with the Jewish politics and theology that had gained ascendancy. Like Josephus, so too the Jewish Christian made use of Daniel in order to interpret the situation, and in doing so made some claim to a prophetic role. While Josephus gives an extended defence of his position as the legitimate heir of Jewish tradition, we catch only a glimpse of this in the brief Judean oracle. Nevertheless, in its use of Daniel and the Maccabean notion of godly flight from the city, it too lays claim to being the legitimate heir and interpreter of these Jewish writings.

There are therefore some subtle but important similarities between Josephus and the author of the Judean oracle which make Josephus not simply an acceptable, but in fact an indispensable adjunct to an investigation of the meaning of τὸ βδέλυγμα τῆς ἐρημώσεως in the Judean oracle. Josephus and the Jewish-

---

[42] Van Unnik, 'Josephus', 15.   [43] *Ibid.*, 45–53.

Christian author are not united in their choice of action, but they share a common attitude to ascendant Jewish politics and theology, namely that of the Zealots: the Zealots cannot claim to be the legitimate heirs of Judaism.

It seems that the formulator of the Judean oracle was in sufficient sympathy with the Maccabean flight from Jerusalem to use that flight as a model for his or her own call to flight, though there is no evidence of any thought of guerrilla resistance similar to that of the Maccabees. Josephus, too, was in sympathy with the Hasmonean position, despite his speech cited above to the effect that taking up arms bespoke a lack of trust in God. (He himself, of course, had initially taken up arms.) In Josephus' case, his sympathy is largely due to the fact that he was descended directly from the Hasmonean dynasty, and traced his genealogy back to Jonathan, son of Asmoneus, by the marriage of Jonathan's daughter to his great-great-grandfather, Matthias Ephlias (*Life* 2–6). Moreover, his sympathy for the Hasmoneans is reflected in his account of the struggle against Antiochus Epiphanes. In the opening of the first book of *The Jewish War*, he notes on more than one occasion that the Hasmoneans were, like himself, friends of Rome (*J.W., I.38, 48*). So it is not surprising that Josephus focusses much of his attack on the Zealots' cultic offences, and in particular on their ousting of the high-priestly families and installing of their own high priest. The passage in which this is described deserves particular attention (*J.W., IV.147–57*), not least because of its use of the language of sacrilege:

> [The Zealots] boasted of their crimes as if they were benefactors and saviours of the City. The result was that the people became so cowed and abject, and the terrorists so rabid, that they actually got control of the appointment of high priests. Setting aside the families which provided them in succession, they appointed obscure persons of no family, to gain partners in crime; those who without deserving it found themselves in the highest office were inevitably the creatures of those who had put them there. Again, they sowed dissension between their rulers by various tricks and scandalous stories, turning the squabbles of those who might have restrained them to their own advantage, till, sated with their crimes against men, they transferred their insolence (τὴν ὕβριν) to the Deity and

entered the Sanctuary with their polluted feet (καὶ μεμιασ-
μένοις τοῖς ποσὶ παρῄεσαν εἰς τὸ ἅγιον).

The populace were now seething with discontent, urged on
by the oldest of the high priests, Ananus, a man of the
soundest judgement who might have saved the City if he
had escaped the hand of the plotters. These made the
Temple of God their stronghold and refuge from popular
upheavals, and the Sanctuary became the centre for their
illegal operations. Through their atrocities ran a vein of
ironic pretence more exasperating than the actions themselves. For to test the submissiveness of the people and
prove their own strength, they attempted to appoint the
high priests by lot, though as we said before the succession
was by birth. The excuse given for this arrangement was
ancient custom; they said that from time immemorial the
high priesthood had been conferred by lot. In reality this
was a reversal of the regular practice and a device for
consolidating their power by arbitrary appointments. As-
sembling one of the clans from which high priests were
chosen, a clan called Eniachin, they drew lots for a high
priest. The luck of the draw furnished the clearest proof of
the depths to which they had sunk. The office fell to one
Phanias, son of Samuel, of the village of Aphtha, a man
not only not descended from high priests but too boorish
to have any clear notion of what the high priesthood might
be. Anyway they dragged him willy-nilly from his holding
and disguised him from head to foot like an actor on the
stage, robing him in the sacred vestments and teaching him
his cues. To the perpetrators this shocking sacrilege (τὸ
τηλικοῦτον ἀσέβημα) was the occasion for ribald mirth,
but the other priests, watching from a distance this
mockery of their law, burst into tears, cut to the heart by
this travesty of the sacred rites (κατέστενον τὴν τῶν ἱερῶν
τιμῶν κατάλυσιν).

Shortly after this, Ananus addresses the crowds:

How wonderful it would have been if I had died before
seeing the house of God full of countless abominations
(τοσούτοις ἄγεσι καταγέμοντα) and its unapproachable,
sacred precincts crowded with those whose hands are red
with blood!   (*J.W.*, IV.163).

To Josephus, who was himself a member of one of the ruling families that were displaced by the Zealot appointment of Phanias, son of Samuel, this action constituted a shocking sacrilege. In Josephus' view, this appointment was a device for consolidating the Zealot power, for rendering the people more submissive and for ensuring that the high priests were under the control of those who had put them there. On the other hand, something of the Zealot perspective is apparent in this account. For them, it returned the system of high-priestly appointments to what it had been prior to the Hasmonean dynasty, and separated the political seat of power from the cultic one. The Zealots presumably saw themselves as restoring the Temple cult, which had been compromised by the Hasmonean accrual of kingly and high-priestly power. In effect, the 'restoration' stripped the high-priestly role of its political power. It was this that the Zealots intended, and it was this that Josephus decried.

In installing their own appointed high priest, the Zealots upset what had been an uneasy balance of power between the ruling conservative high-priestly families and the radical nationalists. The installation of Phanias, though he himself was politically insignificant, constituted a key shift in the balance of power.

It is this shift, I propose, that is reflected in the Judean oracle.[44] The reference to τὸ βδέλυγμα τῆς ἐρημώσεως standing where *he* should not be is, as I have pointed out, a cryptic reference to a man who begins a process of standing where he should not be. Every indication is that this is a cultic reference, and that the place is the Temple, or more specifically, the Sanctuary. The installation of Phanias was the point at which the balance of power shifted in such a way that the former acceptable diversity of political opinion was replaced by a political situation in which the nationalists' viewpoint was dominant. From this point onwards, those who did not share their convictions were increasingly at risk. Much of Josephus' account describes the increasing tyranny which the nationalists exercised over the inhabitants of Jerusalem, as in the following passage:

---

[44] Sowers, in his important article 'Circumstances', 318–19, suggested Phanni (*sic*) as the possible referent behind the abomination (Mark 13:14), but he did not explore the possibility in detail. In the late nineteenth century, Pfleiderer proposed that τὸ βδέλυγμα τῆς ἐρημώσεως could refer to the desecration of the Temple by the Zealots ('Komposition'), though he saw this as deriving from a Jewish *Flugblatt*. He subsequently took a different position (*Urchristentum*), 380.

there was no section of the people for whose destruction they did not invent an excuse. Those with whom any of them had quarrelled had long ago been put away; those who had not collided with them in peacetime were subjected to carefully chosen accusations: if a man never came near them at all, he was suspected of arrogance; if he approached them boldly, of contempt; if he was obsequious, of conspiracy.   (*J.W.*, IV.363–4)

Against this background, the position of the Jewish Christians was becoming untenable. There are certain indications within the New Testament that the (Jewish) Christians of Jerusalem were an identifiable group with a regular meeting place within the Temple precincts, namely in Solomon's Portico. The reference in Acts 5:12–13 to Solomon's Portico as a meeting place of the church, along with Acts 3:11 and the reference in John 10:22–3 to Jesus' choice of these porticoes as a meeting place, lends weight to the notion that the Jewish Christians of Jerusalem were an identifiable group which congregated in Solomon's Portico and which had not felt it necessary to conceal their allegiance to the crucified Messiah. If, as I assume, the majority of Jewish Christians shared a passivist stance which went back to Jesus himself, this would have rendered them particularly unpopular with the Zealots, who sought to make the population take up arms.[45]

The rise of the Zealots to power must have been observed by all the inhabitants of Jerusalem. The uncertain factor, however, was whether the Zealots and their supporters would succeed in wresting power from the high-priestly families; if this took place, then all restraints upon the Zealots would be swept away. It was in this situation of uncertainty, I suggest, that the Judean oracle was formulated. It accounts for the cryptic formulation, which could be interpreted as referring to the Romans. It accounts for the reference to the cult, and for the man beginning to stand where he should not be. It accounts for the injunction to flight being coined in Maccabean terms, as the reference was thus sufficiently ambiguous to allow it to imply a call to a Maccabean-style resistance against foreign powers. It also accounts for the urgency which this installation triggers, for the Zealots would lose no time in further consolidating their power once the restraints had been removed.

[45] Contra Brandon, *Fall*. See esp. 87, 121.

To claim that the installation of a puppet high priest lies behind the phrase τὸ βδέλυγμα τῆς ἐρημώσεως is *not* to assert that Phanias himself was viewed as 'the antichrist'. As mentioned previously, I am of the opinion that a fully fledged notion of 'the antichrist' was a later development.[46] Rather, at the stage when the Judean oracle was formulated, the puppet high priest had not yet been chosen. It wasn't until the puppet high priest was chosen by lot from the clan of Eniachin, as quoted above, that the oracle came into effect. The offence of his installation for the Jewish Christians of Jerusalem did not lie primarily in his person, which was, as all could see, harmless enough, but in the political shift that it represented. By his installation, the Zealots both proclaimed and consolidated their power. It was this power, in the Jewish Christians' view as well as in that of Josephus, which not only violated the Sanctuary directly because of its blood-shedding and impious actions, but also destroyed the universality of the Temple by ensuring that the Jewish diversity over which the Temple had presided was now outlawed. This rendered the Temple desolate.

The phrase προσεύχεσθε δὲ ἵνα μὴ γένηται χειμῶνος gives some indication of the timing of the oracle. According to the chronology of *The Jewish War*, the installation of Phanias as high priest took place in late 67, in winter.[47] This would therefore mean that winter was upon them, or nearly upon them, when the oracle was formulated, and the prayer was to be that God would delay the foreseeable rise in Zealot power until the weather conditions were more favourable to flight. The beginning of the campaigning season in 68 CE is indicated in *J.W.*, IV.413, with the reference to the 4th Dystros (March/April). In a passage which comes after the account of Phanias' installation and before the beginning of the spring campaign, we read:

> a steady stream of deserters eluded the Zealots. But flight was difficult as every exit was guarded and anyone caught going out, whatever the reason, was assumed to be on his

[46] See Gnilka, *Matthäusevangelium II*, 322–3, for whom the term antichrist is a later systematization. Most recently Beasley-Murray writes: 'I cannot see how Mark himself could have viewed the abomination of desolation as the last antichrist. The concept in 2 Thessalonians 2 is in the nature of an expansion of the earlier tradition in Mark 13 . . .', *Last Days*, 414.

[47] Cf. notes 3 and 4, 441–2 of Williamson's translation of *The Jewish War*. His dating is based on the chronology of the war, as described in *J.W.*, IV.120 and 130.

way to the Romans and dispatched forthwith. However, if he paid enough they let him go, and only if he failed to pay was he a traitor, so that the rich purchased their escape and only the poor were slaughtered.   (*J.W.*, IV.377–379)

Under such circumstances, it may have been possible for some Jewish Christians to escape, but it is difficult to envisage a larger group managing to flee. For this reason, it would be more likely that a flight of Jewish Christians occurred immediately upon the shift of power to the Zealots.

According to Josephus' account, the installation of Phanias led directly to a concerted effort by Ananus and his supporters to rouse the people to resistance. In this way, the installation of Phanias as high priest became the spark which ignited an armed struggle between the people loyal to Ananus and the high priestly families on the one hand, and the Zealots and their sympathizers on the other (*J.W.*, IV.193–207). The upshot of this struggle was that the Zealots were temporarily confined to the inner court of the Temple. If any time was suitable for escape in late 67, it was then. This makes sense of the great urgency of the Judean oracle; once the installation of the puppet high priest had been successfully carried out, there was no time to begin packing – it was time to flee, for it was unclear whether the resistance offered by the high-priestly families and their supporters would last a matter of days, hours or only minutes.

One further reference in Josephus is worth noting, for it describes what both Ananus' supporters and the Zealots knew to be at stake: 'the former [Ananus and his supporters] were convinced that *it was impossible to stay in the City* unless they rid her of the terrorists, the Zealots that unless they triumphed they would be spared no punishment' (*J.W.*, IV.199, emphasis mine). If Josephus is reliable at this point, the Jewish Christians were not the only group which perceived that its position would no longer be tenable under a Zealot regime. However, the Jewish Christians chose flight rather than armed resistance.

Much of this reconstruction of events depends upon the reliability of Josephus' account of the Jewish War, and I have cautioned against an uncritical reading of Josephus, or one which accords him an aura of omnipresence. Nevertheless, this reconstruction is founded in the *Lebens- und Gedankenkomplexe* of Josephus as well as in the details of his account, and for this reason can claim a greater degree of probability than other historical reconstructions.

Under the circumstances described above – as the Zealot groups vied for power with the aristocratic leadership – it would have been possible for a Jewish-Christian prophet to formulate an oracle such as the reconstructed Judean oracle, with its cryptic reference to τὸ βδέλυγμα τῆς ἐρημώσεως standing where he ought not to be, its urgent call to flight, coined in Maccabean terms, and its call to prayer that the flight might not have to take place in winter, or in a storm. This reconstruction develops the suggestion of S. Sowers that the appointment of a puppet high priest may be the referent behind the phrase τὸ βδέλυγμα τῆς ἐρημώσεως. The use of Josephus in this reconstruction was devised independently of Breytenbach, but agrees in many respects with his interpretation.[48] I am of the opinion that it is the most convincing explanation of the historical background to the material found in Mark 13:14ff.

I have argued that there was indeed a flight of Jewish Christians from Jerusalem in the winter of 67 CE. I have also argued that the Pella flight tradition did not originate with Eusebius nor with Epiphanius, and that Epiphanius' sources included a source other than Eusebius and Eusebius' source. These traditions associate the flight both with Pella specifically, and with Perea more generally. This information, combined with the fact that Mark and his community gained early access to the Judean oracle, permits me to postulate that a single unified flight to Pella was a piece of systematizing fiction behind which a true historical kernel is evident. There was indeed an exodus of at least a considerable number of Jewish Christians from Jerusalem; some of those who escaped went to Pella, some to other localities in Perea, and some north to Syria. The remembrance of the flight was preserved because it was regarded as a concrete and miraculous instance of God's mercy to the Christians of Jerusalem, but this remembrance took various forms. In the synoptic tradition it was preserved as a version of the oracle itself, with no mention made of destination. In the tradition which reached Eusebius, presumably via Hegesippus, the remembrance was preserved in the form of a report, which included the detail of the Pella destination. Epiphanius' source (possibly Tertullian or Hippolytus) included the more accurate reminiscence that

---

48 Breytenbach, *Nachfolge*, 314–15. Breytenbach identifies the desecration of the Temple as stemming from the Zealots' actions, but does not associate the installation of Phanias with a power shift, as I have done. Breytenbach also differs from the position I have argued in that he attributes the formulation of Mark 13:14ff to the evangelist, rather than to a Judean oracle.

Pella was not the only destination of the fleeing Jewish Christians by mentioning the region of Perea. Thus the synoptic flight oracle (the Judean oracle) and the Pella flight tradition permit a glimpse of the way in which a historical event gave rise to a variety of traditions.

This historical scenario, as set out in my doctoral dissertation, has been favourably discussed by J. Murphy O'Connor in his recent article 'The Cenacle – Topographical Setting for Acts 2:44–45' cited above. Despite his defence of Ariston as the source of Eusebius,[49] he finds it 'a most plausible *Sitz im Leben* for the oracle'.[50]

[49] Cf. esp. note 13 above with regard to the difficulties of claiming Ariston as Eusebius' source. The view which favours Hegesippus is not fraught with these difficulties. Murphy O'Connor's continuing claim that Epiphanius is dependent on Eusebius alone is not justified in the face of the above arguments.

[50] Murphy-O'Connor, 'Cenacle', 317.

5

MATTHEW 24: ESCHATOLOGICAL EXPECTATION AFTER THE JEWISH WAR

Let us now turn our attention to the eschatological discourse in Matthew's Gospel, of which one section (Matt. 25:1–13) has already been examined. The primary focus of this chapter will be upon the material that has direct parallels to Mark 13, as it provides the opportunity to examine the distinctive redactional and compositional techniques by which the evangelist appropriated and reshaped the Markan discourse. It is necessary to give attention first of all to the wider context in which this material is situated.

All scholars who accept Markan priority note that Matthew has significantly extended the eschatological discourse *vis-à-vis* the Markan source. J. Dupont notes that Matthew's last great discourse is almost three times as long as Mark's and Luke's, comprising ninety-four verses, as opposed to Mark's thirty-three and Luke's twenty-nine.[1] The contrast between Matthew's eschatological discourse and those of Mark and Luke is even more striking when one considers that Dupont's reckoning only takes Matthew 24 and 25 into consideration, for there are weighty reasons for including chapter 23 as integral to Matthew's conception of this final discourse. I will therefore begin by considering the question of the status of Matthew 23; is it to be understood as the opening of the eschatological discourse, or rather as a separate discourse in its own right?

1. Is Matthew 23 part of the eschatological discourse?

In J. Gnilka's opinion, the evangelist Matthew has clearly indicated that Matthew 23 and Matthew 24–5 are separate discourses by giving each a distinct audience and narrative setting (23:1 – disciples

---

[1] Dupont, *Trois Apocalypses*, 49.

and people; 24:1–3 – only the disciples).[2] He then proceeds to give an overview of the narrative audiences of the various discourses. However, Gnilka does not give sufficient weight to the fact that in the parable discourse of Matthew 13, a similar shift in both audience and scene takes place: τότε ἀφεὶς τοὺς ὄχλους ἦλθεν εἰς τὴν οἰκίαν. καὶ προσῆλθον αὐτῷ οἱ μαθηταὶ αὐτοῦ λέγοντες· διασάφησον ἡμῖν τὴν παραβολὴν τῶν ζιζανίων τοῦ ἀγροῦ (Matt. 13:36).

In chapter 13, Jesus is depicted as leaving the crowds who are not able to comprehend and going away with the disciples to a private place, and that becomes the occasion for the disciples' questions and further instruction. Similarly, at the beginning of Matthew 24, after having addressed a discourse both to the crowds and to the disciples (τοῖς ὄχλοις καὶ τοῖς μαθηταῖς αὐτοῦ, 23:1), Jesus withdraws from those who do not comprehend, namely the scribes and Pharisees. They too, like the crowds of the parable discourse, have been accused of blindness (Matt. 23:16, 17, 19, 24, 26). U. Luz discusses this movement away from the crowd and towards the disciples in relation to Matthew 13,[3] and indicates that the history of Matthew's own community *vis-à-vis* its Jewish neighbours is also apparent here. Matthew tells the story of Jesus and simultaneously invites the readers to look through the window of the text to see their own story at work. At these points in the story (Matthew 13 and 23–5), Matthew allows the readers to glimpse their struggle with the Jewish authorities and the resulting movement apart.

In Matthew 13, a contrast between the understanding of the disciples and the lack of understanding of the crowds is made, and the key to the widening gulf between the disciples and the crowds is characterized by the bearing of fruit or the lack of it. It appears that for Matthew, understanding must be expressed in the bearing of fruit, or else it is not understanding.[4] This Matthean theme is also apparent in Matthew 23, particularly in the call in verse 3 to 'do whatever they teach you and follow it; but do not do as they do, for they do not practise what they teach'. The scribes and

---

[2] Gnilka, *Matthäusevangelium II*, 522.

[3] Luz, *Matthäus II*, 294–5. Note that Luz considers chapters 23 and 24–5 as a single discourse because of their intrinsic links and because no narratives have been placed between them; *Matthew*, 44.

[4] Cf. Luz's comment: 'Offensichtlich ist das Fruchtbringen das Entscheidende, das zum Verstehen gehört', in *Matthäus II*, 295.

Pharisees do not bear the fruit of what they teach, and in this they show their lack of understanding. Just as in chapter 13, where a division between crowds and disciples occurs because of the former's lack of understanding, so too is there a comparable division between Matthew 23 and 24. These apparent divisions in both discourses graphically illustrate the parting of ways between the two groups (the disciples and those who lack understanding) on the level of the narrative.

For these reasons, it is preferable to interpret the discourse of Matthew 23 as integral to chapters 24 and 25. There is not the scope within the parameters of this Chapter to undertake a full analysis of Matthew 23.[5] Instead, I will offer some possible implications of interpreting Matthew 23 as part of the wider eschatological discourse.

The first of these is that the link between eschatology and ethics – which is evident throughout the Gospel,[6] and particularly clearly in chapter 25 – effectively frames the final great discourse. The Pharisees are reproached not for their teaching but for their actions, and the results of their actions are viewed against the backdrop of the coming judgement. This backdrop is set by the repeated woes which are pronounced against them. Like the beatitudes, where the horizon of the pronounced 'happiness' is both the eschatological future and to some extent the eschatological present which has arrived in the person of Jesus, the horizon of the pronounced woes against the scribes and Pharisees is both the eschatological future judgement and the (for Matthew) present destruction of the Temple by which they swore, according to Matt. 23:16–22.

A second implication of interpreting Matthew 23 as part of the final discourse is that the eschatological fate of the 'hypocrites', those who wear the mask of serving God but whose actions contradict this, becomes much more prominent. Towards the end of the Sermon on the Mount we are told that 'not everyone who says to me, 'Lord, Lord,' will enter the Kingdom of Heaven, but only the one who does the will of my Father in heaven' (Matt. 7:21). Matthew 23 forms an extended counterpart to this, whereby those saying 'Lord, Lord' (to God) but not doing God's will are

---

[5] See Newport's recent monograph, *Sources*. He sees the passage beginning at 23:33 as having more in common with the eschatological discourse than with the preceding material, 150.

[6] See section 2 of this chapter.

the scribes and Pharisees. As will be shown below in the discussion on John the Baptist, Matthew feels free to apply the same accusations that are levelled at 'outsiders' (scribes and Pharisees) to members of the evangelist's own community. For this reason, Matthew 23 need not be understood as included for the 'benefit' of Jewish scribes and Pharisees, nor even as ammunition against them, but, just as possibly, directed on the Matthean level of the story to the 'hypocrites' within the Matthean community, the apparently successful prophets reflected in Matt. 7:15–23 and 24:5, 11, 24.[7]

A third implication of interpreting Matthew 23 together with the following two chapters is that the final crescendo of accusation which 23:29–39 represents is not interpreted as finished at verse 39, with a new start made at 24:1. Rather, when read together, their essential integrity becomes apparent. In both Matt. 13:36 and Matt. 24:3 the disciples seek further clarification of the teaching Jesus gave in the preceding section of the discourse. If chapters 23 and 24 are interpreted separately, it might seem that the disciples' question in 24:3 relates only to Jesus' comment of 24:2, but in fact the desolation of the Temple (ὁ οἶκος ὑμῶν) has already been brought into view in 23:38. The following verse, verse 39, explicitly associates the desolation of the house with seeing Jesus again and acknowledging him as 'the one who comes in the name of the Lord': ἰδοὺ ἀφίεται ὑμῖν ὁ οἶκος ὑμῶν ἔρημος. λέγω γὰρ ὑμῖν, οὐ μή με ἴδητε ἀπ' ἄρτι ἕως ἂν εἴπητε· εὐλογημένος ὁ ἐρχόμενος ἐν ὀνόματι κυρίου (Matt. 23:38–9). Whereas the Markan Jesus, as discussed in chapter 3, treats this link between the destruction of the Temple and the End as an instance of the disciples' misunderstanding, the Matthean Jesus himself effectively sets up the link between the destruction of the Temple and his own 'coming'. Matthew's reformulation of the Markan question in 24:3, adding the reference to παρουσία, must therefore be understood in the context of the link between this coming and the destruction of the Temple made in 23:38–9. In Matthew's Gospel, the disciples' question accurately reflects the implication of Jesus' own words.

This raises some important questions as to how Matthew, whom

---

[7] Cf. two studies which examine the way in which Matthew directs many apparently outwardly directed sayings and parables at internal issues of the community: Freyne, 'Vilifying', especially 137–8 and Appendix B, and Roloff, 'Kirchenverständnis'.

I understand to have been writing later than Mark and with a greater time lapse from the destruction of the Temple, could have apparently strengthened the links between the destruction of the Temple and the parousia. Are there other indications in the discourse that this is the case? I am of the opinion that there are, and I will therefore return to these questions after setting the discourse within its wider context.

2. The prominence of eschatology in Matthew's Gospel

If it is accepted that the final great discourse of Matthew's Gospel encompasses not only chapters 24 and 25, but 23 as well, the contrast between Matthew's eschatological discourse and those of Mark and Luke is even more striking than Dupont allowed: it is more than four times the length of the equivalent discourses of the other synoptic Gospels. The length of the final discourse in Matthew's Gospel gives us an indication of the importance which this evangelist attached to eschatology and its ramifications. This is borne out by an examination of the Gospel as a whole, as G. Bornkamm's important article 'Enderwartung und Kirche im Matthäusevangelium' demonstrated. It is worth reiterating and elucidating some of the features of this article which show the importance of eschatology for Matthew, and the way in which it is constantly linked to ecclesiology in this Gospel.

(a) The figure of John the Baptist

Unlike in the Gospels of Mark and Luke, the preaching of John the Baptist in Matthew's Gospel is closely associated with that of Jesus. Only in Matthew is the Baptist's preaching and that of Jesus summarized by the same saying: μετανοεῖτε· ἤγγικεν γὰρ ἡ βασιλεία τῶν οὐρανῶν (Matt. 3:2, 4:17). The proclamation of the coming Kingdom, of imminent judgement and of the need for repentance characterizes both the Baptist's and Jesus' message; the saying about the unfruitful tree which is cut down and thrown into the fire is found both in the Baptist's preaching (3:10) and on Jesus' lips, both in the Sermon on the Mount (7:19), and again in a variant version of the saying at 12:33. While the Pharisees and Sadducees are addressed by the Baptist and the Pharisees by Jesus in 12:33, it is Christian false prophets who are challenged by Jesus in 7:19. In each case, the sayings warn of a false security, whether it be based in being children of Abraham or in the working of wonders in Jesus' name. All will be judged according to their 'fruit'. The links between the Baptist's preaching and that of Jesus are further apparent in the phrase γεννήματα ἐχιδνῶν, used by the Baptist to speak of the Pharisees and Sadducees (3:7) and in Jesus' mouth to speak of the Pharisees (12:34) and again of the scribes and Pharisees (23:33). It is probable that Matthew found the Q saying of John the Baptist (cf. Luke 3:7–9) a particularly appropriate warning against complacency and false security for the community's own situation, and thus incorporated the two further versions of it on the lips of Jesus. It is notable that in each case the vituperation is reserved for religious leaders in Matthew, rather than being addressed more generally to the crowds, as we find in Luke.

In these ways, Matthew has strengthened the links between the proclamation of John the Baptist and Jesus; the Baptist has been co-opted as a 'Christian' preacher, though his function is a preparatory one. One result of this is to heighten the prominence of the coming eschatological judgement and its significance for the church; it will be a time of trial for believers and unbelievers alike.

(b)   The eschatological perspective of the Sermon on the Mount

H. Windisch described the Sermon on the Mount as the 'proclamation of the God-given entry requirements [into the Kingdom] in the mouth of Jesus'.[8] This rather provocative encapsulation of the first Matthean discourse correctly indicates that the 'Kingdom of Heaven' is often depicted by Matthew as a future reality which the community will enter if it walks in the way of righteousness.[9] The Sermon is framed by references to the kingdom (5:3, 10; 7:21), and

---

[8] Windisch, *Bergpredigt*, 9 (translation mine).
[9] Cf. Luz, *Matthew*, 217. The only instances of sayings in Matthew's Gospel which seem to depict the presence of the Kingdom of Heaven are the Q sayings found in 11:12 and 12:28. However, the contexts of the sayings maintain the futurity of judgement (cf. 11:22, 12:27, 36). Hiers, in *Kingdom* argues that these sayings should be interpreted as referring to the future coming. Not all scholars agree that Matthew's conception of the kingdom is primarily as future reality; cf. Kingsbury, *Matthew*, 128–49, who interprets present and future aspects as being of equal weight for Matthean eschatology, and sees the Kingdom as growing from the time of Jesus' birth until the parousia. Matthew's understanding of the relationship between future and present aspects of the Kingdom receives further attention in section 5.4 of this chapter.

at the centre of the Sermon, in the Lord's Prayer, is the petition for its coming. The eschatological significance of one's actions is constantly in view throughout this first Matthean discourse, either explicitly, as in the references to reward (μισθός, 5:12, 46; 6:1, 2, 5, 16), or as the implicit foundation of the teaching. The conclusion of the Sermon, with its warning against false prophets (whose appearance belongs to the signs of the End times, 24:4ff), with its depiction of the final judgement (7:21ff) and with the concluding parables, makes the eschatological perspective of the Sermon on the Mount unmistakable.

(c) Matthew's mission discourse

In the mission discourse, the content of the disciples' proclamation is the nearness of the Kingdom of Heaven: πορευόμενοι δὲ κηρύσσετε λέγοντες ὅτι ἤγγικεν ἡ βασιλεία τῶν οὐρανῶν (Matt. 10:7). The content of their proclamation is thus formulated in the same terms as John the Baptist's (3:2) and Jesus' (4:17). The disciples are to perform the signs of its nearness in healing the sick, raising the dead and casting out demons. These signs in turn reflect Jesus' own actions, in which the coming Kingdom is made present (cf. Matthew 8 and 9, esp. the summary statements at 8:16–17 and 9:35). The disciples' mission is set squarely in the context of the coming judgement (Matt. 10:15) and of the coming of the Son of Man (Matt. 10:23). The eschatological nature of their mission is also apparent in the material Matthew has borrowed from the Markan eschatological discourse and relocated to this point (10:17–22). The disciples' mission will entail persecution, but this is not to be feared (10:26–31). Rather it is to be understood as necessary to the End times. Their mission is in fact portrayed as a beginning of the eschatological harvest (9:37–8), for the manner in which the disciples are received has eschatological implications (10:40–2). The discourse concludes with a promise of heavenly reward.

(d) The parable discourse

The composition of the seven parables of the Kingdom in chapter 13 shows the conjunction of eschatological and ecclesiological/paraenetic motifs. The unifying aim of the discourse is the significance of the coming judgement for the church. Towards the end of the discourse is a picture of the eschatological judgement, in which the angels separate the evil from the righteous (13:49–50), and the conclusion about the scribe who is trained for the Kingdom is linked closely with the preceding picture of judgement. In some sense, to bring out of one's treasure what is new and what is old is linked with understanding the nature of the coming judgement.[10]

(e) The community discourse

The fourth major discourse, found in chapter 18, is also concerned with the church in the light of the coming Kingdom. Once again there are references to entry into the Kingdom and also the prospect of eschatological punishment that form the two horizons against which the ethical commandments are to be understood. The parable of the unforgiving servant concludes the discourse, again shifting the focus towards the judgement that awaits church members who are not prepared to forgive.

(f) The parables of the wicked tenants and the wedding banquet

Both of these parables (21:33–45, 22:1–14) are told in the first instance against the chief priests and Pharisees. Matthew emphasizes at two points in the first parable that the vineyard will be taken from them and given to those who will produce fruit (οἵτινες ἀποδώσουσιν αὐτῷ τοὺς καρπούς, 21:41; δοθήσεται ἔθνει ποιοῦντι τοὺς καρποὺς αὐτῆς, 21:43), and, by implication, indicates that no one, not even those of his own community, can expect to be exempt from this responsibility. In this way, the evangelist makes it clear that the same criterion according to which everyone will be judged will also apply to the church.

The final scene which the evangelist has appended to the parable of the wedding banquet makes this point once again. The man without the wedding robe has not prepared himself to attend the banquet and is thrown into the outer darkness. Once again it is Matthew's community which is warned to take heed.

If eschatological reward and punishment are the two horizons of Matthew's paraenesis, one notices that each of the discourses

---

[10] This is discussed further in the following section (5.3).

concludes with reference to these horizons. The more prominent of the two is the horizon of punishment, which concludes the first, third, fourth and final discourses (cf. 25:31–46). The second discourse, with its emphasis on what the disciples must suffer, concludes with the promise of reward. As can be seen from the preceding overview, the eschatological judgement is given great prominence in this Gospel. U. Luz observes that most of the teaching about the coming judgement is found in parable form, with the exception of the sayings in 7:21–3 and 10:32–3, and 24:29–31.[11] Matt. 25:31–46, though not strictly a parable, gives in story form an exposition of the Gospel's teaching on the coming judgement.

Given this Matthean emphasis upon the coming judgement under which all stand, what is the function of Matthew's eschatology?

3. The function of Matthew's eschatology

To begin to address this question, I will take up a passage which has already been mentioned, namely the conclusion of the parable discourse, 13:47–53. In verses 51–2 there is a short parable about the householder who brings out of the store what is new and what is old. It is not immediately apparent what the relevance of this parable is at this point, nor why the focus should shift from the disciples to scribes who have been trained for the Kingdom of Heaven. Most interpretations have read 'scribe' as a reference to Matthew himself, or more generally to Christians who were schooled in the Old Testament. But the primary level of the text suggests that all who judiciously teach *just as Jesus has done* are intended. Jesus has just concluded an extended discourse to the crowds and later to the disciples alone. The theme of the teaching was the Kingdom of Heaven, particularly from the perspective of its eschatological claim upon the hearer. Those schooled in the Kingdom of Heaven, as the disciples have been, share in its secrets (13:11), and are therefore equipped to bring their knowledge judiciously out of their store at the appropriate time.

Much has been made of the reference to the 'new and the old' in these verses, as meaning the 'new' of Jesus' proclamation and the 'old' of the law and the prophets. While this may reflect the

---

[11] Luz, *Matthäus II*, 374.

evangelist's understanding, it is useful to ponder whether the parable can function without recourse to allegory. Interpreters have found the picture of a householder bringing out from the store both new and old illogical, as one would rather expect the householder to bring out produce – fruit and vegetables, wine, corn – or such items as clothes and tools.[12]

I would suggest, however, that the role of a judicious householder was to bear in mind the variety of produce stored, with an awareness that different foods last for different periods of time. In a hot climate prior to refrigeration, it required considerable skill to manage a food store in such a way that a variety of foods was kept, but only so long as they were still good (= the 'old'), for the use of the foods had to be 'budgeted', so that not all of the fresh seasonal foods (= the 'new') were eaten immediately, leaving none for later. The picture is of a careful householder who knows what is in the store and the 'shelf-life' of each item, and who can estimate accurately the future needs of the household. According to this interpretation, the scribes trained for the Kingdom of Heaven would judiciously bring from their store of understanding the appropriate teaching, just as Jesus did in the preceding discourse.[13] Not every piece of information was given to everyone, but Jesus gave further understanding to those who already possessed some (13:12). In this way, these verses may make a similar point to the otherwise cryptic saying found in 7:6: μὴ δῶτε τὸ ἅγιον τοῖς κυσὶν μηδὲ βάλητε τοὺς μαργαρίτας ὑμῶν ἔμπροσθεν τῶν χοίρων, μήποτε καταπατήσουσιν αὐτοὺς ἐν τοῖς ποσὶν αὐτῶν καὶ στραφέντες ῥήξωσιν ὑμᾶς. 'That which is holy', τὸ ἅγιον, and 'pearls', οἱ μαργαρίται, would therefore also refer to the secrets of the Kingdom of Heaven. If this interpretation of 13:51–53 is accepted, it means that the parable discourse, which begins with the parable of the sower and teaching about the secrets of the Kingdom of Heaven, is concluded with a piece of

---

[12] Cf. *Ibid.*, 362.

[13] For a recent interpretation which differs from the one presented here, cf. Orton, *Scribe*, 137–53. Orton seeks to interpret this passage against the background of Dan. 12:10. When the disciples identify themselves as *maskilim* who 'understand', this is to be understood as an eschatological event, in direct fulfilment of scripture (147). Thus for Orton the disciples are the scribes referred to in Matt. 13:52, though this does not exclude the role of Jesus: 'If the Teacher's disciples are *maskilim*, the disciples' Teacher is bound to be a Maskil!' (150). Although this does not contradict the position set out here, Orton's interpretation of the *Bildhälfte* of the saying is, in my opinion, inadequate.

teaching about what to do with these secrets: how to administer them judiciously.

What are the secrets of the Kingdom of Heaven? The plural formulation leads me to interpret the secrets not simply as the secret of Christ's own person, but rather as analogous to the phrases 'the Gospel of the Kingdom' (9:35) and the 'word of the Kingdom' (13:19).[14] It therefore refers to the coming eschatological kingdom, which has drawn close in the person of Jesus, and to its ethical dimension; these 'secrets' have remained hidden from the crowd, who have shut their eyes and stopped their ears against them (13:15). These 'secrets' are in a sense not secret at all, but rather the proclamation of the Gospel. However, they have become secret, in that they have been rejected (cf. the whole of chapter 13). They are now to be brought out judiciously, just as Jesus himself is shown to have done in this chapter.

The reference to 'all this', ταῦτα πάντα, in verse 51 therefore refers not only to the *content* of the preceding discourse, but also to the *manner* in which the appropriate teachings for the crowds and for the disciples were selected. The structure of the discourse makes clear that not all teaching is appropriate for the crowds:

13:1–9	Address to the crowds, concluding with a call for hearing: ὁ ἔχων ὦτα ἀκουέτω.
13:10–23	Teaching and interpretation of the parable of the sower, addressed to the disciples, who hear: verse 16: ὑμῶν δὲ μακάριοι οἱ ὀφθαλμοὶ ὅτι βλέπουσιν καὶ τὰ ὦτα ὑμῶν ὅτι ἀκούουσιν.
13:24–34	Parables addressed to the crowds.
13:35	Fulfilment formula.
13:36–53	Interpretation and further parables addressed to the disciples.

The interpretations are reserved for the disciples alone. Verses 36–50, addressed to the disciples, are structured in such a way that two judgement scenes frame two short parables about the overwhelming preciousness of the kingdom and how one's response to the opportunity of the kingdom must be total and unreserved. Once again one can see the way in which the eschatological horizon, here represented by the judgement scenes, gives urgency to the call for

---

[14] Cf. Luz, *Matthäus II*, 312.

action which is inherent in the parables of the treasure and the pearl.

Therefore, when Jesus asks the disciples in verse 51 if they have understood all this, his question also includes the eschatological horizon as necessary to the other teaching of the Kingdom, because of the way in which it lends urgency and an ethical imperative to the promise of salvation. The disciples affirm that they do indeed understand. 'Those who have been trained in the Kingdom of Heaven' presumably included a self-reference, and the way in which Matthew has structured not only the preceding discourse, but each of the discourses, as set out above, shows the evangelist at work judiciously selecting the appropriate teaching from the store: *the appropriate teaching for Matthew constantly includes the horizon of judgement.* Matthew is aware that a scribe trained in the Kingdom of Heaven could bring out a different configuration of teaching; indeed, the Gospel of Mark would have been a concrete example of this. However, the teaching appropriate to this situation and this community included, in Matthew's opinion, a heightened emphasis upon the coming judgement.

It is notable that the coming judgement is not portrayed primarily as a teaching appropriate to 'the crowds', even though it is not altogether absent from the teaching addressed to them (cf. 13:30). Rather, it is the disciples, and through them the members of Matthew's community, that are to take particular note of the significance of the coming judgement. So the evangelist does not consider the coming judgement in the first instance as an 'evangelistic' tool. Rather, the eschatological horizon is part of the tradition which is of particular relevance to the Matthean situation.

I have noted the close association between eschatology and ethics in the Gospel; for Matthew, eschatology is inextricably bound together with concern for the church and its ethics. One might be inclined to regard ethics as the evangelist's primary concern, and eschatology simply as the 'stick' with which to discipline the church.[15] Or alternatively, one could seek to interpret the Gospel as

---

[15] Cope, in an article entitled '"To the close of the age"', also takes up Bornkamm's thesis, seeking to show that he understated his case. Cope argues that 'the dominant role which the apocalyptic expectation plays in the Gospel of Matthew is the role of avoiding punishment for misdeeds and receiving reward for good deeds' (118). I differ from the position taken in this article, in that Cope sees Matthew and the Matthean community as having embraced a heightened

having such an overwhelming sense of the imminent End that an 'interim ethic', suited only to the short intervening period before the End, was called for.

I suggest that neither of these positions is adequate. Both positions to some extent represent a modern 'domestication' of Matthew's theology: the former by interpreting the eschatological perspective as of secondary importance and thus ridding the modern reader of a stumbling block to contemporary appropriation, and the latter by regarding the ethics set out in the Sermon on the Mount as interim, that is, fundamentally unworkable for long-term practical application. In my view, Matthew's eschatological perspective was not of secondary importance nor simply a disciplinary stick, but integral to this evangelist's theology. For Matthew, the nature of the coming judgement was one of the secrets of the Kingdom which were vouchsafed to the disciples: the surprise will be that it will be the *righteous* who will shine like the sun (13:43), not necessarily all those who call Jesus 'Lord'. This teaching is also vouchsafed to the crowd in the parable of the wheat and the tares, but they are not entrusted with the interpretative key as to who the wheat and the tares will be.

Matthew's ethics are eschatologically orientated, but there is no evidence that they were intended to be 'interim' ethics, in the sense propounded by J. Weiss and A. Schweitzer. Matthew did not rank ethics above eschatology, nor eschatology above ethics. Rather, the two are inextricably interwoven. It is no coincidence that the prominent Matthean motif of bearing fruit (ethics) also has associative links with the motif of harvest (eschatology).

It is in the bearing of fruit that one shows oneself to be a 'child of the Kingdom', which is also portrayed as a present reality (cf. 13:38). Let us therefore consider for a moment the relationship between present and future Kingdom for Matthew. As I have already stated, the primary conception of the Kingdom for Matthew is as future reality. However, it has drawn near (ἤγγικεν γὰρ ἡ βασιλεία τῶν οὐρανῶν), and it is worth asking in what sense this was understood. The verb ἐγγίζω has both spatial and

apocalyptic hope in the decades following the fall of Jerusalem (120); I am of the opinion that Matthew is not simply reflecting the community's outlook but rather, like a preacher and pastor, seeking to direct attention back to the eschatological horizon. I will endeavour to show within the scope of this chapter why the evangelist considered this to be the appropriate message for the Matthean community.

temporal connotations, and in exploring Matthew's conception of the relationship between future and present Kingdom, both should be borne in mind.

4. The relationship between the present and the future Kingdom of Heaven in Matthew: a comparison with Berakoth 61b

P. Achtemeier, in an article entitled 'An Apocalyptic Shift in Early Christian Tradition', argued that there was a shift in the understanding of the Kingdom of God and the notion of the two ages between Paul and the deutero-Pauline epistles towards an emphasis on present reality. He claims that an analogous shift can be observed from Mark's 'resolutely future' orientation[16] towards a perspective in Matthew in which the coming age is shown to be already present. As evidence, Achtemeier cites the resurrection appearances, the apocalyptic motifs of the earthquake (Matt. 27:52, 28:1–4) and the resurrection of saints (27:53), as well as the final pronouncement of the Gospel which promises the continuing presence of Jesus. Achtemeier, however, acknowledges that the references to the Kingdom of Heaven maintain its futurity.[17] The evidence does not unequivocally point to a shift in early Christian tradition towards a more present or realized understanding of the Kingdom in Matthew's Gospel, but rather to a conception whereby the future reality bursts in upon the present at particular moments of significance.

It is relevant to observe that the problem of the relationship between present and future Kingdom is not simply confined to Christian traditions. It is evident in intertestamental and pseudepigraphical writings, as well as in the early traditions of the Talmud. There is not the scope to give a full account of the way each corpus deals with the question of God's present 'kingship' and its relation to the future Kingdom. Rather, I will examine a particular passage from the Talmud, Berakoth 61b, which reflects this question of the relationship between present and future Kingdoms, and which may offer a useful comparison with Matthew's conception. In doing so, I acknowledge that the tradition as it stands is considerably later than Matthew; nevertheless, the interest of the following comparison does not depend upon a precise dating of the talmudic

---

[16] Achtemeier, 'Shift', 240.   [17] See note 9 above.

tradition, for it illustrates that a tension between present and future Kingdom is not reflected solely in Christian writings.

Berakoth 61b in the Babylonian Talmud gives an account of the martyrdom of Rabbi Akiba, which took place *c.* 135 CE. The relevant section reads as follows:

> When R. Akiba was taken out for execution, it was the hour for the recital of the *Shema'*, and while they combed his flesh with iron combs, he was accepting upon himself the kingship of heaven. His disciples said to him: Our teacher, even to this point? He said to them: All my days I have been troubled by this verse, *'with all thy soul'*, [which I interpret,] 'even if he takes thy soul'. I said: When shall I have the opportunity of fulfilling this? Now that I have the opportunity shall I not fulfil it? He prolonged the *ehad* until he expired while saying it. A *bath kol* went forth and proclaimed: Happy art thou, Akiba, that thy soul has departed with the word *ehad*! The ministering angels said before the Holy One, blessed be He: Such Torah, and such a reward? [He should have been] *from them that die by Thy hand, O Lord*. He replied to them: *Their portion is in life*. A *bath kol* went forth and proclaimed, Happy art thou, R. Akiba, that thou art destined for the life of the world to come. (Seder Zeraim, Soncino translation, 386–7)[18]

[18] The text of the Palestinian Talmud is briefer:

> R. Aqiba [*sic*] was being tortured [lit.: being judged] by the evil Tinneius Rufus. When [he was close to death,] the time to recite the *Shema'* approached. He began to recite the *Shema'* and he smiled. He [Tinneius] said to him, 'Elder, either you are a sorcerer [who does not feel pain] or you mock the torture [that I inflict upon you]'. He [Aqiba] said to him, 'Woe unto you. I am neither a sorcerer, nor a mocker. But [I now was thinking,] all my life when I recited this verse, I was troubled and wondered when I would be able to fulfil all three aspects [of this verse]: "And you shall love the Lord your God with all your heart, and with all your soul, and with all your might" (Deut. 6:5). I have loved him with all my heart. And I have loved him with all my wealth. But I did not know how I would [fulfil the verse and] love him with all my soul. And now the time has come [for me to love him] with all my soul, and the time has come to recite the *Shema'*. It is now clear to me [how I shall serve him with all my soul]. For this reason I now am reciting and smiling'. And just as he said this, his soul passed from him. (Yerushalmi Berakhot 9:3, in *The Talmud of the Land of Israel*, 346).

In this version, the interest lies primarily with the Torah faithfulness of R. Akiba, and how Deut. 6:5 might be fulfilled. There is no apparent tension between the present and future reign of God, no questioning by the ministering angels. The nature of God's kingdom is not raised.

Here, as in other rabbinic writings, the action of taking upon oneself the Kingdom, or Kingship, of Heaven means reciting the *Shema*.[19] Earlier in this passage one reads that these events took place under 'the wicked [i.e. the Roman] government', and so when R. Akiba takes upon himself the Kingship of Heaven by reciting the *Shema*, he effectively transfers himself from their domination. It is an act of piety and is recorded as such, but it is also a political act which declares that he is not under the rule of the heathen, but under the rule of God. Although he remains physically under the kingship of the Romans, he has invoked the rule of heaven and belongs to that Kingship.

The ensuing question of the ministering angels is instructive. They question why R. Akiba, transferred as he was to the Kingship of Heaven, should be permitted to die at the hands of the heathen; if he was to die, then surely it should have been at the hands of God, under whose kingship he stood at the time of death. God replies that he intends not death but life for those such as R. Akiba, making his death a 'door' to the life of the world to come.

In this passage we see the age to come as the time when God's Kingship will be fully apparent. However, God does rule in the present and this rule can be apparent when people open themselves to it, as R. Akiba did in reciting the *Shema*. The reality of the present Kingship of Heaven is shown not in political changes – R. Akiba still dies at the hands of the Romans – but in the defiantly faithful actions of those who take it upon themselves. God's rule invades earthly rule through a person's consciously taking it on.

Some comparisons between the view of God's Kingship expressed in this passage and that of the Gospel of Matthew can be made. In both, God's Kingship will only become fully apparent in the age to come. Nevertheless, both view God as presently King, and God's rule can become apparent in the present. For both Berakoth 61b and Matthew's Gospel, a person's action in opening himself or herself to God's rule is crucial. As has been seen in the preceding discussion of Matthew's Gospel, right action is not understood as an optional extra, but essential to the better right-

---

[19] Cf. Str-B I, 172ff, and also the parallel passage in the Palestinian Talmud cited above, in which it explicitly refers to R. Akiba's recital of the *Shema* at the corresponding point. In pursuing these reflections, I am aware that the rabbinic reflection upon the *Shema* may not correspond to first-century understanding and practice.

eousness required for entry into the Kingdom of Heaven. The right action for Matthew is not focussed upon the recital of the *Shemaᶜ*, but it would be wrong to draw too sharp a distinction between Berakoth and Matthew at this point, as R. Akiba's recital of the *Shemaᶜ* in the talmudic passage is understood as a reflection of his commitment to the study and practice of the Torah, as the statement of the angels implies.

As in Berakoth 61b, God's rule invades earthly reality in Matthew's Gospel. There is no miraculous rescue for R. Akiba; the reality of his taking upon himself the Kingship of Heaven is vouched for not by a miraculous rescue, but by a *bath kol*. By contrast in Matthew's Gospel, the reality of God's Kingship invades the present age in the person and work of Jesus, through the miracles he performs and also through the miracles the disciples are enabled to perform (10:8). Achtemeier is right that the apocalyptic signs at the crucifixion, including the earthquake and the resurrection of the saints, show that the coming age is present; however this presence is not the continuous realized presence of John's Gospel, but a bursting into the present of God's Kingdom which has been allowed or occasioned by some event within the human sphere. The most obvious event is the crucifixion itself, but in exorcisms and healings, God's Kingdom is made present. This is the reason for the close association between the proclamation of the Kingdom and the curing of disease and casting out of demons (cf. Matt. 4:23, 9:35, 10:7–8).

John the Baptist, Jesus and the disciples proclaim that the Kingdom of Heaven has drawn near (ἐγγίζω). As was noted above, this verb has both temporal and spatial connotations. This 'nearness' is generally understood as temporal: Matthew expected the Kingdom *soon*. While this may be correct – and I shall argue later that this is in fact the case – nevertheless the nearness can also be conceptualized spatially: the Kingdom of Heaven is near and is in fact bearing in upon the present age.[20] At particular points, the Kingdom not only bears in but breaks in. This does not mean that the present age has as yet come to an end, but rather that it is hard pressed by the encroaching reality of God's Kingdom.

This interpretation of Matthew's understanding of the Kingdom

---

[20] Cf. Aalen's 'Reign', 215–40 and Witherington's discussion of this and other positions in *Jesus*, 61–2.

of Heaven may shed light on the strong eschatological motifs present in the passion narrative, such as the shaking of the earth, the splitting of the rocks, the opening of the tombs and the raising of many saints at the moment of Jesus' death (Matt. 27:51bff). At this central eschatological moment, the present age is so hard pressed by the encroaching reality of the Kingdom of Heaven that the eschatological future breaks into the present, though the present age does not yet pass away.

This interpretation may also shed light upon another problematic passage of the Gospel, Matt. 11:12, which was mentioned above: ἀπὸ δὲ τῶν ἡμερῶν Ἰωάννου τοῦ βαπτιστοῦ ἕως ἄρτι ἡ βασιλεία τῶν οὐρανῶν βιάζεται καὶ βιασταὶ ἁρπάζουσιν αὐτήν. The term βιάζομαι can mean 'occupy a territory by force',[21] and a spatial interpretation of the nearness of the Kingdom, which bursts in and occupies the 'foreign kingdom', is in keeping with this. John the Baptist is the first to proclaim the nearness of the Kingdom in Matthew's Gospel, and its nearness was then proclaimed by Jesus and the disciples; this would account for the time designation ἀπὸ δὲ τῶν ἡμερῶν Ἰωάννου τοῦ Βαπτιστοῦ ἕως ἄρτι. It is true that βιάζομαι generally has negative overtones, as one would expect of a term that means 'to occupy a territory by force', for the territory is clearly not welcoming its occupiers. The Beelzebul controversy in chapter 12 makes it clear that the 'territory' which is being occupied is not welcoming its 'occupation', According to this interpretation, this saying could be translated as follows:

> From the days of John the Baptist until now
> the Kingdom of Heaven has been occupying enemy territory [bursting in] and the occupiers [i.e. the people through whom this occupying takes place, the disciples] claim it for themselves [perhaps like R. Akiba claimed it, or took it upon himself].

In this way, the above interpretation may clarify Matthew's use of this Q saying.

Against the background of these reflections about the prominence of eschatology in Matthew's Gospel, and about the way in which eschatology and ethics are inextricably interwoven, let us now turn to an examination of Matthew 24.

---

[21] BAGD cites Appian, *The Civil War*, 3, 24 no. 91 as an example of this usage.

5.   Matthew 24: is there a chronological sequence?

Of particular interest to an examination of Matt. 24:4–31 is the question of chronology: how did the evangelist understand the sequence of events portrayed in these verses, and at what point did the evangelist consider the Matthean community to be? Many exegetes have recognized that the chronology of Matthew 24 presents difficulties; verses 9–13 apparently reflect the current situation of the Matthean community, several years after the destruction of the Temple in Jerusalem.[22] In the following section, verses 15ff, Matthew includes the Markan prophecy of the Temple's destruction and of the ensuing tribulation, and, most intriguingly, the evangelist then binds this period of tribulation more closely to the End (verses 29ff) by the addition of εὐθέως, verse 29. G. Strecker comments that this chapter shows on the one hand a 'zeitliche Periodisierung' – a temporal periodisation – but that on the other there is a lack of 'grundsätzliche Abgrenzung' – fundamental division – in it.[23]

For the reasons outlined above, it is difficult to understand Matt. 24:4–31 as a single chronological sequence. It is possible to interpret the chapter as a series of loosely connected oracles which are not to be understood chronologically. However, there are some indications that Matthew may have had a scheme in mind which reflected the evangelist's own understanding of the interrelationship and chronology of the events described in this chapter.

5.1   The two-sequence schema

The first indication of a schema can be discerned from the prominence given to the coming of false prophets who will lead many astray. Although this theme was already prominent in Mark, as has been shown in Chapter Three, it receives greater emphasis in Matthew by the addition of a third reference to them. They are now referred to at the opening of the discourse, verses 4–5, in the central section on the internal strife within the church, verse 11, and again in verses 23–4, by means of some Q material. As in my interpretation of Mark 13, I will assume that these references refer not to three unrelated instances, but to a current threat facing the

---

[22] Cf. Matt. 21:41, 22:7. Some dissenting voices as to this post-seventy dating of Matthew's Gospel, including J. A. T. Robinson, Ellis, Moule, Reicke, Maier and Gundry, are noted and discussed by Davies and Allison, *Matthew*, I, 127ff.

[23] Strecker, *Weg*, 239.

Matthean community. The verbal similarity between these three references with respect to the effect which these false leaders have lends weight to this position: in verses 4–5 one reads that πολλοὺς πλανήσουσιν; in verse 11, πλανήσουσιν πολλούς, and in verse 24, one reads that they perform signs and wonders ὥστε πλανῆσαι, εἰ δυνατόν, καὶ τοὺς ἐκλεκτούς.

Having noted these references as oracles pertaining to the present experience of Matthew's community, I can also note that, prior to the latter two references, the term θλῖψις is used (verses 9 and 21). Although the θλῖψις of verse 21 is accompanied by the adjective μεγάλη, the phrase is anarthrous and need not necessarily be understood as referring to a period distinct from the earlier reference. If one assumes for a moment that they do in fact refer to the same tribulation, one begins to have the impression that two parallel sequences within this chapter are emerging.

Verses 13 and 14 refer to the completion of the Gentile mission, and then to the End. It is striking that the End should be referred to in what is essentially the middle of the chapter, but, if one has been alerted to the possibility of two parallel sequences within this chapter, then these verses would form the end of the first sequence. Their counterpart in the second sequence would be verses 29ff, which elaborate 'the End' and the effect upon the Gentiles (αἱ φυλαὶ τῆς γῆς, verse 30). The perspectives on the End given in verses 13–14 and verses 29ff are, of course, quite distinct; the former focuses on the immediate inner-worldly precursor to the End, the completion of the Gentile mission, while the latter's focus is the cosmic unsettling immediately prior to the End. Nevertheless, both refer, from different perspectives, to the End.

In the light of these features, I locate the beginning of the two sequences as follows: the first sequence begins at verse 6, and refers to wars, and rumours of wars. They are not to be understood as the End itself (οὔπω ἐστὶν τὸ τέλος), but they herald the beginnings of the birthpangs (πάντα δὲ ταῦτα ἀρχὴ ὠδίνων, verse 8). The beginning of the parallel sequence is at verse 15; this verse and the following ones also refer to war, namely the Jewish War of 66–70 CE. From Matthew's own perspective, the Jewish War was not the End, as many who had been touched by the Zealot expectations hoped,[24] but for Matthew, one may assume that it constituted a beginning. I may therefore set out this hypothesis of two parallel sequences as follows:

Table 4. *The two-sequence schema*

	First sequence	Second sequence
A: 66–70 CE		
	verses 6–8 wars/rumours	verses 15–20 desolating sacrilege
	οὔπω ἐστὶν τὸ τέλος	ἐν τόπῳ ἁγίῳ [war!]
	famines	flight
	earthquakes	
	πάντα δὲ ταῦτα	
	ἀρχὴ ὠδίνων.	

B: Matthew's situation post-70 CE characterized by suffering, false prophets, persecution by the Gentiles and the Gentile mission

	verse 9 θλῖψις	verses 21–2 θλῖψις μεγάλη
	death	
	hatred ὑπὸ πάντων τῶν ἐθνῶν	
	verse10 disintegration of community, falling away, betraying and hating one another	

verses 4–5; 'Many will come in my name saying ἐγώ εἰμι ὁ χριστός'	verse 11 many false prophets will arise	verses 23–8 false christs, false prophets
καὶ πολλοὺς πλανήσουσιν	καὶ πλανήσουσιν πολλούς	ὥστε πλανῆσαι καὶ τοὺς ἐκλεκτούς
	wickedness multiplied love grows cold	verses 26–8 where not to seek Christ (verse 27–8: sayings asserting that Christ's coming will be apparent to all)

C: The End, with its accompanying signs: completion of the Gentile mission, the sign of the Son of Man seen by all and the gathering-in of those who have remained faithful

verses 13–14	verses 29–31 (εὐθέως μετὰ τὴν θλῖψιν)
Salvation of 'faithful'	
Gentile mission completed (earthly perspective)	Sun darkened etc. (cosmic perspective)
. . εἰς μαρτύριον πᾶσιν τοῖς ἔθνεσιν	τότε φανήσεται τὸ σημεῖον τοῦ υἱοῦ τοῦ ἀνθρώπου . . . καὶ τότε κόψονται πᾶσαι αἱ φυλαὶ τῆς γῆς . . .
. . . τότε ἥξει τὸ τέλος	. . . gathering in of the elect (= salvation of 'faithful')
Answers the first part of the disciples' question: πότε ταῦτα ἔσται; with τότε ἥξει τὸ τέλος, verse 14	Answers the second part of the disciples' question: τί τὸ σημεῖον τῆς σῆς παρουσίας καὶ συντελείας τοῦ αἰῶνος; with τὸ σημεῖον τοῦ υἱοῦ τοῦ ἀνθρώπου, verse 30.

As can be seen from the table, verses 6–31 can be set out in columns as two parallel chronological sequences. Verses 4–5 form a prologue, by which the following sequences are grounded in the 'present' of Matthew's community. I have divided the chart horizontally into three sections, marked A, B and C. Section B, the longest section in both sequences, is the implied present for the Matthean community. Section A is the implied past, and section C, the implied future.

The strengths of this schema are apparent.[25] First of all, it makes sense of the chronological position of the oracle about the Jewish War (verses 15ff). If the War did indeed lie in the past for Matthew and the evangelist's community – which the vast majority of scholars hold – the position of this oracle renders an interpretation of the chapter as a single chronological sequence extremely difficult.[26]

[25] In his recent book *The Theology of the Gospel of Matthew*, 127, Luz incorporates with acknowledgement this aspect of the present study, observing that 'there is nothing in the text to suggest that verse 15 recounts the chronological continuation of the events given in verses 4–14. On the contrary, I feel that the same period of time is reported in 24:4–14 as in 24:15–28, albeit from a different perspective.'

[26] Broer calls verses 15ff the 'Achilles' heel' of any interpretation that sees the

Second, the redactional addition in verse 29 of εὐθέως, which binds the description of the End more closely to the tribulation described in verses 21–8, no longer defies interpretation. If verses 21–8 are understood as describing the present tribulation of Matthew's community, then it is perfectly comprehensible that Matthew could view the coming End as following immediately upon the period of tribulation. This addition gives the impression of a heightened expectation of the End, which finds support in heightened prominence of eschatology within this Gospel, as discussed above.

Third, this interpretation can make sense of the future tense of κολοβόω in verse 22, which in the Markan *Vorlage* was aorist:

> Matt. 24:22 καὶ εἰ μὴ ἐκολοβώθησαν αἱ ἡμέραι ἐκεῖναι, οὐκ ἄν ἐσώθη πᾶσα σάρξ· διὰ δὲ τοὺς ἐκλεκτοὺς κολοβωθήσονται αἱ ἡμέραι ἐκεῖναι.

> Mark 13:20 καὶ εἰ μὴ ἐκολόβωσεν κύριος τὰς ἡμέρας, οὐκ ἄν ἐσώθη πᾶσα σάρξ· ἀλλὰ διὰ τοὺς ἐκλεκτοὺς οὓς ἐξελέξατο ἐκολόβωσεν τὰς ἡμέρας.

It is likely that for Mark, the days of tribulation referred to the Jewish War and the upheavals it brought. It is possible that for Matthew, verse 22 also refers back to the tribulation of the Jewish war, and that the future tense of κολοβόω should simply be understood as a *futurum propheticum* on the lips of Jesus. This would mean that it should be part of Section A, the implied past for Matthew. However, the redactional change of tense encourages me to think that in Matthew's reinterpretation of the material, the great tribulation was present reality, characterized by false prophets, internal strife and betrayal within the community, and growing lawlessness. It is this tribulation that will be cut short by the coming End.

The use to which Matthew has put the Markan material on persecution (Mark 13:9–13) is relevant in this context. Matthew has transposed much of the material about external persecution to the mission discourse, chapter 10. In that particular context, it describes what the disciples (and through the 'window' of the text, the

destruction of the Temple as a past and no longer pressing event, 'Aspekte', 217, n. 28. Broer himself comes to the conclusion that verses 15ff do not refer to the destruction of the Temple, which he concludes has been alluded to in verses 6–8. However, he is not able to offer a convincing interpretation of ἐν τόπῳ ἁγίῳ (222–3).

church) will experience at the hand of the Jewish authorities (Matt. 10:17) and the Gentile rulers (10:18). By placing it within this context, this persecution is shown to be in the very nature of discipleship; it is not in itself a sign of the End. Nevertheless, it is of eschatological significance, in the sense that it will bear witness to the Gentile authorities and to the nations (καὶ ἐπὶ ἡγεμόνας δὲ καὶ βασιλεῖς ἀχθήσεσθε ἕνεκεν ἐμοῦ εἰς μαρτύριον αὐτοῖς καὶ τοῖς ἔθνεσιν, 10:18). In chapter 24 it is affirmed that this witness to the nations will be borne in all the world, and then the End will come (24:14).

In the context of Matthew 24, the evangelist seems to be more interested in the tribulation that arises from *intracommunity conflict* rather than what results from external persecution. It is true that 24:9 reiterates that external persecution will take place, and forms a doublet to 10:22, though with the addition that they will be hated by all *the nations*. However, in the context of Matthew 24, the attention immediately shifts to the strife within the community, implying that the pressure of the external hatred prompts and feeds the internal divisions. The conjunction καὶ τότε in verse 10 strengthens this impression. It seems, then, that Matthew understands external persecutions to be part of the nature of discipleship, but that internal conflict, hatred, lawlessness and love growing cold are directly associated with the tribulation of the End.

From the schema outlined above, I draw the following inferences for a reconstruction of the way in which the evangelist viewed the present: it was a time characterized by the rise of leaders who promised much and sought to lead the community astray. The exact nature of their pretensions could be discussed at length, but it is clear that they were religious (cf. ἐγώ εἰμι ὁ χριστός, verse 5, in the sense either of the one anointed by God, or as a charismatic prophet speaking in the name of the Risen Lord). That they had charismatic, or perhaps more accurately thaumaturgic, leanings is evident in 24:24 (cf. also 7:22). Most disturbing for Matthew, however, seems to be the division that they foster, because the resulting lawlessness and lovelessness is for Matthew the very negation of the Gospel (cf. 22:37–40). Matthew viewed the present, then, as a time of θλῖψις, of which a major part was the disintegration of the community. There was also some persecution by the Gentiles (24:9), but this was not viewed as a phenomenon exclusive to the present; indeed, they looked back on the recent past in which wars, and the Jewish War in particular, had occasioned conflict with the Gentiles. The present was also the time of the Gentile mission; the conflict with the Gentiles would be the occasion for bearing witness to the Gospel of the Kingdom, and then the End would come. The schema thus supports a situation of the post-seventy period in which the community is going through a period of pressure, both internal and external. The evangelist maintains an imminent expectation of the End, both in terms of a fervent hope that these days of tribulation would be shortened, and also as a point of orientation for those who are under pressure to fall away.

5.2   What distinguishes the two sequences?

Until this point I have examined the sequences together in order to draw out the parallels between them. It is now relevant to examine the sequences individually; are they intended to give a different perspective upon the same period of time?

The first sequence seems to take the perspective of the Matthean community. If, as I assume, the most probable location of the community was in a Syrian city, possibly Antioch,[27] then the events of the Jewish War would indeed have been heard of rather than experienced (μελλήσετε δὲ ἀκούειν πολέμους καὶ ἀκοὰς πολέμων, verse 6). Similarly, the famines and earthquakes occurred κατὰ τόπους, not directly affecting the community. Although it is possible to trace specific famines and earthquakes which may be alluded to in verse 7 (e.g. the famine under Claudius, Acts 11:28, the earthquake in Asia Minor, Tacitus, *Annal.* 14.26), these references are in the first instance to be understood as apocalyptic *topoi*. The presence of these apocalyptic *topoi* in verses 6–8 implies that some indeed considered this period to be the direct precursor to the End. Both Matthew and Mark before him considered it necessary to recognize these expectations, but to emphasize that these were not the End, but the beginning (πάντα δὲ ταῦτα ἀρχὴ ὠδίνων, Matt. 24:8).

The first sequence continues with material which focusses on the perspective of the Matthean community. The implied reader of this section, verses 9–12, would share the evangelist's perspective on the persecution and strife within the community, though the actual readers of the Gospel may not have viewed the intracommunity

---

[27] Cf. the discussion of this issue in Davies and Allison, *Matthew*, I, 138–47.

conflict or the 'opposing leaders' (Matthew's false prophets) in as dire a light.

The first sequence finishes with the reference to the Gentile mission, after which the End will come. It is widely recognized that the question of the Gentile mission was a significant issue for the Matthean community, which, in its recent past, had maintained a Jewish-Christian perspective.[28] It is therefore striking that, for Matthew, the Gentile mission had become an eschatological imperative: only upon the completion of this 'commission' would the End come. The eschatological nature of the commission is also apparent when the commission is explicitly given, in Matt. 28:19–20, for the final sentence sets the eschatological context for the command: καὶ ἰδοὺ ἐγὼ μεθ' ὑμῶν εἰμι πάσας τὰς ἡμέρας ἕως τῆς συντελείας τοῦ αἰῶνος. A concern for the συντελεία τοῦ αἰῶνος is voiced by the disciples in 24:3, when they question Jesus as to what its sign will be. The nature of the disciples' question will be discussed further below, but it is evident that, to the evangelist, the Gentile mission was closely associated with the close of the age.

The second sequence opens with explicit reference to the events associated with the war in Jerusalem and Judea. Unlike the opening of the first sequence, the perspective is of those who have first-hand experience of the war and who were resident in Judea at the time (cf. verse 15, ἴδητε, verse 16, οἱ ἐν τῇ Ἰουδαίᾳ). It was possible for Matthew, using the device of the two parallel sequences, to present the same period from a different perspective.[29] This does not, however, explain *why* the evangelist would have chosen to do so. The possible explanations seem to fall into two categories; either the second perspective was 'preserved' by the evangelist, although it was not directly relevant to the Matthean community, or the second perspective did have some relevance to the experience of the community.

Matthew may have retained this oracle despite the fact that the

[28] I share the opinion of Luz, *Matthew*, 84ff, that the Gentile mission was not taken for granted by the Matthean church, but that it is a deliberate new venture, commissioned by the Risen Lord himself (Matt. 28:19–20). An opposing thesis, that the Gospel of Matthew in its final redaction comes from a Gentile-Christian community and from a Gentile-Christian author, is maintained by Clark, 'Gentile Bias', Nepper-Christensen, *Matthäusevangelium*, 202–8, Strecker, *Weg*, 15–35, *et al.*

[29] Broer, without discerning two parallel sequences, nevertheless suggests that verse 15 begins a new section, and that verses 15–28 at least partially echo the same themes as the previous section. 'Aspekte', 210–11.

community did not share its Judean perspective because of the
evangelist's attitude to the Markan *Vorlage*. U. Luz argues that
'the evangelist was not a "free" author but *willingly* let himself be
influenced to a large extent by his main source, Mark', and discerns
that 'Matthew knows the Gospel of Mark so well, that he antici-
pates future material in his redaction, and that he reuses in other
places sayings from omitted verses of Mark. It is as if the evangelist,
despite his considerable condensations, wanted to use as much of
the text of Mark as possible!'.[30] It is therefore possible that 24:15ff
was retained out of respect for the importance of the oracle.
However, the opposite tendency is also apparent in the Gospel:

> Our redactor has omitted sayings and incidents that appar-
> ently held no meaning for him. There are, for example, no
> parallels to Mark 9.49–50 ('everyone will be salted with
> fire', followed by two non-sequiturs); 11.16 ('and he would
> not permit anyone to carry a vessel through the temple');
> and 14.51–2 (the flight of the naked young man).
> Matthew's faithfulness to his tradition did not include the
> passing on of incomprehensible matter.[31]

It is therefore necessary to consider whether the 'Judean oracle' was
indeed in some sense relevant to Matthew or the Matthean community. If so, its relevance may have been symbolic. Flight from
the Temple and from Judea could have represented a turning away
from the old order of Judaism, as symbolized by the Temple and its
cult. Matthew's community was to cling no longer to the old order,
but to open itself to the new challenge of the Gentile mission. It is
possible that this oracle was retained in order to strengthen the
legitimacy of the Gentile mission.

It is also possible that there were some members of the community for whom this oracle had been of great significance, namely
some refugees from Judea. This explanation is necessarily speculative, but it could have been a motivating factor. I am aware that the
Matthean community was not one which had escaped all outside
influences. Indeed, Matthew's use of the Gospel of Mark and of Q
as well as the special M material suggests to me that the community
had undergone some expansion concurrent with the prompting to
produce a new version of the Gospel story more suited to the
community needs.

[30] Luz, *Matthew*, 73.   [31] Davies and Allison, *Matthew*, 74.

A choice as to whether Matthew has retained this material primarily out of respect for the Markan source, or whether it was understood as relevant either because of its symbolism of departure from Judaism or because of the influence of some Judean refugees rests largely upon the interpretation given to certain striking additions to the oracle in verse 20, namely προσεύχεσθε δὲ ἵνα μὴ γένηται ἡ φυγὴ ὑμῶν χειμῶνος μηδὲ σαββάτῳ. So resolving this question will be deferred until after the discussion of these additions.

6. How can the additions to 24:20 (ἡ φυγὴ ὑμῶν and μηδὲ σαββάτῳ) be explained?

In incorporating the material of the Judean oracle from the Markan source, two striking features not found in Mark are added, namely the phrases 'your flight' and 'nor on a sabbath'. Does this imply that Matthew had access to a form of the Judean oracle independent of Mark, or are these additions to be explained on the redactional level? An answer to these questions will enable the function of the oracle in the Matthean discourse to be clarified.

These two phrases are not the only additions to this material in Matthew's Gospel, but the other ones are readily explicable as redactional clarifications of the Markan *Vorlage*. Matt. 24:15 reads: ὅταν οὖν ἴδητε τὸ βδέλυγμα τῆς ἐρημώσεως τὸ ῥηθὲν διὰ Δανιὴλ τοῦ προφήτου ἑστὸς ἐν τόπῳ ἁγίῳ . . . By noting that the prophet Daniel is the source of the cryptic reference to the desolating sacrilege, Matthew's characteristic interest in how the Hebrew Scriptures are fulfilled in the person and story of Jesus is apparent. The evangelist then 'corrects' the Markan ἑστηκότα, and makes 'where he should not be' more explicit, namely ἐν τόπῳ ἁγίῳ. Given this tendency to 'correct' and make more explicit, the phrase ἡ φυγὴ ὑμῶν may simply be such a clarification, intended to specify that the prayer was not about the circumstances of the installation of the βδέλυγμα τῆς ἐρημώσεως, but rather about the difficulty of flight under these circumstances. Thus this phrase may be no more than a clarification of the Markan *Vorlage*, such as the other clarificatory additions; this might suggest a redactional origin for ἡ φυγὴ ὑμῶν.

However, the phrase μηδὲ σαββάτῳ is no mere clarification, but definitely an expansion. Part of the problem in attributing this phrase to the redactional level is uncertainty as to the Sabbath observance of Matthew's own community. This verse seems to provide some evidence that the Matthean community observed the Sabbath,[32] though Matt. 12:1–8 leaves this open. All 'redactional' explanations necessitate interpreting this phrase as somehow relevant for the Matthean community, but it is by no means obvious why this phrase should be added to a flight that the evangelist explicitly ties to the Temple – ἐν τόπῳ ἁγίῳ.

Bearing in mind the findings of the previous chapter, in which it was shown that the literary deposits occasioned by the flight of Jewish Christians from Jerusalem during the Jewish War were quite diverse and did not necessarily conform in terms of their wording, it might be the case that Matthew had access to a version of the oracle which included these additions.

One verse which might support this theory – by indicating that the evangelist had access to recent information from Jerusalem via the Q prophets – is Matt. 23:35, with its enigmatic reference to the blood of Zachariah, son of Barachiah, who was slain between the sanctuary and the altar. Although it is now common to interpret this as referring to the death of Zechariah son of Jehoida in 2 Chr. 24, the difficulties with this interpretation are sufficient to warrant the consideration of a view which identifies the Zachariah of Matt. 23:35 with the Zachariah son of Bariscaeus/Baruch/Bareis whose murder is recounted in Josephus' *J.W.,* IV.334ff. According to the dating set out in the previous chapter, the beginning of the campaigning season of 68 CE is mentioned in *J.W.,* IV.413, which would set the assassination of Zachariah in late 67, not long after the installation of Phanias as high priest. The association between the Zachariah of Matt. 23:35 and of Josephus enjoyed some popularity in the eighteenth century, and may go back as far as John Chrysostom, according to J. Wellhausen.[33] It is Wellhausen, most recently, who championed this association.

One objection to the association is the fact that the saying is found upon the lips of Jesus;[34] this is not a weighty objection, in my opinion. Another is that one would have to suppose that this Zachariah must have been a Christian to have occasioned this saying, yet one might expect that such a Christian martyr would

---

[32] Cf. *Ibid.,* 27.   [33] Wellhausen, *Einleitung,* 118.

[34] E.g. Lagrange, *Matthieu,* 456: 'It would require more persuasive circumstances to oblige us to suppose that the tradition has placed this precise allusion to a future event upon the lips of Jesus' (translation mine).

have been more famous.[35] Despite these objections, the interpretation linking Matthew's Zachariah son of Barachiah with Josephus' Zachariah son of Bariscaeus has found some support by H. Falk, who emphasizes the link between the Bet Shammai Pharisees and the Zealots, and argues that Bet Shammai is the primary target of Matthew 23.[36]There is not scope within the parameters of this study to evaluate the evidence in detail, but I wish to note that this saying may represent a late addition to Q with a notable Jewish-Christian flavour.[37] It suggests that Matthew had access to information about Jerusalem in 67 CE from a source not available to Mark. If this were so, it would be likely that the bearers of this information also knew the Judean oracle, with slightly different wording. The most straightforward explanation of the additions is that they reflect a variant version of the Judean oracle.

However, in an article entitled 'Pray that your Flight may not be in Winter or on a Sabbath (Matthew 24:20)', G. N. Stanton reviews the possible explanations which can be given for these additions, and rejects any interpretation which shies away from regarding the additions as due to redactional activity. To him, claims of an earlier, original form preserved here look like 'special pleading'.[38] Instead, he regards them as redactional additions which indicate Matthew's concern that the Christians of the Matthean community recognize that they, too, may be called upon to flee. This point is also made in Matt. 10:18 and 22, as well as in the example of the wise men of Matt. 2:12.

According to Stanton's interpretation, the evangelist is seeking to indicate that current persecution of the disciples will lead to their flight, though no specific flight is in view.[39] The addition of 'on a Sabbath' would denote not the scruples of the Christian community about fleeing on a Sabbath, but rather the concern that such a flight would further antagonize some of those who were persecuting them. Of the redactional explanations, Stanton's is the most convincing.

---

[35] For this and other objections, cf. Chapman, 'Zacharias'.

[36] Falk, *Jesus the Pharisee*, 124–5: 'A major objection to Wellhausen's interpretation has been that Jesus is speaking here to the Pharisees, and not to Zealots. However, since we have established a direct link between Bet Shammai and the Zealots, Wellhausen may be vindicated.'

[37] Such an evaluation would be in keeping with the hypotheses of Luz, as set out in *Matthew*, 78 etc.

[38] Stanton, 'Flight'. The reference to 'special pleading' is on page 19 of the article in *JSNT*.

[39] *Ibid.*, 24.

A basic assumption of Stanton's interpretation is that the additions are intended to refer to the future rather than to the past.[40] By contrast, my interpretation of the chapter has argued that the flight in question was specifically in the past, namely the flight from Jerusalem at the time of the Jewish War. If the flight referred to in verses 15ff was understood as a past event, it could nevertheless have had a current symbolic meaning, just as the departure of the wise men was at once viewed as past, but with implications for the present. As argued in Chapter 4, the Maccabean flight also served as a model for later flights.

The result of this discussion is that while the additions to Matt. 24:20 can be accounted for on a redactional level, as Stanton demonstrates, it is more straightforward to allow that Matthew could have had access to a variant version of the Judean oracle. It is my opinion that the evangelist intended the implied reader to understand Matt. 24:15–20 as a past event. For Matthew, however, past events could and did have present significance, so that these verses invite a symbolical reading as advocating departure from the Temple and all it represents as well as from the rabbinic requirements of Sabbath observance. The alternative interpretations set out at the end of the previous section are therefore not mutually exclusive. Matthew could and in my opinion did conserve the Judean oracle from Mark, with some additions made available by certain Jewish Christians fleeing Judea, but allowed the oracle to function symbolically to show the necessity of parting ways with the old order.

There are three further matters about my interpretation of two sequences within Matt. 24:6–31 that need to be addressed: are there any precedents to this interpretation; what evidence is there that such a literary technique was known at the time when the Gospel was written; and if this interpretation is plausible for Matthew, why not also for Mark?

7.   Precedents for the two-sequence interpretation

The two-sequence interpretation outlined above is an independent contribution to the exegesis of Matthew 24. Nevertheless, since I formulated this hypothesis, two comparable interpretations have come to light. The earlier one, upon which the latter is based, is

---

[40]   *Ibid.*, 21.

found in a nineteenth-century commentary by J. P. Lange, entitled *The Gospel According to Matthew*. In his section on Matthew 24, Lange writes as follows:

> In harmony with apocalyptical style, He [Matthew's Jesus] exhibited the judgements of His coming in a series of cycles, each of which depicts the whole futurity, but in such a manner that with every new cycle the scene seems to approximate to, and more closely resemble, the final catastrophe.[41]

According to Lange, there are three cycles:

> Thus the first cycle delineates the whole course of the world down to the end, in its general characteristics (vers. 4–14). The second gives the signs of the approaching destruction of Jerusalem and paints this destruction itself as a sign and a commencement of the judgement of the world, which from that day onward proceeds in silent and suppressed days of judgement down to the last (vers. 15–28). The third describes the sudden end of the world and the judgement which ensues (vers. 29–44).[42]

In my opinion, Lange correctly perceived that the chronology of Matthew 24 is best understood as 'cycles' or sequences, and he rightly interpreted verses 15ff as the beginning of the second cycle. These cycles he interpreted as encompassing the whole of human history, in keeping with his theological/homiletic interests and with the methodology available to him. He did not interpret them from the viewpoint of the evangelist or the Matthean community, which the present study has sought to do. He did not draw parallels between the cycles, nor did he further discuss the claim that such cycles are in keeping with apocalyptic literature. Nevertheless, his interpretation is, to my knowledge, the first to account for the chronology of Matthew 24 by means of cycles or sequences.

Lange's interpretation was taken up in a recent, unpublished doctoral thesis entitled 'A Chronology of Matthew 24:1–44', by J. F. Hart. Hart belongs to a conservative school of exegesis which does not use the historical-critical method or any of the newer interpretative methodologies, but rather a 'grammatical-historical-theological' style of analysis.[43] There is some interaction between

---

[41] Lange, *Matthew*, 418.   [42] *Ibid.*, 418.   [43] Hart, 'Chronology', 27.

Hart and critical scholarship reflected in this thesis, but it is for the most part negative (i.e. why these scholars are mistaken). Hart endeavours to read Matt. 24:1–44 purely eschatologically, viewing it 'as containing predictions of predominantly or exclusively future events'.[44] Even verses 15ff, which, he admits, refer to the destruction of the Temple in Jerusalem, are interpreted as pertaining to a rebuilt Jerusalem Temple.[45] Hart's interests are in fact more systematic that exegetical. He constantly measures Matthew 24 against the 'program' of Revelation, 2 Thessalonians, and other scriptural passages, and harmonizes the meanings, for his assumption is that prophetic scripture is unified.[46] He interacts frequently with premillenial and pretribulational interpretations, as well as those of dispensationalists. Moreover, he makes no distinction between the original meaning and the hermeneutical task. For these reasons it is not profitable to the purposes of this study, which takes a primary interest in the redaction-critical question of the evangelist's own conception, to engage further with Hart's interpretation. Let us now therefore turn to the second issue raised above, namely the evidence for such a two-sequence technique.

8. Evidence for a literary technique using multiple chronological sequences: Revelation

As mentioned above, J. P. Lange made the comment that a model which divided Matthew 24 into cycles was quite in keeping with apocalyptic techniques. Although he gave no further substantiation for this, the intervening century of scholarship would seem to affirm rather than overturn his assumption. Progress has been made on the techniques whereby the apocalypticists interpolated and reshaped material.[47] The material closest to hand which affords the opportunity to compare the function of cycles and their relation to a writing's overall chronological conception is the Revelation to John. The visions of the seven trumpets (chapters 8–9) and the seven bowls (chapters 15–16) have long been recognized as being in many respects parallel,[48] and the vision of the seven seals, including its relationship to the other sequences of seven, is crucial for understanding the overall conception of the

---

[44] *Ibid.*, 39.   [45] *Ibid.*, 147.   [46] *Ibid.*, 143.

[47] Cf. the proceedings of the International Colloquium on Apocalypticism, Uppsala, August 12–17, 1979, in Hellholm, *Apocalypticism*.

[48] Cf. Bornkamm, 'Komposition', who cites earlier studies of this parallelism.

work. R. H. Mounce put the problem in the following way: 'The basic structural question is whether John intended his readers to understand the visions recorded in his work in a straightforward chronological sense or whether some form of recapitulation is involved'.[49] In seeking to draw any useful comparison between this issue in Revelation and in Matthew 24, it must be recognized that the problem of the overall structure of Revelation is far more complex than can be dealt with fully in this context, and also considerably more complex than the structure I have proposed for Matt. 24:6–31. Moreover, there is no question of any direct literary association between the two writings, so that any comparison must remain at the level of the literary techniques available to the respective authors.

J. Lambrecht, in an article entitled 'A Structuration of Revelation 4,1–22,5', takes up the question of the interrelationship between the visions and their contexts. Lambrecht seeks to show that the successive visions are to be understood as both recapitulation and intensification: 'There certainly is much recapitulation in Rev. (e.g. trumpets and bowls), but not pure, simple repetition. We have a type of recapitulation which at the same time manifests intensification . . . yet does not exclude progress.'[50] Lambrecht sets out a structuration of Revelation which, rather than seeing the three series of seven as discrete units, shows them to 'encompass' one another, partly through the fact that they overlap, and partly because the first two series are open-ended, finding their resolution only in the final series. Their open-endedness is made more vivid by the intercalation of material pertaining to the protection of persecuted Christians, for the seventh seal and trumpet are dramatically deferred by these insertions.

Lambrecht's position is that the elements of the series are related both through repetition and intensification. On the question of the implied chronology of Revelation, he answers as follows:

> Are not the three septets of increasing plagues, precisely because of both their frequency and their repetitive character, meant by the author to suggest that his literary presentation does not equal literal concretization in future history? If the answer to this question is yes – and we think it is – the repetition feature is intended by John to weaken

[49] Mounce, *Revelation*, 45.   [50] Lambrecht, 'Structuration', 81.

the straightforwardness of his presentation. Through this feature he warns as it were his readers that future historical realization will not necessarily follow his literary artificial prophecy.[51]

One might perhaps explain John's intention in somewhat different terms, namely as a dramatic shaping of the material in order to 'perform' the retarding and speeding of time, which, in being given a public dramatic reading, could engender in the audience a sense of the possibility of endurance.[52] Nevertheless, Lambrecht's point about the series as being at once recapitulation and intensification is relevant to this present study of Matt. 24:6–31.[53]

According to my interpretation of how Matthew structured this section of the eschatological discourse, there is indeed recapitulation evident between the two sequences. There may be a certain intensification from the first to the second sequence, not so much in the description of tribulation, but in the description of the End. In the first sequence, it is simply mentioned, verse 14. The first sequence in no way describes the features of the End; it is simply the horizon against which the time of the community's tribulations and of the Gentile mission are measured. In the second sequence, however, verses 29–31 elaborate upon the nature of the End. Thus the focus of the second sequence is more squarely upon the End. However, it is not clear that the second Matthean sequence is to be interpreted as a dramatic heightening of the first in the same way that the seven series in Revelation are. Rather, as has been shown above, the perspective of the first is primarily upon the community's own experience, whereas the second sequence's perspective is wider, embracing the experiences of the fleeing Jewish-Christian

---

[51] *Ibid.*, 104.

[52] This explanation is comparable to the 'creative envisioning' function of apocalyptic imagination referred to by Horsley in *Violence*, 144.

[53] On the interrelationship between the series in Revelation, see also the controversial study by Corsini, *Apocalypse*, who argues on page 63 that:

> although the account is often read as a continual progression, this is not the case. Like the Gospel of John, the same theology is repeated over and over again, each time going a little deeper, and carrying the message further, like waves on a seashore. It is a story of sin and redemption, of suffering and hope, told four times – the number four (four corners of the earth) representing the whole of the earth and its history. This story is dominated by the first coming of Jesus, the 'Revelation of Jesus Christ' (1:1) central yet culminating in its role in salvation history both before and after the actual presence of Jesus of Nazareth among us.

refugees, the situation of the elect (more generally), and the vision of the End.

It is possible that the two sequences are intended to reply more clearly to the (redactionally modified) question of the disciples in verse 3: πότε ταῦτα ἔσται καὶ τί τὸ σημεῖον τῆς σῆς παρουσίας καὶ συντελείας τοῦ αἰῶνος; If one compares this question to its Markan counterpart (πότε ταῦτα ἔσται καὶ τί τὸ σημεῖον ὅταν μέλλῃ ταῦτα συντελεῖσθαι πάντα;), one notices that here, too, Matthew has sought to clarify the latter part of the question, making Christ's coming the explicit focus of the End of the age. I have argued that the Markan Jesus did not answer the question in the terms in which it was asked. For Matthew, however, whose interest does not lie in the misunderstanding of the disciples, the twofold question may in fact correspond to the two sequences. 'When will this be?', which refers in the first instance to the destruction of the Temple, is addressed in both sequences by the positioning of the references to the destruction at the beginning. More generally, however, the question of 'when' is answered by the end of the first sequence: once the Gentile mission is complete, the End will come. The πότε of the question seems to find its answer in the τότε of verse 14. The second sequence addresses the question of a sign, showing that neither the destruction of the Temple, nor even the period of great tribulation and false prophets, is the *sign* of Christ's coming. The only sign is to be the 'sign of the Son of Man', verse 30. Although there have been various proposals as to what this sign is, I maintain that it is the coming itself, which will be apparent to all.[54]

In summary, then, I have demonstrated that a literary technique

---

[54] Contra Higgins, 'Sign'. Higgins is certainly right that a strictly chronological reading of verse 30 seems to imply that they first see the sign of the Son of Man, then mourn, and only subsequently see the Son of Man coming on the clouds. This seems to favour an understanding that the sign of the Son of Man is something other than his coming, and early interpretations (Did. 16,6; Gos. Pet., 10, 39–42; Apoc. Pet.) pursue this distinction, though in ways more varied than Higgins allows. However, it is not clear that the two additional Matthean phrases, which do, as Higgins rightly states, reflect the testimonies of Deut. 7:13 and Zech 12:10ff, are meant to be understood as chronological stages. 'The sign of the Son of Man', drawing as it does on a Q tradition (Luke 11:29–30/Matt. 12:39–40), may be a clarificatory addition which is intended to make Jesus' reply to the disciples question in verse 3 more explicit. If this is so, verse 30 a and c may be describing the same event, and are separated by verse 30 b simply owing to the evangelist's compilation of the sources. Other indications within the chapter, esp. verse 27, support the idea that there will be no sign other than the coming itself.

of parallel sequences which both recapitulate and shift the perspective of the reader was open to Matthew. Moreover it has been argued that it is possible, though not altogether certain, that the sequences may correspond to the evangelist's interpretation of the twofold question in verse 3, which itself seeks to make more explicit the central role of Christ's coming in the close of the age.

Let us now turn to the question of why I maintain a two-sequence structure for Matthew, but not for Mark.

9. Two sequences in Matthew, but not in Mark?

It might seem that a two-sequence structure could be applied just as well to Mark's eschatological discourse as to Matthew's. In the preceding study of the Markan discourse, I proposed that the two references to false prophets are best understood as a type of *inclusio*, whereby Mark indicates the 'present' nature of all the intervening material. The other obviously redactional feature, the βλέπετε references, fall within these parameters, and indicate current concerns facing Mark's community; these imperatives do not seem to point to two parallel sequences. I will therefore set out in point form some further reasons why the two-sequence structural model is convincing for Matthew, but not for Mark.

(a)   As set out above, it seems that the disciples' question in Matt. 24:3 finds an answer in the two sequences. The question when – πότε – is answered at the end of the first sequence by the τότε of verse 14, and the requested sign is explicitly addressed at the end of the second sequence (verse 30) in the reference to τὸ σημεῖον τοῦ υἱοῦ τοῦ ἀνθρώπου.

In Mark, however, the question of 'when' does not find an answer until verse 32, and this answer is emphasized in verses 33 and 35: you do not know when. In Mark, the disciples' question is to be understood against the wider theme of the misunderstanding of the disciples, and Jesus does not give them a reply in the terms that they ask for it.

(b)   The word θλῖψις occurs in Matthew 24 at verses 9 and 21. By contrast, in Mark's Gospel only the second of the two references is found. There is therefore no verbal indication at this point in Mark that there could be some sort of parallelism at work.

(c)   There are three references in Matthew to false prophets (24:5, 11, 23–4), whereas in Mark there are two (13:6, 21–2); the two seem to indicate an *inclusio* rather than two sequences. The verbal parallels between the three references in Matthew are more apparent than in Mark:

Matt. 24	Mark 13
v.5 πολλοὺς πλανήσουσιν	v. 6 πολλοὺς πλανήσουσιν
v.11 πλανήσουσιν πολλούς	
v.24 ὥστε πλανῆσαι . . . καὶ τοὺς ἐκλεκτούς	v.22 πρὸς τὸ ἀποπλανᾶν . . . τοὺς ἐκλεκτούς

The addition of the second reference in Matthew heightens the possibility of parallelism.

(d) Matthew changes the Markan aorist verb ἐκολόβωσεν (Mark 13:20) to the future form κολοβωθήσονται in Matt. 24:22b. Whereas for Mark, the shortening of the tribulation seems to have already taken place,[55] for Matthew, it is still to be shortened, which allows it to be understood as a present reality. This supports the two-sequence model for Matthew, but not for Mark.

(e) A further indication that the tribulation is understood by Matthew as present reality is the addition of εὐθέως in verse 29; Matthew expects the End to follow immediately upon this period of tribulation. There is no comparable reference in Mark, who does not consider the Markan community to be in a 'historical caesura' between verses 23 and 24, but in the whole period indicated by the *inclusio*. The fact that the tribulations of Matt. 24:9–12 and 21–6 are the implied present means that a two-sequence model is the most appropriate way to explain the structure of this section of Matthew's discourse.

(f) Matthew finishes the first sequence with a sentence that has a conclusive air about it: καὶ τότε ἥξει τὸ τέλος (verse 14). At the equivalent place in Mark is the sentence ὁ δὲ ὑπομείνας εἰς τέλος οὗτος σωθήσεται, which Matthew included in verse 13. In Mark, therefore, there is no equivalent conclusive sentence which might point to a two-sequence structure.

(g) Matthew includes the saying about the Gentile mission at the close of the first sequence, indicating a close association between the Gentile mission and the End. Mark, by contrast, has this saying in the middle (verse 10) of the persecution passage (13:9–13). For

---

[55] It might of course be possible to interpret the Markan reference as pertaining to the apocalyptic notion that the times have already been fixed by God, and that the shortening has been preordained. However, I have suggested that Mark associated this tribulation with the flight from Judea, and that it was, for this reason, already past.

Matthew, then, verses 9–14 refer to the Gentile mission, as shown by the addition of an explicit reference to them in verse 9 (ἔσεσθε μισούμενοι ὑπὸ πάντων τῶν ἐθνῶν). Thus Matthew frames the present as the time of the Gentile mission (verses 9 and 14). For Mark, there does not seem to be a comparably strong distinction between Jewish and Gentile persecution; the opening of the equivalent passage (verse 9) refers to both Jewish and Gentile persecution. In Mark, the specific reference to the Gentile mission (verse 10) interrupts rather than frames the section. The way in which Matthew frames the section indicates that the following material is not to be understood as part of the present, and this supports the two-sequence model for Matthew, but not for Mark.

(h)   At the end of both sequences, Matthew shows an interest in the fate of the Gentiles. A parallel is not found in Mark.

For these reasons, I maintain that a two-sequence model best explains the Matthean redaction of this section of the eschatological discourse, but that there are no indications that such a model was used by Mark. In the light of this, I can draw some inferences about Matthew's *Naherwartung* or expectation of the imminence of the End.

10.   Did Matthew expect an imminent End?

The evidence of the Gospel as a whole reveals that Matthew gives particular prominence to the eschatological horizon of judgement, especially in comparison with the Markan *Vorlage*. With regard to the eschatological discourse itself, Matthew has lengthened it significantly. In terms of redactional tendencies, I have shown that Matthew often seeks to clarify what may be obscure to the Matthean community, making the Markan material more explicit and grammatically correct. Moreover Matthew shapes the material to reflect the community situation more clearly, using, as I have argued, a two-sequence technique. This situation includes false prophets, intracommunity conflict, the rise of wickedness and the cooling of love, as well as some persecution, first at the hands of fellow Jews (chapter 10) and then at the hands of the Gentiles (24:9, 14). This is not the picture of a community with a uniformly high eschatological hope; if anything, the opposite seems to be true. In the face of this, the evangelist emphasizes the eschatological perspective of their faith and reiterates the imminence of the parousia.

I have argued that the eschatological horizon is not simply to be explained as a tool in the service of ethics. In my opinion, the evangelist really did believe that they were currently living in the last days. Matthew does not comfortably fit our understanding of an author seeking to come to terms with the delay of the parousia, for the imminence of expectation is heightened by such an addition as εὐθέως in verse 29.

In considering the question of whether Matthew really thought that the Matthean community was living in the last days, let us consider Matt. 16:28 and its parallels.

Matt. 16:28	**Mark 9:1**	**Luke 9:27**
	καὶ ἔλεγεν αὐτοῖς·	
ἀμὴν λέγω ὑμῖν ὅτι	ἀμὴν λέγω ὑμῖν ὅτι	λέγω δὲ ὑμῖν ἀληθῶς,
εἰσίν τινες τῶν ὧδε	εἰσίν τινες ὧδε τῶν	εἰσίν τινες τῶν αὐτοῦ
ἑστώτων	ἑστηκότων	ἑστηκότων
οἵτινες οὐ μὴ	οἵτινες οὐ μὴ	οἳ οὐ μὴ
γεύσωνται θανάτου	γεύσωνται θανάτου	γεύσωνται θανάτου
ἕως ἂν ἴδωσιν	ἕως ἂν ἴδωσιν	ἕως ἂν ἴδωσιν
τὸν υἱὸν τοῦ ἀνθρώπου		
ἐρχόμενον		
ἐν τῇ βασιλείᾳ	τὴν βασιλείαν	τὴν βασιλείαν
αὐτοῦ.	τοῦ θεοῦ	τοῦ θεοῦ.
	ἐληλυθυῖαν ἐν δυνάμει.	

If one begins by looking at Mark, one finds the claim that some of those present would not taste death until they saw the Kingdom of God having come in power. Mark has followed this claim with the account of the transfiguration, which leads many scholars to see this as the intended referent. Luke abbreviates at this point so that the reference is simply to the 'Kingdom of God'. Although Luke does not do away with the future aspect of the Kingdom, the emphasis is given to the presence of the Kingdom in Jesus' own preaching and presence and subsequently in the work of the disciples. It is only Matthew who heightens this logion with a specific reference to the parousia of the Son of Man. It is logical to assume Matthew did so because this evangelist understood Mark in this sense and believed it to be the case. This is not to claim that Matthew was not an heir to certain traditions which recognized a delay in the parousia – the study of Matt. 25:1–13 has shown that this was indeed the case. Nevertheless, the evangelist did not see this as the central issue facing the Matthean community. Rather, the experience of tribulation, particularly within the community, confirmed for Matthew that they were living in the last days.

Could Matthew's Gospel have a heightened expectation of the parousia if it were really written later than Mark's? Some will seek to solve this conundrum by means of an alternative-source hypothesis, such as the Griesbach hypothesis. However, my position is that the models that have been used for reconstructing the development of eschatology need revision. If Matthew's Gospel shows a more heightened expectation of the parousia than Mark's and yet was written later than Mark, it calls into question the form-critical assumption which dates the relative age of certain sayings according to the imminence of their eschatological expectation. In my opinion, the fact that Matthew displays a more imminent expectation of the End than Mark does not negate the validity of the two-source hypothesis as the best working hypothesis for the explication of synoptic relations, but rather calls for a more nuanced understanding of the factors governing eschatological expectation and for a greater appreciation of the diversity of early Christianity.

The diversity of early Christianity is best grasped against the background of the diversity of Judaism, even post-70 CE. I will conclude this chapter by comparing some of the Jewish apocalyptic responses to the destruction of Jerusalem with the response of Matthew as reflected in the eschatological discourse.

11. Matthew compared with other Jewish apocalyptic responses to the Jewish War

Some scholarly attention has already been devoted to a comparison of Jewish apocalyptic responses to the fall of Jerusalem,[56] and this present contribution cannot attempt to deal with the subject comprehensively. Rather, I will limit myself to the material which affords opportunity to compare and contrast Matthew with contemporary Jewish apocalyptic writings.

The four apocalypses which address the problems created by the destruction of Jerusalem and the Temple are 4 Ezra, 2 Apoc. Bar., the Apocalypse of Abraham (Apoc. Ab.) and 3 Apoc. Bar. The literary relationship between these works, which is particularly

---

[56] Cf. Stone, 'Reactions', also *Fourth Ezra*, esp. 35ff. A comparative study which includes Matthew is found in Nickelsburg, *Jewish Literature*, 277–309. For further references, see Nickelsburg's bibliography, 307ff.

close between 4 Ezra and 2 Apoc. Bar., cannot be dealt with here.[57]

Each of these works seeks to deal with the question of theodicy: why has a just God allowed sinful Gentiles to prevail against the covenant people and to destroy the Temple? At the time of the destruction of the Second Temple in 70 CE, these issues were by no means new; the Babylonian exile had similarly raised them. The answers given during the Second Temple period maintained that the justice of God was evident in these events, and linked Israel's suffering to Israel's sin. The profound effect that the destruction of the First Temple had is reflected in the way the Jewish writers sought to recount, examine and evaluate the events of the past in order to find a basis for understanding the present.[58] It is therefore not surprising that three of the four apocalypses are fictitiously set against the background of the first destruction.

Each of the apocalypses links the destruction of the Temple to the sins of the people. 2 Apoc. Bar. opens with God's announcement that the city will be destroyed because of the people's sin. 3 Apoc. Bar., too, in chapter 16, depicts God as loosing wrath upon the people because of their sin. In the Apoc. Ab., God permits the destruction of Jerusalem and the burning of the Temple as punishment for cultic abominations (chapter 27), and thus gives more specific content to the nature of the sin for which Israel, in this apocalyptic seer's opinion, was being punished. It is, however, 4 Ezra which gives the most comprehensive reflections upon the question of Israel's sin. In this work, the seer 'Ezra' is not content with the explanation of the justice of Israel's punishment, for it is due, at least in part, to the burden of 'an evil heart' which God has not removed (3:20–7). For Ezra, this is a universal problem of humanity, but most acute in the case of Israel, for it has not allowed God's chosen people to bear the fruit of the Torah. Moreover, Ezra does not see in what way God's justice is expressed in the desolation of Israel, for 'the deeds of Babylon', if weighed in the balance, would be shown to be far more iniquitous (3:28–36). Thus each of the apocalypses allows the question of God's justice to be, at least in part, answered by reference to Israel's sin. In the case of 4 Ezra, the initial response to Ezra's misgivings about God's justice is that God's deeper wisdom necessarily eludes those who are

---

[57] For a discussion of this issue, cf. Stone, *Fourth Ezra*, 39–40, 41–2.
[58] Cf. Stone, 'Reactions', 196, who cites Ackroyd, *Exile*, 63–102.

tainted by the corrupt world (4:10–12). This is more like salt in the wound to Ezra than comfort, yet it asserts that despite all appearances, God's justice is at work and has not failed.

An interrelated issue of theodicy is the question of God's covenant relationship with Israel and the issue of God's holy name. How can God allow the covenant people to be trampled underfoot, and thus bring the holy name into disrepute before the Gentiles? The reproach before their victors is that their God is no god, namely one who has no power to save (cf. 2 Apoc. Bar 21:21ff, 3 Apoc. Bar. 1:2, Apoc. Ab., esp. chapters 27–9, and most eloquently, 4 Ezra 4:22–5, 5:21–30, 6:55–9).

If one examines Matthew for comparable concerns, one is not disappointed. While it is true that Matthew does not offer the sort of extended laments which are found in the apocalypses, the issues of theodicy which they raise – God's justice, Israel's sin, what has become of God's relationship with the covenant people and the reproach before the Gentiles – are all addressed. I do not therefore share the opinion of Nickelsburg that Matthew does not write 'with an eye towards the problem of theodicy, as do all the contemporary apocalyptists in their own ways'.[59] In opening the eschatological discourse with chapter 23, Matthew at once affirms the importance of Moses' seat and the ongoing pre-eminence of the Torah, while at the same time making clear that the scribes and Pharisees[60] are disqualified in their leadership of God's people. According to Matthew 23, it is due to their own sin and hypocrisy – which has repercussions not only on the individual but also on the community level (verses 4, 13) – that the culmination had to be the desolation of their house (verse 38). Matthew maintains that God's covenant relationship with Israel is expressed in the way in which God has constantly sought them (Matt. 23:34, 21:33–43, and in the depiction of Jesus' mission to the lost sheep of the house of Israel). Indeed, the whole Gospel sets out to show the way in which Israel has been sought, and the way in which it progressively turns away. Matthew seeks to show that it is in the face of this turning away, constantly repeated, that God justly punishes Israel for its sin. Matthew does not consider God's relationship with the covenant people cut off and offered instead to the Gentiles, though some

---

[59] Nickelsburg, *Jewish Literature*, 304.

[60] I acknowledge Orton's distinctions between various scribes, as set out in *Scribe*. Here it is apparent that the scribes of the Pharisees are in view.

might read Matt. 21:41 this way. The vineyard – rather than the tenants – represents the covenant relationship; the tenants are those who administer it. Matthew does view the Jewish leadership as unfit for this administration, and the transfer is to those who will produce the fruits of the Kingdom of God (21:43). Against the wider background of this Gospel, this refers to those who practise the 'better righteousness' (5:20), referring thus to Christians, Jewish and Gentile, though not all qualify (7:21ff).[61] The reproach before the Gentiles is thus forestalled, for the Gentiles themselves, at least in part, are drawn into God's wider plan (Matt. 2:1–12, 27:54, etc.). Even the frustrating reply given to Ezra about God's deeper wisdom has a counterpart in Matthew, in the Matthean notion of 'understanding' discussed above. Unlike in 4 Ezra, where the issue of understanding exacerbated rather than relieved the questions of theodicy, in Matthew 11:25–6 the effect is indeed to offer comfort, as the reader by implication shares in this deeper wisdom.

These reflections are offered in order to show that Matthew was by no means writing in a vacuum. The Jewish apocalyptic answers, in addressing the pressing issues of their day, vary in the way they deal with questions of theodicy. Similarly Matthew, in addressing the issues which were pressing for the Jews of the post-70 period, offers a distinctive Jewish theological response. The implications of the destruction were, in Matthew's case, much more mixed than they were for the authors of the apocalypses in question. There *is* lament over the destruction of Jerusalem in the Gospel (cf. 23:37), and yet it has caused the evangelist to dwell in such a way upon Jewish sin that a vindication of Christ could be seen in the destruction. Read through the lenses of subsequently triumphalist Christian responses to the destruction of the Temple, this might imply an anti-Jewish and pro-Gentile perspective. However, although Gentiles are countenanced and are part of God's eschatological schema, Matthew's response is a *Jewish* response.[62] In that sense, Gentile Christians cannot simply appropriate it and level it back at Jews, as has often been done throughout history. Rather, one must respect and not misuse the fact that each Jewish response acknowledged a role which Jewish sin had played; each struggled to find God's justice and covenant faithfulness through this most

---

[61] On the issue of the nature of the new covenant people, cf. Stanton's discussion of the title of his book *A Gospel for a New People*, 10–12.

[62] Cf. Segal, 'Voice'.

devastating of events – the destruction of Jerusalem and the Temple.

If Matthew did indeed adapt Mark 13 to the Matthean community situation by means of a literary technique using two chronological sequences, as I have argued, this was a remarkable scribal achievement. It means that the evangelist adopted a *literary* solution to the problem of how to adapt the Markan text, and a solution that was both conservative of the traditions and flexible in their application. It is also a solution that reflects some familiarity and facility with techniques known and used by apocalyptic streams within Judaism. My findings support the study of D. E. Orton which situates Matthew squarely in the tradition of the apocalyptic scribes, and calls for a new recognition and appreciation of the 'quasi-prophetic creative authority of the insightful scribe'.[63]

[63] Orton, *Scribe*, 175.

6

DIDACHE 16 AS A DEVELOPMENT IN CHRISTIAN ESCHATOLOGY

As the final aspect of this study, let us now turn our attention to the eschatological traditions preserved in the last section of the Didache, chapter 16. In examining this material, I hope to be able to gain some clues as to the factors influencing the development of eschatology in the early church. The passage in question reads as follows:

1. Γρηγορεῖτε ὑπὲρ τῆς ζωῆς ὑμῶν· οἱ λύχνοι ὑμῶν μὴ σβεσθήτωσαν, καὶ αἱ ὀσφύες ὑμῶν μὴ ἐκλυέσθωσαν, ἀλλὰ γίνεσθε ἕτοιμοι· οὐ γὰρ οἴδατε τὴν ὥραν, ἐν ᾗ ὁ κύριος ἡμῶν ἔρχεται. 2. πυκνῶς δὲ συναχθήσεσθε ζητοῦντες τὰ ἀνήκοντα ταῖς ψυχαῖς ὑμῶν· οὐ γὰρ ὠφελήσει ὑμᾶς ὁ πᾶς χρόνος τῆς πίστεως ὑμῶν, ἐὰν μὴ ἐν τῷ ἐσχάτῳ καιρῷ τελειωθῆτε. 3. ἐν γὰρ ταῖς ἐσχάταις ἡμέραις πληθυνθήσονται οἱ ψευδοπροφῆται καὶ οἱ φθορεῖς, καὶ στραφήσονται τὰ πρόβατα εἰς λύκους, καὶ ἡ ἀγάπη στραφήσεται εἰς μῖσος. 4. αὐξανούσης γὰρ τῆς ἀνομίας μισήσουσιν ἀλλήλους καὶ διώξουσι καὶ παραδώσουσι, καὶ τότε φανήσεται ὁ κοσμοπλανὴς ὡς υἱὸς θεοῦ καὶ ποιήσει σημεῖα καὶ τέρατα, καὶ ἡ γῆ παραδοθήσεται εἰς χεῖρας αὐτου, καὶ ποιήσει ἀθέμιτα, ἃ οὐδέποτε γέγονεν ἐξ αἰῶνος. 5. τότε ἥξει ἡ κτίσις τῶν ἀνθρώπων εἰς τὴν πύρωσιν τῆς δοκιμασίας, καὶ σκανδαλισθήσονται πολλοὶ καὶ ἀπολοῦνται, οἱ δὲ ὑπομείναντες ἐν τῇ πίστει αὐτῶν σωθήσονται ὑπ᾿ αὐτοῦ τοῦ καταθέματος. 6. καὶ τότε φανήσεται τὰ σημεῖα τῆς ἀληθείας· πρῶτον σημεῖον ἐκπετάσεως ἐν οὐρανῷ, εἶτα σημεῖον φωνῆς σάλπιγγος, καὶ τὸ τρίτον ἀνάστασις νεκρῶν· 7. οὐ πάντων δέ, ἀλλ᾿ ὡς ἐρρέθη· **Ἥξει ὁ κύριος καὶ πάντες οἱ ἅγιοι μετ᾿ αὐτοῦ.** 8. τότε ὄψεται ὁ κόσμος τὸν κύριον ἐρχόμενον ἐπάνω τῶν νεφελῶν τοῦ οὐρανοῦ . . . [1]

---

[1] The text is that of Codex Jerusalem 54, the only comprehensive extant copy of the

1. Watch over **your** life. Do not let **your** lamps be extinguished and do not let **your** waist be ungirded, but be ready, for you do not know the hour in which our Lord is coming.

2. Assemble yourselves regularly, seeking out the things that are proper for **your** inner-selves, for the whole time of your faith will not be of any use to **you** if, in that last moment, you are not perfected.

3. For, in the last days, false prophets and corrupters will be multiplied, and the sheep will be turned into wolves, and love will be changed to hate.

4. For, as lawlessness increases, people will hate, persecute and betray one another. And then the world-deceiver will appear as a son of God: and will do signs and wonders, and the world shall be handed over into his hands and he will commit abominations which have never happened before.

5. Then the creation of humans will pass through the testing fire, and many will fail and perish, but those who have persevered in their faith will be saved from the grave (*katathematos*) itself.

6. And then the signs of truth will appear: first the sign of an opening in the heaven, then the sign of the sound of the trumpet, and thirdly, the resurrection of the dead:

7. [The resurrection] not of all [the dead], but as he [the Lord] said, 'The Lord will come and all his saints [will come] with him'.

8. Then the world will see the Lord coming upon the clouds of heaven . . .[2]

This passage of the Didache may well be able to yield some useful information about the development of early Christian eschatology, whether one perceives the material common to the synoptic Gospels and the Didache as evidence of literary dependence by the Didache on one or more of the synoptic Gospels, or whether the parallels between Matthew 24 and Didache 16 are thought to be better accounted for by reference to the use of a common source.

Greek original. The ending, however, is presumably incomplete, as the versions include a picture of the final judgement. Wengst reconstructs the missing ending with the words ἀποδοῦναι ἑκάστῳ κατὰ τὴν πρᾶξιν αὐτοῦ (to requite each person according to his/her deeds). *Schriften*, 90.

[2] Translation by Milavec in 'Pastoral Genius'. Bold script indicates plural.

The question of the literary relationship between the texts has largely dominated the discussion of Didache 16, and at present one can by no means speak of a consensus with regard to this important question. For this reason it will be necessary to offer a critique of certain contemporary positions in order to reach a basis upon which further exploration can be founded. The complex questions of the literary unity of the Didache and the stages of its redaction have been much debated. However, for the purposes of this study, I will limit myself to Didache 16, where the parallels to the synoptic eschatological material are prominent.

The support for an explanation of the literary relationship between the synoptic Gospels and the Didache via the use of common sources has been growing in recent years.[3] The influence of the major works by H. Koester,[4] and J.-P. Audet[5] accounts in part for this. It has been argued by C. N. Jefford that one can speak of three dominant approaches aligned according to the three dominant languages of the primary individual researchers.[6] However, with respect to the question of literary relations, support comes from all three dominant languages for an explanation which looks to a source or sources common to both Matthew 24 and the Didache.[7] Similarly, one can cite support for the theory that the Didache made use of one or more of the synoptic Gospels from each of these language groups, though contemporary German-speaking scholars are perhaps better represented here.[8] It seems that the dividing line does not lie according to language groups, but rather according to two interrelated factors. The first is whether the scholars consider themselves to be in the first instance 'Didachists' or 'New Testament scholars',[9] and the second is the criteria upon

---

[3] The various sources of the Didache, such as the widely accepted 'Two-Way' source, cannot be examined within the scope of this chapter. Rather, I will confine my attention to sources behind Did. 16.

[4] Koester, *Überlieferung*.   [5] Audet, *Didachè*.   [6] Jefford, *Sayings,* 4ff.

[7] In addition to those already cited, cf. Glover, 'Quotations', 12–29; Giordano, 'L'escatologia', 121–39; Rordorf and Tuilier, *Doctrine*; Kloppenborg, 'Didache 16 6–8', 54–67; Rordorf, 'Problème', 499–513, and his more recent article 'Does the Didache Contain Jesus Tradition?', 394–423; Draper, 'Tradition', 269–287, and more recently his article, 'Torah Apostles', 347–72. German support for this position was strong among the earlier studies: Drews, 'Untersuchungen', 53–79; Seeberg, *Didache*; Knopf, *Lehre*.

[8] Cf. Massaux, 'Influence'; Butler, 'Relations', also 'Two Ways'; Vielhauer, 'Apocalyptic', 628–9; Layton, 'Sources'; Giet, *Enigme*; Wengst, ed., *Schriften*; Köhler, *Rezeption*; Knoch, 'Kenntnis'; Stanton, 'Flight'; Tuckett, 'Tradition'.

[9] Such a distinction is voiced by Tuckett, 'Tradition', 206–7.

which source interrelationship is assessed. I will examine these two factors in turn.

1. Methodological divergence between 'Didachists' and 'New Testament scholars'

When considering the question of whether the Didache reveals knowledge of Matthean redaction, which would indicate that the Didachist had access to the Gospel of Matthew rather than to a source which Matthew also used, the two groups differ methodologically. 'New Testament scholars' maintain that the question of Matthean redaction should be primarily one of synoptic relations, while 'Didachists' dispute this.

This methodological divergence is demonstrated in a scholarly interchange between C. M. Tuckett and W. Rordorf. Tuckett writes:

> If the existence of these parallels [between Matthew and the Didache] is universally accepted, their significance is disputed. Much depends on one's beliefs about the origin of the material in Mt 24,10–12. Methodologically, the problem should perhaps be one of synoptic study before one considers the Didache itself. Within Matthean scholarship there is widespread agreement that these verses are due to MattR [Matthean redaction]. If this is the case, then it would appear to provide clear evidence of the Didache's presupposition of Matthew's redactional activity and hence of Matthew's gospel. This conclusion has however been disputed from the side of Didachean scholarship . . . [10]

W. Rordorf, in his article entitled 'Does the Didache contain Jesus Tradition independently [*sic*] of the Synoptic Gospels?', questions Tuckett's methodology: 'if any statement at all is to be made about use of sources in Mt. 24.10–12, it is possible only in view of the parallels in the *Didache*. H. Köster makes precisely this analysis . . .'[11] Both scholars proceed to debate the strength of two methodological steps which H. Koester took with regard to this passage. The first is Koester's claim that the verbal agreement between Matthew 24 and the Didache is insufficient to show

---

[10] *Ibid.*   [11] Rordorf, 'Jesus Tradition?', 417.

dependence on Matthew; rather, both depend on common tradition. Moreover Didache 16 itself, in Koester's view, may provide evidence that Matt. 24:10–12 is a piece of pre-Matthean tradition.[12] Tuckett disputes this reasoning: 'the measure of verbal agreement between the Didache and Matthew cannot be used to determine whether that agreement is due to direct dependence of one on the other or to common dependence on a prior source'.[13]

W. Rordorf does not choose to take issue with this, and indeed it would be difficult to do so. Rather, Rordorf indicates that another argument which Koester gives is far weightier, namely that the Didache seems to consider only this one passage which was inserted by Matthew into the synoptic apocalypse.[14] This is in fact the very issue which Tuckett seeks to re-examine in his article and about which he draws quite different conclusions from those of scholars such as Koester, Rordorf and Kloppenborg. Thus this is not yet the heart of the matter.

The second methodological objection which Tuckett raises with regard to Koester's analysis is as follows:

> Second, and more important, the claim that Did. 16 itself may provide evidence that Mt 24,10–12 is pre-Matthean is a case of petitio principii here. If the question is whether the Didache depends on Matthew's Gospel or on a pre-Matthean source, one cannot use the evidence of the Didache itself to solve the source problem of Matthew's text. Koester's argument is thus dangerously circular.[15]

Rordorf's reply indicates the nature of the methodological divergence between himself and Tuckett: 'I cannot see this. The *only procedure possible for me* is to ask the question whether Mt. 24.10–12 can be a self-sufficient Matthaean [*sic*] composition *based on Mk 13:9–13*' (emphasis mine).[16]

Rordorf shows himself thus to be fundamentally a source-critic; if Matt. 24:10–12 is not obviously based on Mark 13:9–13, then he moves immediately to search for another source, and in doing so draws upon the Didache parallel. Tuckett, however, and most Matthean scholars with him, pursues the redaction-critical question of whether this material could be Matthean redaction. As Tuckett's

---

[12] Koester, *Überlieferung*, 181.   [13] Tuckett, 'Tradition', 207.
[14] Koester, *Überlieferung*, 183–4.   [15] Tuckett, 'Tradition', 207–8.
[16] Rordorf, 'Jesus Tradition?', 418.

lengthy footnote 43 indicates,[17] the majority of Matthean scholars, weighing the conceptual and linguistic considerations of these verses, argue that they are indeed best accounted for as Matthean redaction. For Matthean scholars steeped in redaction criticism, this step has methodological priority over any further source considerations. This is what Tuckett meant by his statement 'the problem should perhaps be one of synoptic study before one considers the Didache itself'. Rordorf, Koester and others who share their method therefore postulate a shared source, whereas Matthean scholars do not find the evidence pointing in that direction to be nearly as compelling.

In the light of the preceding study of Matthew 24, I am inclined to share the view of the majority of Matthean scholars that Matt. 24:10–12 has been formulated by the evangelist. The importance of verse 11 in Matthew's schema, indicating as it does the present situation of the Matthean community, favours an interpretation of it as redaction rather than tradition. Moreover the close parallel between this verse and verse 5, and also the reference in verse 24 to the false christs and false prophets engaged in leading astray the elect, is not easily explained as having been drawn from a distinct source. Typical Mattheanisms are present in verse 10: καὶ τότε, σκανδαλίζομαι, and in verse 12: ἀνομία. Furthermore, the motif of 'love', verse 12, when considered against the background of such passages as Matt. 19:19 and 22:40, must be recognized as reflecting the evangelist's own concerns, and not simply relaying those of the tradition. For these reasons, these verses are better accounted for as Matthean redaction, and the Didachean parallel is then evidence for the Didachist's use of the Gospel of Matthew.

Let us now turn to a second factor upon which the two groups of scholars diverge, namely the criteria upon which source interrelationship is assessed.

2. Divergence of criteria upon which source interrelationship is assessed

As the arguments of W. Rordorf have demonstrated, 'Didachists' work in the first instance with source-critical criteria. In New Testament scholarship, in addition to redaction-critical consider-

---

[17] Tuckett, 'Tradition', 206–7.

ations, the types of source-critical criteria applied to a case such as this have been devised and shaped through the careful study of the interrelationship between the three synoptic Gospels, and then applied in turn to the study of extra-canonical material. However, the synoptic parallels in the Didache do not follow the 'canons' of synoptic source-criticism. When there are parallels between the Didache and the synoptic Gospels, these are not generally 'quotations', but are more analogous to allusions or reminiscences. To put it another way, the Didache's use of synoptic traditions does not show nearly as many verbal parallels as are found in parallel synoptic passages. This raises the question of whether the Didachist could have known and used one or more synoptic Gospel, or whether the sources for these loose parallels was something other than our canonical Gospels. I will illustrate this once again with reference to W. Rordorf:

> I pose now only the basic, and for me in the last analysis the decisive question: is it conceivable that the Didachist culls the double command of love from a passage in Matthew (there is no question of it being Luke), namely Mt. 22.36–40, which he then quotes in a remarkably different form? Furthermore does he draw the Golden Rule from Mt. 7.12, but express it in the otherwise normal negative form, and subsequently add the Synoptic material about love of enemies and retribution in a form and order different from those both of Matthew and of Luke? It seems to me that to put this question is to provide an answer to it.[18]

These are indeed weighty considerations for those who are persuaded that the Didache knew Matthean redaction, as I am. Criteria of form and order (so central to the study of Q material, for instance) would seem to be totally disregarded by the theory that the Didache knew and used one or more of the synoptic Gospels in their present form. Those who maintain the theory that the Didache did indeed know and use the Gospels of Matthew and possibly Luke need to postulate a qualitatively different type of usage from that which is reflected in synoptic interrelationship. Tuckett does indeed argue this case, and he maintains that the

---

[18] Rordorf, 'Jesus Tradition?', 411.

Didache's use of the synoptic tradition must be understood on its own terms.[19]

Rordorf is aware of Tuckett's argument, and is not convinced. To his mind, the variants are too striking to be accounted for as reminiscence or allusion. What this stalemate between the two scholars illustrates is the need for a methodology appropriate to the type of use which the Didache makes of the synoptic tradition. In searching for a methodology appropriate to the type of use which Tuckett postulates, it is necessary to turn elsewhere. A recent monograph by W.-D. Köhler, *Die Rezeption des Matthäus-evangeliums in der Zeit vor Irenäus*, sets out to devise criteria suitable to describe the type of usage to which the Gospel of Matthew was put in the early church, usage which differs significantly from the interrelationship between the synoptic Gospels. Köhler makes the following differentiations between possible types of reception on pages 7–12 of his monograph (translation mine).

i.   (a)   Use which is identified as such, e.g. quotations;

     (b)   Use which is not identified as such, e.g. allusion.

ii. (a)   The use of distinctive wording/phrasing/formulation

         (α)   With explicit reference to a specific pericope/ verse;

         (β)   Without explicit reference to a specific pericope/ verse (= reception of Matthean language).

     (b)   Use of contents/concepts

         (α)   Use of narrative details;

         (β)   Use of statements which, with regard to their

---

[19] Tuckett argues as follows:

> One further preliminary point to be made is that it is quite clear that, for the most part, the Didache does not 'quote' the synoptic tradition. There are a few instances where the Didache clearly indicates its intention to quote something (from whatever source): cf. Did. 1,6; 8,2; 9,5; 16,7. Elsewhere there are references to a εὐαγγέλιον (8,2; 11,3; 15,3.4) which may be a written source. However, the remaining links between the Didache and synoptic tradition are at the level of allusion only. It is thus inappropriate to judge the Didache's use of synoptic tradition as if it were a case of explicit quotation and to expect exact agreement between the quoted version and the source used. The Didache's use of synoptic tradition is more one of free allusion. Hence disagreements between the Didache and the Gospels in, for example, the context and application of synoptic tradition need not imply that the Didache cannot have known our gospels. Indeed it can be argued that precisely such freedom in the use of synoptic tradition is to be expected if the Didache is using our gospels as, in some sense, authoritative texts. ('Tradition', 198–9.)

      contents, allow the discernment of particular
      Matthean themes.

iii. Some differentiations as to the function of the Matthean
    material in its new context:
    (a) Use which corresponds to Matthean material;
    (b) Use which extends/carries forward Matthean
        material;
    (c) Use which rejects Matthean material.

By means of these differentiations, Köhler seeks to categorize the
variety of usages to which the Gospel of Matthew could be and was
put by early Christian writers. In doing so, he opens a much wider
range of possibilities than traditional source-criticism allows, and
makes allowance for different types of reception. While common
sense has long since recognized that the use to which a Gospel may
be put in a sermon or in an exhortatory letter may vary widely, and
one may not expect quotations to be cited explicitly or allusions to
reflect the corresponding passage word-perfectly, Köhler seeks to
achieve some formal scholarly recognition of such facts. In the
cases where the reception of Matthean material is either explicit or
obvious, few problems arise. It is, however, in the many cases
where possible Matthean reception is neither explicit nor obvious
that criteria for weighing the probabilities become crucial. Köhler
sets out his criteria as follows on pages 13–14 (translation mine):

    Reference to Matthew's Gospel is *probable*, if
    (a) the wording of a particular passage clearly (i.e. not
        only in the choice of a few single words) corresponds
        to Matthew's Gospel;
        and at the same time
    (b) the similarity to other passages is less than to
        Matthew;
        and in addition
    (c) the wording of the passage in question, including its
        deviations from Matthew, can be well explained by
        the assumption that it made direct use of Matthew.

    Reference to Matthew's Gospel is *certainly possible*, if,
    (i)   when factors (b) and (c) remain the same,
        the wording of a particular passage corresponds
        only slightly with Matthew,
            or if

(ii) when factors (a) and (c) remain the same,
      the similarity to other passages is just as strong as
      to Matthew.

Reference to Matthew's Gospel is *at best theoretically
possible, but by no means obvious,* if
(i)   when factors (a) and (c) remain the same,
      the similarity to other passages is greater than to
      Matthew,
          or if
(ii) when factors (a) and (b) remain the same,
      the wording of the passage in question cannot be
      well explained by the assumption that it made direct
      use of Matthew.

Köhler recognizes that the problem of special Matthean tradition is
not adequately dealt with by means of these criteria, since it was
presumably handed on independently of Matthew's Gospel for
some time, and he offers some evaluative considerations based on
the provenance of the writing in question. Interestingly, he does not
refer at this point to the evidence of Matthean redaction as giving
an important indication that the writing in question used the
finished Gospel. If it could be shown that the Didache made
reference only to special M material, the case that the Didache did
not know the canonical Matthew, but rather knew Matthean
tradition, would be irrefutable, as indeed Kloppenborg considers it
to be.[20] However, if Matt. 24:10–12 is indeed redactional formulation, as discussed above, the case that Didache 16 knew only
special M cannot be upheld.

Having given in some detail the ways in which Köhler seeks to
differentiate and evaluate Matthean reception, let us now turn to
his discussion on Didache 16 itself, in order to see how these
distinctions are applied.

3.   W.-D. Köhler's discussion of Didache 16

Although Köhler's overall assessment of the evidence indicates that
it is highly probable that the Didachist knew and used Matthew's
Gospel, his analysis of Didache 16 leads him to view the notion
that this chapter drew its main orientation from Matthew as

---

[20] Kloppenborg, 'Didache'.

improbable.[21] Like Koester, Kloppenborg, Rordorf and others, he concludes that the Matthean parallels in chapter 16 are best explained by postulating that Didache 16 drew on the same traditions as did Matthew 24. Köhler gives us the following assessment of the material:

> In terms of wording, a dependence on one of the synoptic Gospels is at best possible. In terms of individual verses, a dependence on Matthew is certainly possible in 16,4b (Mt 24,10b.c), 16,5b (Mt 24,10a), 16,6a.b (Mt 24,30a), 16,6c (Mt 24,31b), and 16,8a.b (Mt 24,30c.d and 26,64). Dependence on Luke is almost always less probable than dependence on Matthew; only Did. 16,1b.c is an exception, where dependence on Luke appears to be certainly possible; Matthew provides no parallels. Dependence on Matthew is nevertheless theoretically possible in Did. 16,1a (Mt 24,42; 25,13), 16,1d.e.f. (Mt 24,44 and 25,13), 16,3b (Mt 24,11), 16,3c (Mt 7,15), 16,3d (Mt 24,12b), 16,4d (Mt 24,24b) and 16,5c.d (Mt 24,13a; 10,22b). Reference to Matthew is improbable in Did. 16,7b (Mt 25,13).[22]

Köhler's criteria have introduced a gradation of probability into the study of possible literary dependence, based on wording. The results of this aspect of his analysis have been ambivalent: in many cases, it is 'certainly possible' that Didache 16 used Matthew's Gospel; in many others, it is 'theoretically possible'. It is not clear that Köhler's criteria have in fact made any contribution over and above the more traditional procedures; the hoped-for allowance for the less easily assessable types of usage such as allusion has not eventuated. Ultimately Köhler makes his assessment on grounds other than those of wording, namely:

(i)   the Didachist does not adopt the structure of Matthew;
(ii) Didache 16 contains many traditions that have no parallel in a synoptic Gospel.

It is on the basis of these factors that Köhler states: 'Dependence of the Didache on one of the synoptic Gospels, in the sense of deriving its orientation from them, is to be rejected.'[23] The traditional

---

[21] Köhler, *Rezeption,* 54–5.   [22] *Ibid.,* 54 (translation mine).
[23] *Ibid.,* 53 (translation mine).

criteria of form (wording) and order (structure/internal logic) thus undergird Köhler's approach as well.

It is interesting that on the basis of the evidence, Köhler is not prepared to say that Didache 16 did not *know* Matthew's Gospel: rather, he states that it is clear that Didache 16 did not *orientate itself* on Matthew's Gospel. According to his own differentiations – iii.b and c as set out above – a text may extend/carry forward or even reject Matthean material, that is, show a different orientation, and still have made use of a synoptic Gospel. To say that Didache 16 did not 'orientate itself' on Matthew's Gospel is by no means the same thing as saying that it did not know the Gospel. However, Köhler does not seem willing to explore this further with regard to Didache 16. Rather, he is content to rest his conclusions on the two grounds listed above. I will examine in turn the strength of these two factors.

4. Is it the case that the Didachist did not adopt the structure/internal logic of Matthew?

Didache 16:1–2 opens the eschatological material with paraenesis. It is a call for vigilance and preparedness, given that the hour of the Lord's return is unknown. This concern for vigilance and preparedness on the basis of the unknown hour of the parousia is also the central concern of Matthew's eschatological discourse. These introductory verses of Didache 16, when one focusses not on the minutiae of wording but on the wider question of the overall unifying themes, show that both the Didache and Matthew's eschatological discourse are shaped towards paraenetic application. These verses are thus in keeping with the overall structure of Matthew's eschatological discourse.

The opening phrase γρηγορεῖτε ὑπὲρ τῆς ζωῆς ὑμῶν (Did. 16:1a) tends to be interpreted individualistically by scholars,[24] but when one considers the concern of verse 2, it more probably refers to the common life of the communities.[25] This impression is strengthened by the plural of the imperative and pronoun. The threat to the communal life is also of central interest to Matthew,

---

[24] E.g. Niederwimmer, *Didache*, 256: 'Doch ist γρηγορεῖτε ὑπὲρ τῆς ζωῆς ὑμῶν eine ungewöhnliche Verbindung. Gemeint ist wohl "über seinem Leben wachen", was bedeutet: Leib und Leben in Zucht halten gegenüber dem Bösen.'

[25] In referring to the *Sitz im Leben* of the Didache, I use the plural 'communities', which better reflects the rural base of the readership (see below, n. 32).

as is seen with particular clarity in the specific verses which Matthew has in common with the Didache, namely 24:10–12. If, as I have argued in the previous chapter (Chapter 5.1), Matthew incorporated the material of chapter 23 for the benefit of the community itself, the function of the warning to the community with which Didache 16 opens is not dissimilar to the function which Matthew 23 has in relation to the material of Matthew 24.

I will set out the apocalyptic section of Didache 16 (verses 3–8) in order, so as to facilitate a comparison of its structure/internal logic *vis-à-vis* that of Matt. 24:4b–31.

(i)   The apocalyptic section of Didache 16 begins at verse 3 with the warning against false prophets and seducers. Similarly, the apocalyptic section of Matthew's eschatological discourse, which begins at 24:4, opens with a warning about those who would seek to lead the disciples astray. The fact that both texts open this section of their material with reference to such figures is, in my opinion, a strong indication of congruence between their respective structures.

(ii)   The Didache then moves on to material about the perversion of community life (verses 3c–4b). This corresponds to Matt. 24:10–12, and as shown above, the Didache seems to be making use here of Matthean redactional material.

(iii)   Did. 16:4c moves immediately to the appearance of the world deceiver (ὁ κοσμοπλανής) as a son of God. In terms of the Matthean structure, this corresponds to the βδέλυγμα τῆς ἐρημώσεως standing in the holy place (Matt. 24:15). As mentioned in chapter 3 (p. 92), an individual antichrist figure, such as ὁ κοσμοπλανής, seems to have developed from the βδέλυγμα τῆς ἐρημώσεως, and so this once again represents a congruence in structure between the Didache and Matthew.

Up to this point, the order of Didache 16 and that of Matthew 24 have been strikingly similar. At this point, however, although there continue to be parallels between the texts, the order no longer fully corresponds. If one were to assume that the individual antichrist figure had accrued the characteristics of the third Matthean reference to false christs and false prophets, obviating the need for them, the order of point (v) below still corresponds to the Matthean order. Points (v) and (vi) refer to a period of great tribulation, and point (vii) to endurance in the face of it; these correspond in a general way to the Matthean period of great tribulation and the need to endure, though the order of the parallel sayings does not correspond.

(iv) The world deceiver is to perform signs and wonders, just as the false christs and false prophets of Matt. 24:24 are described as doing.

(v) The wanton or lawless acts (ἀθέμιτα) which he will commit are described in a way that resembles the Matthean description of the great tribulation in conception though not in wording:

Did. 16:4–5 reads καὶ ποιήσει ἀθέμιτα, ἃ οὐδέποτε γέγονεν ἐξ αἰῶνος.

Matt. 24:21 reads ἔσται γὰρ τότε θλῖψις μεγάλη οἵα οὐ γέγονεν ἀπ᾽ ἀρχῆς κόσμου ἕως τοῦ νῦν οὐδ᾽ οὐ μὴ γένηται.

(vi) Did. 16:5 proceeds to describe further tribulation, and the way many will fall away in the face of it. Although there is no parallel to Did. 16:5a in Matthew, the description of falling away, Did. 16:5b, is paralleled by Matt. 24:10a.

(vii) Did. 16:5c refers to those who endure in their faith being saved, as does Matt. 24:13 (as well as Matt. 10:22b).

After this point, the order of the two texts once again resumes its congruence.

(viii) Did. 16:6 begins the denouement of the eschatological drama with the reference to the signs of truth. The obvious interest that the Didache shows in the nature of the signs is, in my opinion, a significant link to Matthew 24. The reference to the sign of the Son of Man in heaven in Matt. 24:30 should be understood as a redactional addition by Matthew to the Markan *Vorlage* in order to give a more explicit reply than Mark does to the disciples' question about signs. In my opinion, the Didache's interest in signs at this point gives a strong indication that the Didachist was familiar with Matthew 24, and was not simply using a pre-Matthean source. In elaborating and explicating the signs of truth at this point, the Didachist is developing the Matthean reference, as Matthew had already developed the Markan discourse.

(ix)   On a literal reading of Matt. 24:30–1, the sign of the Son of Man in heaven and the coming of the Son of Man on the clouds of heaven appear to be two distinct events, with the first preceding the second. As set out in the previous Chapter, I do not understand this redactional reworking of the Markan *Vorlage* to mean two distinct events. However, the Didache splits the two events, first by referring to the σημεῖον ἐκπετάσεως ἐν οὐρανῷ (16:6a) and then by referring to the Lord's coming on the clouds of heaven (16:8a.b): τότε ὄψεται ὁ κόσμος τὸν κύριον ἐρχόμενον ἐπάνω τῶν νεφελῶν τοῦ οὐρανοῦ. In my opinion, this also points to the interpretative use that the Didache made of Matt. 24:30–1, for this splitting of the sign and the coming would otherwise be too great a coincidence.

(x)   In Did. 16:6c.d, the signs of the trumpet and the resurrection of the dead herald the coming of the Lord, Did. 16:8, whereas in Matt. 24:31, the loud trumpet call and the gathering in of the elect from the four winds follow the reference to the Son of Man coming with power and great glory. Although the order is different at this point, it is possible to see how the gathering of the elect from the four winds could be interpreted as the resurrection of the saints, by analogy to Ezekiel's vision of the dry bones: 'Thus says the Lord God: Come from the four winds, O breath, and breathe upon these slain, that they may live' (Ezek. 37:9).

(xi)   Did. 16:8 states that 'the world will see the Lord coming'. This corresponds to the tribes of the earth mourning at the revelation of the Son of Man (Matt. 24:30), though the polemical edge of expected vindication in Matthew is not prominent in the Didache. 'The clouds of heaven' is a direct parallel between them.

The result of the above analysis is that the evidence from the structure/internal logic of Didache 16 is not nearly as clear-cut as Köhler implies. Rather, at certain points, it is difficult to account for the structure of Didache 16 except by reference to the Didachist's knowledge and use of Matthew 24. These points include the shared opening reference to false prophets who seek to lead the people astray, the interest in signs at that point in the material, and the splitting of the sign of the Son of Man and his coming. For these reasons, I do not accept Köhler's first stated reason for rejecting Didache 16's use of Matthew. Let us now turn to his second reason, which can be addressed more briefly.

5. 'The Didache contains many traditions which have no synoptic parallel'

Didache 16 certainly seems to have drawn on traditions other than those found in the synoptic Gospels. The three most striking appear to be:

(i)   the world deceiver, into whose hands the earth will be given and who will commit lawless acts;

(ii) the concept that the human world will enter a trial by fire;

(iii) the three signs of truth, most particularly the first and third of these.

However, as has been shown in the preceding discussion, there is reason to believe that two of these three traditions – (i) and (ii) – may in fact be later extrapolations and developments of the synoptic material. With reference to (iii), the antichrist figure, the synoptic references to the βδέλυγμα τῆς ἐρημώσεως, when supplemented by interpretations of Daniel, the lawless watchers of the Enoch tradition (cf. 1 Enoch 7:2–6, where the watchers bear the name 'the lawless ones') and also the *Nero redivivus* myth,[26] seem to have prompted the development of expectation of an individual personification of evil who masquerades as God's representative. This figure, who is distinct from Satan (cf. 2 Thess. 2:1–12), parodies a number of the features attributed to Christ. The *Traditionsgeschichte* of this figure, as reflected in the Johannine epistles, seems to be bound up with the rise of schism and heresy.[27]

With reference to (iii), the three signs of truth, I have shown that it is difficult to postulate that the first and third of them could have arisen independently of the distinctive redactional features of Matt. 24:30–1.

Moreover, it is incumbent upon those who maintain that Matthew and the Didache drew on a common source for their parallel material to consider whether, had Matthew had access to

---

[26] Cf. Hengel, 'Origin and Situation', 25–7.

[27] Cf. Forsyth, *Enemy*, esp. chapters 14.6 and 17.1. This important work explores, from a literary perspective, the development, variations and reinterpretations that the myths of evil underwent in the literature of the ancient Near East, Judaism and Christianity.

the other traditions, such as those above, the evangelist would have excluded them. This has not, to my knowledge, been addressed by those who maintain the theory of a common source. Those who maintain this theory must at least consider the possibility that the common source reached Matthew and the Didache in forms which already exhibited notable variations. In my opinion, although one may be able to account plausibly for the parallels between Didache 16 and Matthew's Gospel this way, it gives too much weight to a series of source-critical hypotheses.

Only tradition (ii), the trial by fire, can be claimed with some certainty to have no clear synoptic parallel. Although Matthew has a greater interest in eschatological fire than do Mark and Luke, it is primarily portrayed as the fire of Gehenna, into which evildoers will be thrown at the close of the age (cf. 3:10, 12; 5:22; 7:19; 13:40, 42, 50; 18:8, 9; 25:41). Only Matt. 3:11, αὐτὸς ὑμᾶς βαπτίσει ἐν πνεύματι ἁγίῳ καὶ πυρί, drawn from Q, has the notion that the faithful will be subject to fire. This saying may preserve a tradition of a fiery testing, presumably eschatological in nature, to which all will be subjected, but it is clear that the Didache did not draw 16:5a from here. Nevertheless, it is unnecessary to postulate a special source for this tradition, given its wide currency in Jewish and Christian texts (cf. Prov. 17:3; Wis. 3:6; 1 Cor. 3:13; 1 Pet. 1:7, and its prominence in T. Ab. 12–13 and T. Isa. 5:21–25).

In the light of these considerations, the three most striking traditions which have no direct parallel in the synoptic Gospels do not require one to reject the theory that Didache 16 knew and used the Gospel of Matthew. Rather, it seems to me that even these traditions can be well explained by the assumption that Didache 16 made direct use of Matthew's Gospel, elaborating and supplementing it in certain ways. I am therefore of the opinion that Didache 16 fits Köhler's category of 'certainly possible', because:

(i)   an analysis of the wording gives a balance of 'certainly possible' and 'possible';

(ii) the similarity to other passages is less than to Matthew; and

(iii) the wording of the passage, including its deviations from Matthew, seems to assume this usage.

On the basis of this last consideration in particular, I would rate the relationship as 'probable'.

The preceding discussion serves to show that the influence of one text upon another is not limited to direct literary dependence. Although other types of influence are much more difficult to demonstrate, an appreciation of the variety of uses to which a text, particularly an authoritative text, can be put is essential in the study of the relationship between Gospels and other early Christian writings.

I am now in a position, on the basis of the preceding discussion, to examine Didache 16 as a later development within early Christian eschatology which drew upon, at least, the Gospel of Matthew.

6.   Didache 16 as a further development in early Christian eschatology

If the Didachist did know and make use of the Gospel of Matthew, the way in which this use was made is qualitatively different from the sort of use apparent in synoptic relations. A summary statement of Köhler's which he gives at the conclusion of his study is illustrative of the type of use to which the Gospels were put in the post-apostolic era: 'The greatest possible freedom *vis-à-vis* the "text", while maintaining a close connection with the Lord – this was the way in which to apply the written Gospel material to oneself and to one's present situation in the time prior to Irenaeus.'[28]

Didache 16, like other Christian writings from this era, shows a remarkable freedom to rearrange, interpret and omit material drawn from Matthew 24 and elsewhere in the Gospel, as well as the freedom to supplement it from other sources. This seems to be an indication that the function of this chapter, and indeed of the Didache as a whole, was in no way to supplant the written Gospel material. Unlike the way in which Matthew and Luke drew on Mark and Q, which was characterized by a certain comprehensiveness which made the constant use of those earlier texts unnecessary, the Didache does not aspire to comprehensiveness. Rather, its very selectivity presupposes the continued use of the Gospel, and implies that its *function was to serve as an adjunct*.

H. R. Seeliger's article on Didache 16 entitled 'Erwägungen zu Hintergrund und Zweck des apokalyptischen Schlusskapitels der *Didache*' gives some confirmation to this theory on form-critical grounds. He argues that we are not dealing here with an apocalyse

---

[28] Köhler, *Rezeption*, 536 (translation mine).

as such, as it lacks a narrative framework. Rather, we seem to be dealing with a summary and elaboration of apocalyptic revelation that has already been given.[29]

Seeliger's thesis is that this chapter seeks to record and uphold an important aspect of the (true) prophets' proclamation (cf. Did. 11:7) over against the teaching of the false prophets, not least for those communities which have no prophet (cf. Did. 13:4). He thus considers Didache 16 to be an 'Aide-mémoire apokalyptischer Theologie'.[30] This is an interesting theory which well reflects the apparently dependent nature of the Didache 16 material, though without reference to the sources of the apocalyptic theology. In order to be able to evaluate Seeliger's theory and the type of developments this chapter reflects, let us once again turn to the text of Didache 16, this time with a view to assessing its interests *vis-à-vis* those of Matthew's Gospel.

The chapter opens with the call γρηγορεῖτε ὑπὲρ τῆς ζωῆς ὑμῶν, 16:1a. In Matthew's Gospel, γρηγορέω is used without an object being specified, as the appropriate attitude towards the impending eschatological events (cf. Matt. 24:42, 25:13). As in the Gospel of Mark, the narrative of Gethsemane in Matthew illustrates what it is to watch, or fail to watch (Matt. 26:38, 40, 41), as does the parabolic saying of the householder and the thief (Matt. 24:43). In Did. 16:1, the nature of the watching has shifted away from the constant expectation and readiness for the imminent End towards the protection and upbuilding of 'their life', which, as stated above, most probably refers to their communal life. Such a shift away from *Naherwartung* towards a concern about community issues is what scholars have often sought to attribute to the passing of time, but in the light of this study as a whole, one may say that it also reflects the fact that the communities of the Didache were no longer directly pressured by the events surrounding the fall of Jerusalem and its aftermath, nor experiencing a period of persecution. O. Giordano also observes that these events are not reflected in the Didache in his article 'L'escatologia nella *Didaché*', but he takes it as evidence of early composition.[31] Those who maintain the very early dating of the Didache have not reckoned with the fact that though the language of Didache 16 may be similar to that of the

---

[29] Seeliger, 'Erwägungen', 187.   [30] *Ibid.*, 192.

[31] Giordano, 'L'escatologia', 129–30. Giordano shares this view with the early study by Sabatier, *ΔΙΔΑΧΗ ΤΩΝ ΙΒ᾽ ΑΠΟΣΤΟΛΩΝ*, 146.

synoptic tradition (e.g. γρηγορεῖτε), the meaning has shifted away from high eschatological expectation to concerns of maintaining community life.

A second point of comparison between Didache 16 and Matthew's Gospel is their respective understandings of their own position in relation to the 'last days'. As I have sought to demonstrate in the previous chapter, Matthew understood the Matthean community to be living in the last days, which were characterized by false prophets and disintegration of community life. In Did. 16:3 one reads of the last days in the future tense: 'for, in the last days, false prophets and corrupters will be multiplied (πληθυνθήσονται), and the sheep will be turned (στραφήσονται) into wolves, and love will be changed (στραφήσεται) to hate'. The community situation reflected in the exhortation of 16:2 implies a certain apathy, even complacency, about meeting together and maturing in their communal life. If one compares this with the situation predicted for the 'last days' – with many false prophets and deceivers, sheep being transformed into wolves and love into hatred – it seems that the Didachean communities did not perceive themselves as already participating in those last days. Although the use of future tense in apocalyptic writings does not necessarily give an accurate indication of the chronological position of the implied author, in the case of Did. 16:3 the future tense verbs do seem to reflect the Didachist's own perception of the Didachean communities' chronological position.

The impression that the communities behind Matthew and the Didache differ in their perception of the problems facing them is strengthened by their respective uses of the motif of sheep and wolves. In Matthew, the false prophets who are described as wolves masquerading in sheep's clothing (Matt. 7:15) are seen to be a current threat to the community, and the warning against them is given not in an eschatological context, but in the context of the Sermon on the Mount. In Did. 16:3, the warning is an eschatological one, and is somewhat more stylized: ἐν γὰρ ταῖς ἐσχάταις ἡμέραις πληθυνθήσονται οἱ ψευδοπροφῆται καὶ οἱ φθορεῖς καὶ στραφήσονται τὰ πρόβατα εἰς λύκους καὶ ἡ ἀγάπη στραφήσεται εἰς μῖσος. Given that the Didachist has identified this transformation of sheep into wolves not as a present problem, but as one to be associated with the 'last days', it does not seem that it was at that time a pressing concern of the communities, nor that they considered themselves to be already living in those 'last days'.

As I discussed earlier in this chapter, the world deceiver, ὁ κοσμοπλανής, seems to have assumed the function of the Matthean βδέλυγμα τῆς ἐρημώσεως, as well as that of the false christs and false prophets of Matt. 24:24. The appearance of the world deceiver is portrayed as future by Did. 16:4, but for Matthew, ὁ βδέλυγμα τῆς ἐρημώσεως belongs to the immediate past, and the false christs and false prophets to the present.

In these various ways, it is evident that the two writings diverge in their perception of themselves in relation to the End Times. In the light of this, it is necessary to suppose that Didache 16 was written in a context which was somewhat removed from the one in which the Gospel of Matthew was written. This most probably reflects the passing of some decades as well as a provenance not identical to that of Matthew's Gospel.[32] Many intriguing questions as to the nature of the Matthean community's mission, its geographical scope and the success of Matthew's Gospel *vis-à-vis* Mark's and Luke's are raised by these observations, but they are beyond the scope of the present study.

If one takes into account the tendencies which I have just noted, such as the shift away from *Naherwartung* towards concern for community life and the change in their perception of their own position *vis-à-vis* the 'last days', one may say, contra H. R. Seeliger's proposal, that Didache 16 is not simply an 'Aide-mémoire apokalyptischer Theologie'. Seeliger's thesis implies that it is conceived as an 'aide-mémoire' of *correct* apocalyptic theology, as opposed to the theology of the false prophets, whatever that may have been. But there is little evidence in this chapter of a direct polemic against the teachings of false prophets. Indeed, unlike in Matthew, they are assigned to the 'last days', and do not seem to have been a pressing problem for the communities at the time of the composition of this material.

A. Milavec argues that the Didache is intended to offer Gentile converts training in Judeo-Christian ethics and reflects conflict in the communities between Jewish-Christian and Gentile-Christian

---

[32] It is widely accepted that the provenance of the Didache is rural rather than urban, despite the argument of Schöllgen, 'Miszellen', that a rural provenance need not be implied. The itinerant apostles are to be given only enough bread to last until evening, with the implication that the next village is within a day's journey. This, according to Wengst, *Schriften* 33 and others, presupposes a relatively populous rural area with villages and small towns. The Gospel of Matthew, on the other hand, seems to reflect an urban environment, with Antioch as the most likely city; cf. Davies and Allison, *Matthew*, I, 138ff.

members. His proposed *Sitz im Leben* identifies the 'false prophets and corrupters' as those discussed in the previous section of the Didache, and he sees chapter 16 as having been 'deliberately crafted to advance the agenda of the other three parts of the Didache'.[33] In my opinion, the 'false prophets and corrupters' of Didache 16 are portrayed as an End Time phenomenon, and are not identical with the prophets who are abusing their privileges in the communities of the Didache.

I propose that the function of this chapter is to be identified in two areas, the first being paraenesis, and the second being its purpose to clarify and specify certain aspects of Matthew's eschatology. There is no doubt that one of the main foci of this chapter is paraenesis. The chapter introduces the apocalyptic material with paraenesis. The exhortation of 16:2b.c is of particular interest: οὐ γὰρ ὠφελήσει ὑμᾶς ὁ πᾶς χρόνος τῆς πίστεως ὑμῶν, ἐὰν μὴ ἐν τῷ ἐσχάτῳ καιρῷ τελειωθῆτε. This puts in a negative way what is stated positively in 16:5c.d: οἱ δὲ ὑπομείναντες ἐν τῇ πίστει αὐτῶν σωθήσονται ὑπ' αὐτοῦ τοῦ καταθέματος. These two hortatory sentences – the latter based on synoptic material – frame the description of the 'last days' prior to the End, when the signs of truth appear. The earlier sentence warns that, in the last time, it is imperative that one be τελειωθῆναι. Although this may mean nothing more specific than holding fast to the faith, as K. Niederwimmer suggests,[34] the term can have overtones of the mystery religions, for whose adherents it meant being consecrated, initiated. This would tie in with the concept of the fiery trial (16:5), through which the whole of humanity must pass, which could constitute a type of initiation. Whether or not such a concept lies behind the exhortation of 16:2b.c, it is clear that the pastoral interests of maintaining both the corporate life and the faith of the individual are central. O. Knoch, in his essay on the knowledge and use of the Gospel of Matthew in the apostolic Fathers, also supports this view.[35] He argues that the catechetical/pastoral sections of the Didache, including Did. 16:1–8, imply that the Syrian, and presumably also the Palestinian church of this transitional time was primarily interested in the ethical and paraenetical portions of Matthew, which were undergirded by eschatological expectation and were vital for church order.

[33] Milavec, 'Genius', 102.   [34] Niederwimmer, *Didache*, 259.
[35] Knoch, 'Kenntnis', 167.

As Knoch points out, eschatological material came to be used in the interests of ethical and paraenetical concerns as a motivating force. The position of this material as the finale of the Didache as a whole would seem to confirm this. Though Did. 16:8 was presumably not the original end of this chapter, the revelation to the world of the Lord coming on the clouds of heaven and the ensuing judgement – which is widely accepted as having been the original conclusion – are a fitting finale to a chapter which has exhortation as a primary interest.

The other main interest which can be discerned in the chapter is the concern to clarify and specify certain aspects of eschatological expectation, not least those which Matthew's eschatological discourse left open-ended. The structure given to the chronology of the eschatological events is considerably simpler than that of Matthew. The author of this chapter was either not aware of or not interested in the two chronological sequences of Matthew 24. If Didache 16 was composed as an adjunct to Matthew's Gospel rather than as an attempt to supplant it, it seems intended to simplify, summarize and interpret certain aspects of Matthew's eschatological discourse, as well as to elaborate certain features. The structure is simplified, the threats to community life are summarized, and the Matthean βδέλυγμα τῆς ἐρημώσεως is interpreted and elaborated with material drawn from the description of the false christs and prophets.[36] The feature that is most strikingly specified and elaborated is the immediate prelude to the End, the signs of truth. The fact that this was felt to be necessary by the writer of Didache 16 may imply that the Matthean 'sign of the Son of Man in the heavens' was not specific enough for the needs of the communities. Perhaps there were some enthusiasts whose imminent expectation of the End may have led to them seeking to identify the sign themselves, or more probably this simply reflects a midrashic tendency to explicate those points which remain intriguingly obscure.

It was also deemed necessary by the author of this chapter to make explicit something that in Matthew's Gospel is open to interpretation, namely the question of whether the resurrection of the dead would be a general one, or limited to the resurrection of saints. Did. 16:7 maintains that the resurrection will be limited to

---

[36] In the light of this, Milavec may well be correct in highlighting the function of the *Didache* as a training manual for converts.

the saints, which is, as H. R. Seeliger points out, a well-attested Jewish understanding also reflected in the Pauline corpus and in John's Gospel.[37] In Matthew's Gospel, the proleptic resurrection of the saints in the passion narrative, Matt. 27:52–3, could indicate that the evangelist shared this view, but the picture of the great assize in Matt. 25:31–46, if one takes it as a judgement of the dead as well as the living, gives the opposite view. Other texts from Matthew's Gospel which bear upon this question include 7:21–3, 11:20–4, 12:41–2 and 22:23–33. Beginning with 12:41–2, which speaks of the men of Nineveh (ἄνδρες Νινευῖται) and of the Queen of the South as active participants at the judgement, this could either imply that all humanity is pictured as being raised for judgement, or that these very examples are raised because of their righteous attitude (the people of Nineveh repented at the preaching of Jonah, and the Queen of the South came from the ends of the earth to hear the wisdom of Solomon). It is thus possible to interpret this passage both ways.

Matt. 7:21ff, when read in the light of Matthew's imminent expectation of the End, need only apply to those who are living; there is nothing in the material to imply that the people depicted by this passage have been first raised from the dead before this interchange occurs. The fact that the evangelist seems to have had particular people in mind at this point – namely the 'false prophets' who have been troubling the community – supports the interpretation that this judgement scene is, for Matthew, concerned with the living.

In Matt. 22:23–33, Jesus is confronted by Sadducees with a challenge about the resurrection designed to push the doctrine *ad absurdum*. The question evokes a sharp response from Jesus, and a reply that addresses two issues, namely the nature of resurrection existence, and the basis of the doctrine itself. The latter part is of interest in this context: περὶ δὲ τῆς ἀναστάσεως τῶν νεκρῶν οὐκ ἀνέγνωτε τὸ ῥηθὲν ὑμῖν ὑπὸ τοῦ θεοῦ λέγοντος· ἐγώ εἰμι ὁ θεὸς Ἀβραὰμ καὶ ὁ θεὸς Ἰσαὰκ καὶ ὁ θεὸς Ἰακώβ; οὐκ ἔστιν ὁ θεὸς νεκρῶν ἀλλὰ ζώντων (Matt. 22:31–2). Jesus derives the doctrine of the resurrection, via the pentateuchal allusion to the call of Moses, from the very nature of God. In a bold stroke, Jesus extrapolates in rabbinical style that if the living God identifies presently with Abraham, Isaac and Jacob, then they must also be living or be

---

[37] Seeliger, 'Erwägungen' 189–90.

made to live. For the question at hand, this passage speaks in favour of the exclusive resurrection of the saints, for those who will live are those who are identified with the living God, namely the saints.

Matt. 11:20ff is also relevant to a discussion of whether the evangelist envisages a resurrection of saints and sinners alike, or whether the judgement will be of the living, with the saints only raised to participate. Chorazin and Bethsaida are compared unfavourably with Tyre and Sidon, but in each case presumably the inhabitants living at the time are meant.[38] However, the comparison between Capernaum and Sodom goes further: καὶ σύ, Καφαρναούμ, μὴ ἕως οὐρανοῦ ὑψωθήσῃ; ἕως ᾅδου καταβήσῃ· ὅτι εἰ ἐν Σοδόμοις ἐγενήθησαν αἱ δυνάμεις αἱ γενόμεναι ἐν σοί, ἔμεινεν ἂν μέχρι τῆς σήμερον. πλὴν λέγω ὑμῖν ὅτι γῇ Σοδόμων ἀνεκτότερον ἔσται ἐν ἡμέρᾳ κρίσεως ἢ σοί (Matt. 11:23–4). It is clear that the city of Sodom was no longer inhabited at the time. The question is whether verse 24 implies that the land of Sodom will, on the day of judgement, be judged once again, or, on the other hand, if Capernaum will fare worse on that day than the land of Sodom, with its desolate salt plains, now fares. In the Old Testament, Sodom had become the example *par excellence* of a sinful city, but also of the city to which punishment had already been meted out.[39] It seems more likely that Matt. 11:24 is referring not to a further punishment of Sodom on the day of judgement, but to Sodom as an example of the devastating judgement which will face Capernaum on that day. For this reason, this text does not give a clear example of the doctrine that sinners and saints alike are to be raised on the day of judgement.

These passages thus leave the question of who will be raised on the day of judgement open to interpretation. Matthew clearly foresees judgement and condemnation taking place on that day, but may envisage simply those sinners who are living as undergoing this judgement, as indeed Matt. 23:36 implies. Did. 16:7, therefore, is not so much a contradiction of Matthew's doctrine as a particular clarification and concretization of it. In order to illustrate this doctrine of the resurrection of the saints only, the writer of Didache 16 draws upon Zech. 14:5: οὐ πάντων δέ, ἀλλ᾽ ὡς ἐρρέθη·

---

[38] Tyre and Sidon did, however, have a reputation in the Old Testament for wealth and pride, e.g. Isa. 23.

[39] Cf. Isa. 1:9–10, Lam. 4:6, Ezek. 16:50; also Jub. 20:5, 3 Macc. 2:5, T.Naphtali 3:4.

ἥξει ὁ κύριος καὶ πάντες οἱ ἅγιοι μετ᾽ αὐτοῦ. In the Zechariah passage, the holy ones presumably referred to the angels, but they are here interpreted as the Christian saints who have died and been raised again. In this there is no longer any problem reflected as to the issue of Christians dying before the return of Christ, as was seen in the study of Matthew 25 (chapter 2). At the return of the Lord, they will be raised and will return with him. This therefore reveals an eschatology that has confronted and moved beyond the shock of the death of community members, and has embraced a doctrine similar to that which Paul sets out in 1 Thess. 4.

In these ways, the function of Didache 16 includes clarification and specification of certain aspects of Matthean eschatology, as well as an interest in a paraenetic application of eschatology in order to build up both community life and the ethical practice of individuals. Thus eschatological material continues to maintain an important place within the churches of the Didache, even though it no longer reveals an imminent expectation of the End.

CONCLUSION

On the basis of these studies of Matthew 25:1–13, Mark 13, Matthew 24 and Didache 16, I am able to conclude that the widely accepted model of progressive 'de-eschatolization' in the early church due to the passing of time and the disappointment at the delay of the parousia fits the evidence only partially.

Particularly in Matt. 25:5–7a I discerned the literary deposit of a community coming to terms with the delay of the parousia, a problem that had become acute, owing not so much to the passing of time as to the death of community members. This had led to a reworking of eschatological expectation and an incorporation of the possibility that all may die before the expected parousia into their eschatological framework. I tentatively dated the revision of eschatological expectation *within this community* to the forties or fifties, but recognized that not every community necessarily underwent such a process at this time. One could not strictly claim that the process reflected in Matt. 25:1–13 was 'de-eschatolization', for the reworked expectation retained an imminent parousia-hope while at the same time recognizing the experienced delay. By the time this material was incorporated into Matthew's Gospel, I found that the delay of the parousia was no longer a burning issue, as both the possibility of the death of all Christians and the fact of the delay itself had become part of the revised eschatological framework. Unlike such scholars as M. Werner who sought to discern the ongoing influence of the issue of eschatological delay well into the second century and beyond, I find that the indications of Matt. 25:1–13 point to its early importance, but also to its relatively swift acceptance into the eschatology of this community.

The study of Mark 13 found evidence for a heightened expectation of the End within Mark's community, owing to the events concerning the Temple and the influx of Judean Christians and their prophets into the community. This gives support to the scholars who have drawn attention to the correlation between the experience of war or persecution (directly or indirectly) and the heightening of eschatological expectation. I found that the 'present' for Mark lay in Mark 13:5b–23. Verses 14ff, behind which I discerned a 'Judean flight oracle', were thus regarded as present, though the flight itself lay in the immediate past. I gave a tentative dating of the passage to the period immediately following the destruction of Jerusalem. In the face of the heightened expectation of the Markan community and their vulnerability to prophets who spoke with the authority of Christ, Mark sought to move the community away from exultation or apocalyptic fervour at the fate of the Temple back to the way of the cross. The evangelist is critical not so much of the expectation itself as of the power of heightened expectation to distract from, or even seemingly render unnecessary, the way of the cross. I noted certain features of Mark 13 that retard the expectation of an imminent End and others that betray the evangelist's interest in paraenesis.

The study of Mark 13 does not support the theory of a single unified tendency within eschatological development, but rather opposing tendencies: a heightening and a retarding of eschatological hope. This calls for an approach to the development of eschatology that can be sensitive to various trends and recognize the central role that the historical particularities of any given community played in this development. In pursuing the question of the historical circumstances behind Mark 13:14ff, the 'Judean flight oracle', I found that the notion of a single unified flight from Jerusalem prior to the War was probably a systematizing fiction, but behind it lay a historical kernel which gave rise to a variety of traditions.

In the study of Matthew's eschatology, I found that this evangelist gave particular prominence to the eschatological horizon of judgement. I argued that Matthew reinterpreted the Markan discourse for the Matthean community by using a two-sequence technique, which was a remarkable scribal achievement, at once conservative and flexible. I found that Matthew regarded the present as belonging to the last days, which were characterized by false prophets, intracommunity conflict, the 'rise of wickedness and cooling of love', as well as some persecution. Matthew heightens the expectation of an imminent End *vis-à-vis* the Markan *Vorlage*, seeing this reiteration of imminence as the appropriate message for the Matthean community, which presumably did not universally share this outlook. I reviewed some aspects of contemporary Jewish apocalyptic writings, and noted that the issues of theodicy that they raise – God's justice, Israel's sin, the question of what has become of God's relationship with the covenant people and the issue of their reproach before the Gentiles – are also addressed by Matthew. This confirms the view of scholars such as Bauckham who maintain that the issue of eschatological delay, and indeed other issues, were not dealt with in a cultural or theological vacuum by the early church, and also that the devastating events surrounding the fall of Jerusalem were to have profound repercussions in the decades to follow. In summary, I observed once again a diversity in eschatological reflection, fuelled by various attitudes within a community to its historical circumstances.

After reviewing the evidence at some length, I concluded that Didache 16 did know and use the Gospel of Matthew. However, the way in which it used Gospel material is not analogous to synoptic relations; it did not intend to supplant the Gospel, but rather to serve as an adjunct, and for this reason it in no way aspired to comprehensiveness. Didache 16 urges its communities to watch over their communal life, and paraenesis is a primary interest in the use and shaping of eschatological material. The two writings, Matthew's Gospel and Didache 16, diverge in their perception of themselves in relation to the End Times. Unlike Matthew, the author of Didache 16 does not seem to consider the present as part of the 'last days'. This seems to confirm a tendency towards decline in the imminence of eschatological expectation within communities which are not experiencing a period of external or severe internal stress. I noted a second purpose (other than paraenesis) evident in the Didache's reshaping of Matthew's material, namely to clarify and specify certain aspects of Matthew's eschatology. In reworking the Matthean material, a variety of divergent features between Didache 16 and Matthew became apparent. The expectation of the parousia is maintained in Didache 16, but its imminence is no longer prominent, and the function of the reiteration of the parousia-hope is primarily in the interests of paraenesis.

Thus the passing of time and the delay of the expected parousia did not play the major role that has often been assigned to them in the past. This is not because the delay was perceived as insignificant, but because it was recognized and grappled with relatively early. It was not a problem that was 'solved' once and for all. Nevertheless, once having incorporated the delay into their framework of expectation, the communities found themselves confronted with more pressing influences on their eschatology – stresses from without and within, the Jewish War and the destruction of Jerusalem. This study has been able to show that there were various factors involved in the development of early Christian eschatology and to draw attention to a sample of the diversity of Christian responses to the expected return of Christ.

BIBLIOGRAPHY

I Texts and translations of primary sources

Biblia Hebraica Stuttgartensia, ed. K. Elliger, W. Rudolph *et al.*, Stuttgart: Deutsche Bibelgesellschaft, 1984.

Septuaginta, 8th edition, ed. A. Rahlfs, Stuttgart: Württembergische Bibelanstalt, 1965.

Novum Testamentum Graece, 26th and 27th editions, ed. E. Nestle, K. Aland *et al.*, Stuttgart: Deutsche Bibelgesellschaft, 1987 and 1993.

The New Oxford Annotated Bible with the Apocrypha, New Revised Standard Version, ed. B. M. Metzger and R. E. Murphy, New York: OUP, 1989.

The Old Testament Pseudepigrapha, I and II, ed. J. H. Charlesworth, London: Darton Longman and Todd, 1983/85.

Neutestamentliche Apokryphen I, 5. Aufl., ed. E. Hennecke and W. Schneemelcher, Tübingen: J. C. B. Mohr, 1987.

New Testament Apocrypha, II, ed. E. Hennecke and W. Schneemelcher, Philadelphia: Westminster Press, 1965.

Schriften des Urchristentums: Didache (Apostellehre), Barnabasbrief, Zweiter Klemensbrief, Schrift an Diognet, ed. K. Wengst, Munich: Kösel-Verlag, 1984.

The Apostolic Fathers, I, Loeb Classical Library, trans. K. Lake, Cambridge, MA: Harvard University Press, 1912.

The Babylonian Talmud, ed. I. Epstein, London: Soncino, 1948–52.

The Talmud of the Land of Israel: A Preliminary Translation and Explanation, 1 Yerushalmi Berakhot, trans., T. Zahavy, Chicago: University of Chicago Press, 1989.

Epiphanius, in F. J. Klijn and G. Reinink, ed. *Patristic Evidence for Jewish Christian Sects*, NovTSup 36, Leiden: Brill, 1973.

Patrologiae Cursus Completus: Series Graeca, XLIII, ed. J.-P. Migne, Paris, 1858.

Eusebius, *Historia ecclesiastica*, 2 vols., Loeb Classical Library, trans. K. Lake, J. E. L. Oulton, Cambridge, MA: Harvard University Press, 1975.

Josephus, Flavius, *Bellum Judaicum (J.W.), Antiquitates Judaicae (Ant.), Contra Apionem (Ap.), Vita (Life)*, 10 vols., Loeb Classical Library, ed. G. P. Goold, Cambridge, MA: Harvard University Press, 1989.

The Jewish War, trans. G. A. Williamson, ed. E. Mary Smallwood, New York: Dorset Press, 1981.

II Reference Works

Aland, K., ed. *Synopsis of the Four Gospels*, 6th Greek–English edition, Stuttgart: United Bible Societies, 1983.

Aland, K. and H. Werner, *Concordance to the Novum Testamentum Graece*, Berlin and New York: De Gruyter, 1987.

Balz, H. and G. Schneider, ed. *Exegetisches Wörterbuch zum Neuen Testament*, Stuttgart, Berlin, Cologne and Mainz: Verlag W. Kohlhammer, 1980.

Bauer, W., W. F. Arndt, F. W. Gingrich and F. W. Danker, *A Greek–English Lexicon of the New Testament and other Early Christian Literature*, 2nd edition, Chicago/ London: University of Chicago Press, 1958.

Beyer, K., *Semitische Syntax im Neuen Testament*, 1, Göttingen: Vandenhoeck and Ruprecht 1968.

Blass, F., A. Debrunner and F. Rehkopf, *Grammatik des neutestamentlichen Griechisch*, 16th edition, Göttingen: Vandenhoeck and Ruprecht, 1984.

Boismard, M.-E. and A. Lamouille, *Synopsis Graeca Quattuor Evangeliorum*, Leuven/Paris: Peeters, 1986.

Friberg, B. and T., *The Analytical Greek New Testament*, Grand Rapids: Baker Book House, 1981.

Hatch, E. and H. A. Redpath, *A Concordance to the Septuagint and the other Greek Versions of the Old Testament (including the Apocryphal Books)*, Grand Rapids: Baker Book House, 1983 (= Oxford, 1897).

Kittel, G. and G. Friedrich, ed. *Theological Dictionary of the New Testament*, 10 vols., Grand Rapids: Eerdmans, 1964–76.

Klein, O., *Syrisch-griechisches Wörterbuch zu den vier kanonischen Evangelien*, BZAW 28 Giessen: Verlag A. Töpelmann, 1916.

Kloppenborg, J. S., *Q Parallels: Synopsis, Critical Notes and Concordance*, Sonoma: Polebridge Press, 1988.

Lampe, G. W. H., *A Patristic Greek Lexicon*, Oxford: Clarendon Press, 1961.

Liddell, H. G., R. Scott, H. S. Jones and R. McKenzie, *A Greek–English Lexicon*, Oxford: Clarendon Press, 1968.

Payne-Smith, J., *A Compendious Syriac Dictionary*, Oxford: Clarendon Press, 1903.

Rengstorf, K. H. ed. *A Complete Concordance to Flavius Josephus*, I–IV and Supplement, Leiden: E. J. Brill, 1983.

III Commentaries, Monographs, Essays, Dissertations

Aalen, S., 'Reign and House in the Kingdom of God in the Gospels', *NTS* 8 (1961–2), 215–40.

Achtemeier, P. J., 'An Apocalyptic Shift in Early Christian Tradition: Reflections on Some Canonical Evidence', *CBQ* 45 (1983), 231–48.

Ackroyd, P. R., *Exile and Restoration: A Study of Hebrew Thought of the 6th Century B.C.*, London: SCM, 1968.

Aharoni, Y., 'Roads and Highways', *The Land of the Bible*, Philadelphia: Westminster Press, 1979, 43–63, trans. from the Hebrew.

Ambrozic, A. M., *The Hidden Kingdom: A Redaction-Critical Study of the References to the Kingdom of God in Mark's Gospel*, Washington DC: Catholic Biblical Association of America, 1972.

Audet, J.-P., *La Didachè: Instructions des Apôtres*, Paris: Gabalda, 1958.

Aune, D. E., *The Cultic Setting of Realized Eschatology in Early Christianity*, NovTSup 28, 1972.

'The Significance of the Delay of the Parousia for Early Christianity', in G. F. Hawthorne, ed. *Current Issues in Biblical and Patristic Interpretation, Studies in Honor of Merrill C. Tenney*, Grand Rapids: Eerdmans, 1975, 87–109.

Bammel, E., 'Schema und Vorlage von *Didache* 16', in F. L. Cross, ed. *StPatr*, IV, Berlin: Akademie Verlag, 1961, 253–62.

Barrett, C. K., 'Important Hypotheses Reconsidered: V. The Holy Spirit and the Gospel Tradition', *ExpTim* 67 (1955/56), 142–5.

'The Gentile Mission as an Eschatological Phenomenon', in W. Hulitt Gloer, ed. *Eschatology and the New Testament, Essays in Honor of G. R. Beasley-Murray*, Peabody, MA: Hendrickson, 1988.

Bartsch, H.-W., 'Zum Problem der Parusieverzögerung', in *Entmythologisierende Auslegung. Aufsätze aus den Jahren 1940 bis 1960*, II, TF 26, Hamburg, 1962, 69–80.

Bauckham, R. J., 'The Delay of the Parousia', *TynB* 31 (1980), 3–36.

'The Two Fig Tree Parables in the Apocalypse of Peter', *JBL* 104 (1985), 269–87.

Beale, G. K., 'The Use of Daniel in the Synoptic Eschatological Discourse and in the Book of Revelation', in D. Wenham, ed. *The Jesus Tradition Outside the Gospels*, 129–53.

Beare, F. W., 'The Synoptic Apocalypse: Matthean Version', in J. Reumann, ed. *Understanding the Sacred Text, Essays in Honor of M. S. Enslin*, Valley Forge, PA: Judson Press, 1972, 115–33.

Beasley-Murray, G. R., *Jesus and the Future: An Examination of the Criticism of the Eschatological Discourse, Mark 13, with Special Refererence to the Little Apocalypse Theory*, London: Macmillan, 1954.

A Commentary on Mark Thirteen, London: Macmillan, 1957.

'Second Thoughts on the Composition of Mark 13', *NTS* 29 (1983), 414–20.

Jesus and the Last Days: The Interpretation of the Olivet Discourse, Peabody: Hendrikson 1993.

Belo, F., *A Materialist Reading of the Gospel of Mark*, Maryknoll, NY: Orbis, 1981.

Bilde, P., 'The Roman Emperor Gaius (Caligula)'s Attempt to Erect His Statue in the Temple of Jerusalem', *ST* 32 (1978), 67–93.

Blanchetière, F., 'Le "Secte des Nazaréens" ou les Débuts du Christianisme', in F. Blanchtière and M. D. Herr, ed. *Les Origines Juives du Christianisme*, Jerusalem: Pais, 1993, 93–110.

Blanchetière, F. and R. Pritz, 'La Migration des "Nazaréens" à Pella', in F. Blanchtière and M. D. Herr, ed. *Les Origines Juives du Christianisme*, 65–91.

Bordieu, P., 'The Attitude of the Algerian Peasant toward Time', in J. Pitt-Rivers, ed. *Mediterranean Countrymen: Essays in the Social Anthropology of the Mediterranean*, Paris/The Hague: Mouton, 1963, 55–72.

Bornkamm, G., 'Die Komposition der apokalyptischen Visionen in der Offenbarung Johannis', *ZNW* 36 (1937), 132–49.

'Die Verzögerung der Parusie: Exegetische Bemerkungen zu zwei synoptischen Texten', in W. Schmauch, ed. *In memoriam E. Lohmeyer*, Stuttgart: Verlag Katholisches Bibelwerk, 1951, 116–126.

'Enderwartung und Kirche im Matthäusevangelium', in W. D. Davies and D. Daube, ed. *The Background of the New Testament and its Eschatology*, 222–60.

Brandenburger, E., *Markus 13 und die Apokalyptik*, FRLANT 134, Göttingen: Vandenhoeck and Ruprecht, 1984.

Brandon, S. G. F., *The Fall of Jerusalem and the Christian Church: A Study of the Effects of the Jewish Overthrow of A. D. 70 on Christianity*, London: SPCK, 1951.

Breytenbach, C. *Nachfolge und Zukunftserwartung nach Markus: eine methodenkritische Studie*, Zurich: Theologischer Verlag, 1984.

Broer, I., 'Redaktionsgeschichtliche Aspekte von Mt. 24:1–28', *NovT* 35 (1993), 209–33.

Brooks, S. H., *Matthew's Community: The Evidence of His Special Sayings Material*, JSNTSup 16, 1987.

Brown, S., 'The Matthean Apocalypse', *JSNT* 4 (1979), 2–27.

'The Matthean Community and the Gentile Mission', *NovT* 22 (1980), 193–221.

Bultmann, R., *Die Geschichte der synoptischen Tradition*, 9. Aufl., FRLANT 29, Göttingen: Vandenhoeck and Ruprecht, 1979.

Die Geschichte der synoptischen Tradition, Ergänzungsheft, ed. G. Theissen and P. Vielhauer, Göttingen: Vandenhoeck and Ruprecht, 1979.

History and Eschatology: The Presence of Eternity, Edinburgh: Edinburgh University Press, 1957.

Buri, F., *Die Bedeutung der neutestamentlichen Eschatologie für die neuere protestantische Theologie*, Zurich and Leipzig: Max Niehans, 1935.

Burnett, F. W., *The Testament of Jesus Sophia: A Redaction-Critical Study of the Eschatological Discourse in Matthew*, Lanham: University Press of America, 1981.

Busch, F., *Zum Verständnis der synoptischen Eschatologie: Markus 13 neu untersucht*, NTF IV.2, Gütersloh: C. Bertelsmann, 1938.

Butler, B. C., 'The Literary Relations of Didache, Ch. XVI', *JTS* NS 11 (1960), 265–83.

'The Two Ways in the Didache', *JTS* NS 12 (1961), 27–38.

Campenhausen, H. Fr. von, *Aus der Frühzeit des Christentums*, Tübingen: J. C. B. Mohr, 1963.

Chapman, J., 'Zacharias, Slain between the Temple and the Altar', *JTS* 13 (1912), 398–410.

Charlesworth, J. H., *The Pseudepigrapha and Modern Research: New Edition with a Supplement*, Septuagint Cognate Studies Series 7S, MI: Scholars Press for SBL, 1981.

Clark, K. W., 'The Gentile Bias in Matthew', *JBL* 66 (1947), 165–72.

Cohen, S. J. D., *Josephus in Galilee and Rome: His Vita and Development as a Historian*, Leiden: E. J. Brill, 1979.

Collins, A. Y., 'The Early Christian Apocalypses', *Semeia* 14 (1979), 61–121.

'The Eschatological Discourse of Mark 13', in F. van Segbroeck *et al.*, ed. *The Four Gospels 1992*, 1125–40.

Collins, J. J., 'Towards a Morphology of Genre', *Semeia* 14 (1979), 2–20.

Conzelmann, H. 'Geschichte und Eschaton nach Markus 13', *ZNW* 50 (1959), 210–21.

The Theology of St. Luke, London: Faber, 1960.

Cope, O. Lamar, *Matthew: A Scribe Trained for the Kingdom of Heaven*, Washington DC: Catholic Biblical Association of America, 1976.

'"To the close of the age"', The Role of Apocalyptic Thought in the Gospel of Matthew', in J. Marcus and M. L. Soards, ed. *Apocalyptic and the New Testament, Essays in Honour of J. Louis Martyn*, JSNTSup 24, Sheffield: JSOT Press, 1989, 113–24.

Corsini, E., *The Apocalypse: The Perennial Revelation of Jesus Christ*, GNS 5, trans. and ed. F. J. Moloney, Wilmington, DE: Michael Glazier, 1983.

Cousar, C. B., 'Eschatology and Mark's *Theologia Crucis*: A Critical Analysis of Mark 13', *Int* 24 (1970), 321–35.

Cranfield, C. E. B., 'St. Mark 13', *SJT* 6 (1953), 189–96, 287–303; *SJT* 7 (1954), 284–303.

The Gospel According to St. Mark: An Introduction and Commentary, 5th edition, Cambridge: CUP, 1977.

Crawford, B. S., 'Near Expectation in the Sayings of Jesus', *JBL* 101 (1982), 225–44.

Crossan, J. D., *Cliffs of Fall: Paradox and Polyvalence in the Parables of Jesus*, New York: Seabury Press, 1980.

The Historical Jesus: The Life of a Mediterranean Jewish Peasant, Edinburgh: T. and T. Clark 1991.

Cullmann, O., *Christ and Time*, rev. edition London: SCM, 1962.

'Das wahre, durch die ausgebliebene Parusie gestellte neutestamentliche Problem', *TZ* 3 (1947) 177–91.

'Parusieverzögerung und Urchristentum. Der gegenwärtige Stand der Diskussion', *TLZ* 83 (1958), 2–12.

Dalman, G., *Arbeit und Sitte in Palästina*, I and II, Hildesheim: Georg Olms Verlagsbuchhandlung, 1964.

Danker, F. W., 'Double-entendre in Mark XIII 9', *NovT* 10 (1968), 162–63.

Davies, W. D. and C. C. Allison, *A Critical and Exegetical Commentary on the Gospel According to Saint Matthew*, I and II, Edinburgh, T. and T. Clark, 1988, 1991.

Davies, W. D. and D. Daube, ed. *The Background of the New Testament and its Eschatology, Essays in Honour of C. H. Dodd*, Cambridge: CUP, 1956.

Dodd, C. H., *The Parables of the Kingdom*, rev. edition, London and New York: Nisbet and Co., 1936.

'The Fall of Jerusalem and the "Abomination of Desolation"', *JRelS* 37 (1947), 47–54.

Donahue, J. R., *Are You the Christ?*, SBLDS 10, Missoula, MT, 1973.

Draper, J., 'The Jesus Tradition in the Didache', in D. Wenham, ed. *The Jesus Tradition Outside the Gospels*, 269–87.

'Torah and Troublesome Apostles in the Didache Community', *NovT* 33, 4 (1991), 347–72.

Drews, P., 'Untersuchungen zur Didache', *ZNW* 5 (1904), 53–79.

Dupont, J., 'La Parabole du figuier qui bourgeonne (Mc xiii, 28–29 et par.)', *RB* 75 (1968), 526–48.

'La Parabole du maître qui rentre dans la nuit (Mc 13, 34–36), in A. Descamps and A. de Halleux ed. *Mélanges bibliques: en hommage au R. P. Béda Rigaux*, Gembloux: Editions J. Duculot, 1969, 89–116.

'La Persécution comme situation missionaire (Marc 13, 9–11)', in R. Schnackenburg, J. Ernst and J. Wanke, ed. *Die Kirche des Anfangs: Festschrift für Heinz Schürmann zum 65. Geburtstag*, Leipzig: St Benno, 1977, 97–114.

'La Ruine du temple et la fin des temps dans le discours de Marc 13', in L. Monloubou, ed. *Apocalypses et théologie de l'espérance*, Paris: Cerf, 1977, 207–69.

Les Trois Apocalypses synoptiques: Marc 13; Matthieu 24–25; Luc 21, LD 121, Paris: Cerf, 1985.

Dyer, K. D., '"Reader Note Well": Intertextuality and Interpretation in Mark 13', unpublished doctoral thesis, Melbourne College of Divinity, 1991.

Edwards, R. A., *A Theology of Q. Eschatology, Prophecy and Wisdom*, Philadelphia: Fortress Press, 1976.

Eichrodt, W., 'Heilserfahrung und Zeitverständnis im Alten Testament', *TZ* (1956), 103–25.

Elliott, J. H., Review of J. Lambrecht, *Die Redaktion der Markus-Apokalypse*, *CBQ* 30 (1968) 267–69.

Ernst, J., *Die eschatologischen Gegenspieler in den Schriften des Neuen Testaments*, Biblische Untersuchungen 3, Regensburg: F. Pustet, 1981.

Falk, H., *Jesus the Pharisee: A New Look at the Jewishness of Jesus*, New York: Paulist Press, 1985.

Farmer, W. R., *The Synoptic Problem: A Critical Analysis*, New York: Macmillan, 1964.

Farrer, A., 'An Examination of Mark XIII.10', *JTS* 7 (1956), 75–9.

Festinger, L., H. W Riecken and S. Schachter, *When Prophecy Fails*, Minneapolis: University of Minnesota Press, 1956.

Feuillet, A., 'Le Discours de Jésus sur la ruine du temple d'après Marc XIII et Luc XXI,5–36', *RB* 55 (1948), 481–502; 56 (1949), 61–92.

'Le Sens du mot Parousie dans l'évangile de Matthieu. Comparison entre Matth. XXIV et Jac. V.1–11', in W. D. Davies and D. Daube, eds., *The Background of the New Testament and its Eschatology*, 261–80.

Fitzmyer, J. A., *The Gospel According to Luke (X–XXIV)*, AB 28A, New York: Doubleday, 1964.

Fitzmeyer, J. A., ed., *To Advance the Gospel*, New York: Crossroad, 1981.

Flückiger, F., 'Die Redaktion der Zukunftsrede in Mark. 13', *TZ* 26 (1970), 395–409.

Ford, D., *The Abomination of Desolation in Biblical Eschatology*, Washington DC: University Press of America, 1979.

Forsyth, N., *The Old Enemy: Satan and the Combat Myth*, Princeton: Princeton University Press, 1987.

France, R. T., *Jesus and the Old Testament: His Application of Old Testament Passages to Himself and his Mission*, London: Tyndale Press, 1971.

Fredriksen, P., *From Jesus to Christ: The Origins of the New Testament Images of Jesus*, New Haven and London: Yale University Press, 1988.

Freyne, S., 'Villifying the Other and Defining the Self: Matthew's and John's Anti-Jewish Polemic in Focus', in J. Neusner and E. S. Frerichs, ed. *'To see ourselves as others see us': Christians, Jews, 'Others' in Late Antiquity*, Chico, CA: Scholars Press, 1985, 117–43.

Funk, R. W, *Language, Hermeneutic and Word of God: The Problem of Language in the New Testament and Contemporary Theology*, New York: Harper and Row, 1966.

Gaston, L., *No Stone on Another: Studies in the Significance of the Fall of Jerusalem in the Synoptic Gospels*, Leiden: E. J. Brill, 1970.

Geddert, T. J., *Watchwords. Mark 13 in Markan Eschatology*, JSOTSup 26, Sheffield: JSOT Press, 1989.

Gerhardsson, B., 'Mashalen om de tio bröllopstärnorna (Matt. 25:1–13)', *SEÅ* 60 (1995), 83–94.

Geyser, A. S. 'Some Salient New Testament Passages on the Restoration of the Twelve Tribes of Israel', in J. Lambrecht, ed. *L'Apocalypse johannique*, 305–10.

Gibson, J. B., 'The Rebuke of the Disciples in Mark 8:14–21', *JSNT* 27 (1986), 31–47.

Giesen, H., 'Mk 9,1 – ein Wort Jesu über die nahe Parusie?', *TTZ* 92 (1983), 134–48.

Giet, S., *L'Enigme de la Didachè*, Paris: Editions Ophrys, 1970.

Giordano, O., 'L'escatologia nella *Didachè*', in *Oikumene: Studi paleocristiani pubblicati in onore del concilio ecumenico vaticano II*, Catania: Universita di Catania, 1964, 121–39.

Glasson, T. F., *The Second Advent*, London: Epworth Press, 1947.

'Mark xiii and the Greek Old Testament', *ExpTim* 69 (1957/58), 213–15.

'The Ensign of the Son of Man (Matt. XXIV.30)', *JTS* NS 15 (1964), 299–300.

Glover, R., 'The Didache's Quotations and the Synoptic Gospels', *NTS* 5 (1958/59), 12–29.

'Patristic Quotations and Gospel Sources', *NTS* 31 (1985), 234–51.

Gnilka, J., *Das Evangelium nach Markus, Mk 8,27–16,20*, EKKNT II/2, Zurich and Neukirchen-Vluyn: Benziger and Neukirchener Verlag, 1979.

Das Matthäusevangelium, HTKNT I, 2, Freiburg: Herder, 1988.

Gödecke, M., *Geschichte als Mythos: Euseb 'Kirchengeschichte'*, Frankfurt aM: Peter Lang, 1987.

Goldingay, J. E., *Daniel*, WBC 30, Dallas, TX: Word, 1989.

Gollinger, H., 'Ihr wisst nicht, an welchem Tag euer Herr kommt. Auslegung von Mt 24,37–51', *BibLeb* 11 (1970), 238–47.

Grässer, E., *Das Problem der Parusieverzögerung in den synoptischen Evangelien und in der Apostelgeschichte*, 3rd edition, Berlin and New York: de Gruyter, 1977.

Grayston, K., 'The Study of Mark XIII', *BJRL* 56 (1974), 371–87.

Grundmann, W., *Das Evangelium nach Markus*, THKNT 2, 3. Aufl., Berlin: Evangelische Verlagsanstalt, 1965.

Günther, J. J., 'The Fate of the Jerusalem Church. The Flight to Pella', *TZ* 29 (1973), 81–94.

Hahn, F., *Christologische Hoheitstitel: Ihre Geschichte im frühen Christentum*, FRLANT 83, Göttingen: Vandenhoeck and Ruprecht, 1963.

'Die Rede von der Parusie des Menschensohnes Markus 13', in R. Pesch and R. Schnackenburg, ed. in collaboration with O. Kaiser, *Jesus und der Menschensohn: Für Anton Vögtle*, Freiburg: Herder, 1975, 240–66.

'Die eschatologische Rede Matthäus 24 und 25', in L. Schenke, ed. *Studien zum Matthäusevangelium*, 107–26.

Hallbäck, G., 'Der anonyme Plan. Analyse von Mk 13,5–27 im Hinblick auf die Relevanz der apokalyptischen Rede für die Problematik der Aussage', *LB* 49 (1981), 38–53.

Harder, G., 'Das eschatologische Geschichtsbild der sogenannten kleinen Apokalypse Markus 13', *Theologia Viatorum* 4 (1948/49), 71–107.

Hare, D. A., *The Theme of Jewish Persecution of Christians in the Gospel According to St. Matthew*, SNTSMS 6, Cambridge: Cambridge University Press, 1967.

Hart, J. F., 'A Chronology of Matthew 24:1–44', unpublished doctoral thesis, Grace Theological Seminary and College, 1986.

Hartman, L., *Prophecy Interpreted: The Formation of Some Jewish Apocalyptic Texts and of the Eschatological Discourse, Mark 13 Par.*, ConBNT Series 1, Lund: Gleerup, 1966.

Harvey, A. E., *Jesus and the Constraints of History*, London: Duckworth, 1982.

Hellholm, D., ed. *Apocalypticism in the Mediterranean World and the Near East*, Proceedings of the International Colloquium on Apocalypticism, Uppsala, August 12–17, 1979, Tübingen: J. C. B. Mohr, 1983.

Hengel, M., *The Charismatic Leader and His Followers*, Edinburgh: T. and T. Clark, 1981.

'Probleme des Markusevangeliums', in P. Stuhlmacher, ed. *Das Evangelium und die Evangelien*, Tübingen: J. C. B. Mohr, 1983, 221–65.

'The Gospel of Mark: Time of Origin and Situation', in *Studies in the Gospel of Mark*, London: SCM, 1985, 1–30.

The 'Hellenization' of Judea in the First Century after Christ, London and Philadelphia: SCM Press and Trinity Press International, 1989.

The Zealots: Investigations into the Jewish Freedom Movement in the Period from Herod I until 70 A. D., Edinburgh: T. and T. Clark, 1989.

Hiers, R. H., 'Not the Season for Figs', *JBL* 87 (1968), 394–400.
   The Kingdom of God in the Synoptic Tradition, Gainesville, FL: University of Florida, 1970.
Higgins, A. J. B., 'The Sign of the Son of Man (Matt. XXIV. 30)', *NTS* 9 (1963), 380–2.
Holman, C. L., 'The Idea of an Imminent Parousia in the Synoptic Gospels', *Studia Biblica et Theologica* 3 (1973), 15–31.
Hölscher, G., 'Der Ursprung der Apokalypse Mk 13', *TBl* 12 (1933), cols. 193–202.
Hooker, M. D., *The Son of Man in Mark: A Study of the Background of the Term 'Son of Man' and Its Use in St. Mark's Gospel*, London: SPCK, 1967.
   Review of L. Hartman, *Prophecy Interpreted*, *JTS* 19 (1968), 263–5.
   'Trial and Tribulation in Mark XIII', *BJRL* 65 (1982), 78–99.
   The Gospel According to Mark, London: A. and C. Black, 1991.
Horsley, R. A., *Jesus and the Spiral of Violence: Popular Jewish Resistance in Roman Palestine*, San Francisco: Harper and Row, 1987.
Issel, E., *Die Lehre vom Reiche Gottes im Neuen Testament*, Leiden: E. J. Brill, 1891.
Jefford, C. N., *The Sayings of Jesus in the Teaching of the Twelve Apostles*, *VCaro* Supplements 11, Leiden: E. J. Brill, 1989.
Jeremias, J., 'ΛΑΜΠΑΔΕΣ Mt 25 1.3f.7f', *ZNW* 56 (1965), 196–201.
   Jerusalem in the Time of Jesus, Philadelphia: Fortress, 1969.
   The Parables of Jesus, 3rd rev. edition, London: SCM, 1972.
Juel, D., *Messiah and Temple: The Trial of Jesus in the Gospel of Mark*, SBLDS 31, Missoula MT: Scholars Press, 1977.
Jülicher, A., *Die Gleichnisreden Jesu I and II*, Darmstadt: Wissenschaftliche Buchgesellschaft, 1976.
Käsemann, E., 'On the Subject of Primitive Christian Apocalyptic', in E. Käsemann, *New Testament Questions of Today*, Philadelphia: Fortress, 1969, 108–37.
Kee, H. C., *Community of the New Age: Studies in Mark's Gospel*, London: SCM, 1977.
Kelber, W. H., 'The History of the Kingdom in Mark – Aspects of Markan Eschatology', in L. C. McGaughy, ed. *SBL 108th General Meeting Book of Seminar Papers*, I, Los Angeles: SBL, 1972, 63–95.
   The Kingdom in Mark: A New Place and a New Time, Philadelphia: Fortress, 1974.
   The Oral and the Written Gospel: The Hermeneutics of Speaking and Writing in the Synoptic Tradition, Mark, Paul and Q, Philadelphia: Fortress, 1983.
Kilpatrick, G. D., 'The Gentile Mission in Mark and Mk 13,9–11', in D. E. Nineham, ed. *Studies in the Gospels: Essays in Memory of R. H. Lightfoot*, Oxford: Blackwell, 1955, 45–50.
Kingsbury, J. D., *Matthew: Structure, Christology, Kingdom*, London: SPCK, 1976.
   'The Gospel of Mark in Current Research', *RelSRev.* 5 (1979), 101–7.
Klauck, H.-J., *Allegorie und Allegorese in synoptischen Gleichnistexten*, 2.

durchges. Aufl. mit einem Nachtrag, NTAbh., Neue Folge 13, Münster: Aschendorff, 1978.

Kloppenborg, J. S., 'Didache 16 6–8 and Special Matthaean Tradition', *ZNW* 70 (1979), 54–67.

Knoch, O., 'Kenntnis und Verwendung des Matthäusevangeliums bei den apostolischen Vätern', in L. Schenke, ed. *Studien zum Matthäusevangelium*, 157–78.

Knopf, R., *Die Lehre der zwölf Apostel und die zwei Klemensbriefe*, Tübingen: J. C. B. Mohr, 1920.

Koch, D.-A., 'Zum Verhältnis von Christologie und Eschatologie im Markusevangelium. Beobachtungen aufgrund von 8,27–9,1', in G. Strecker, ed. *Jesus Christus in Historie und Theologie, Festschrift für H. Conzelmann*, Tübingen: J. C. B. Mohr, 1975, 395–408.

Koch, K., *The Rediscovery of Apocalyptic*, London: SCM, 1972.

Koester, C., 'The Origin and Significance of the Flight to Pella Tradition', *CBQ* 51 (1989), 90–106.

Koester, H., *Synoptische Überlieferung bei den apostolischen Vätern*, TU 65, Berlin: Akademie Verlag, 1957.

Köhler, W.-D., *Die Rezeption des Matthäusevangeliums in der Zeit vor Irenäus*, WUNT II, 24, Tübingen: J. C. B. Mohr, 1987.

Kolenkow, A. B., 'Beyond Miracles, Suffering and Eschatology', *SBL 109th General Meeting Book of Seminar Papers*, II, ed. G. MacRae, Cambridge, MA: SBL, 1973, 155–202.

Körner, J., 'Endgeschichtliche Parusieerwartung und Heilsgegenwart im Neuen Testament in ihrer Bedeutung für eine christliche Eschatologie', *EvT* 14 (1954), 177–92.

Kühschelm, R., *Jüngerverfolgung und Geschick Jesu: Eine exegetisch-bibeltheologische Untersuchung der synoptischen Verfolgungsankündigungen, Mk 13,9–13 Par. und Mt 23, 29–36 Par.*, ÖBS 5, Klosterneuburg: Österreichisches Katholisches Bibelwerk, 1983.

Kümmel, W. G., *Promise and Fulfilment*, London: SCM, 1957.

'Futurische und präsentische Eschatologie im ältesten Urchristentum', *NTS* 5 (1958/59), 113–26.

Introduction to the New Testament, London: SCM, 1975.

Künzi, M., *Das Naherwartungslogion Mk 9,1 Par: Geschichte seiner Auslegung, mit einem Nachwort zur Auslegungsgeschichte von Markus 13,30 Par*, BGBE 21, Tübingen: J. C. B. Mohr, 1977.

Lacocque, A., *The Book of Daniel*, London: SPCK, 1979.

Ladd, G. E., 'The Eschatology of the Didache', unpublished doctoral dissertation, Harvard University, 1949.

'Eschatology and the Unity of New Testament Theology', *ExpTim* 68 (1956/57), 268–73.

The Presence of the Future: The Eschatology of Biblical Realism, Grand Rapids: Eerdmans, 1974.

Lagrange, M.-J., 'L'Avènement du Fils de l'Homme', *RB* 1906, 382–411.

Evangile selon Saint Matthieu, 8th edition, Paris: Librairie Lecoffre, 1948.

Lambrecht, J., *Die Redaktion der Markus-Apokalypse: Literarische Analyse und Strukturuntersuchung*, AnBib 28, Rome: Päpstliche Bibelinstitut, 1967.

'The Parousia Discourse. Composition and Content in Mt., XXIV – XXV', in D. Didier, ed. *L'Evangile selon Matthieu*, BETL 29, 1972, 309–42.

'A Structuration of Revelation 4,1 – 22,5', in J. Lambrecht, ed. *L'Apocalypse johannique*, 77–104.

Out of the Treasure: The Parables in the Gospel of Matthew, Leuven: Peeters, 1992.

Lambrecht, J., ed., *L'Apocalypse johannique et l'Apocalyptique dans le Nouveau Testament*, BETL 53, Leuven: Leuven University Press, 1980.

Lange, J. P., *The Gospel According to Matthew*, I in P. Schaff, trans. and ed. *Commentary on the Holy Scriptures*, New York: Charles Scribner and Co., 1867. Translation of J. P. Lange, *Das Evangelium nach Matthäus*, in *Theologisch-homiletisches Bibelwerk*, Bielefeld: Verlag von Velhagen und Klasing, 1861.

Layton, B., 'The Sources, Date and Transmission of Didache 1.3b – 2.1', *HTR* 61 (1968), 343–83.

Le Déaut, R., *La Nuit Pascale: essai sur la signification de la Pâque juive à partir du Targum d'Exode XII 42*, Rome: Institut Biblique Pontifical, 1963.

Lee, J. A. L., 'Some Features of the Speech of Jesus in Mark's Gospel', *NovT* 27 (1985), 1–26.

Lightfoot, R. H., *The Gospel Message of St. Mark*, London: Oxford University Press, 1962.

Linnemann, E., *Parables of Jesus: Introduction and Exposition*, London: SPCK, 1966.

Lohmann, H., *Drohung und Verheissung: exegetische Untersuchungen zur Eschatologie bei den apostolischen Vätern*, Berlin and New York: de Gruyter, 1989.

Lohmeyer, E., *Das Evangelium des Markus*, 17th edition, Göttingen: Vandenhoeck and Ruprecht, 1967.

Lohse, B., *Das Passafest der Quartadecimaner*, Gütersloh: C. Bertelsmann, 1953.

Loisy, A., 'L'Apocalypse synoptique', *RB* 1896, 173–98.

Les Evangiles synoptiques I et II, Ceffonds: chèz l'auteur, 1907/8.

Lövestam, E., 'The ἡ γενεὰ αὕτη Eschatology in Mk 13, 30 parr', in J. Lambrecht, ed. *L'Apocalyse johannique*, 403–13.

Lüdemann, G., 'The Successors of Pre-70 Jerusalem Christianity: A Critical Evaluation of the Pella Tradition', in E. P. Sanders, ed. *Jewish and Christian Self-Definition*, 161–73.

'Die Nachfolger der Jerusalemer Urgemeinde. Analyse der Pella-Tradition', in *Paulus, der Heidenapostel*, II, *Studien zur Chronologie*, FRLANT 130, Göttingen: Vandenhoeck and Ruprecht, 1983, 265–86.

Paul, Apostle to the Gentiles: Studies in Chronology, London: SCM, 1984.

Opposition to Paul in Jewish Christianity, Minneapolis: Fortress, 1989.

Lührmann, D., *Das Markusevangelium*, HNT 3, Tübingen: J. C. B. Mohr, 1987.

Luz, U., 'βασιλεία', *EWNT* I, ed. H. Balz and G. Schneider, Stuttgart: W. Kohlhammer, 1980, 481–91.

'The Secrecy Motif and the Marcan Christology', in C. Tuckett, ed. *The Messianic Secret*, London: SPCK, 1983, 75–96.

Das Evangelium nach Matthäus, EKKNT I/1, 2, Zurich and Neukirchen-Vluyn: Benziger and Neukirchener Verlag, 1985, 1990. English translation of vol. I, *Matthew 1–7: A Commentary*, Minneapolis: Augsburg Fortress, 1989.

The Theology of the Gospel of Matthew, Cambridge: Cambridge University Press, 1995.

Maartens, P. J., 'The Structuring Principle in Mt 24 and 25 and the Interpretation of the Text', *Neot* 16 (1982), 88–117.

McCaughey, J. D., 'Three "Persecution Documents" of the New Testament', *AusBR* 17 (1969), 27–40.

Mack, B. L., *A Myth of Innocence: Mark and Christian Origins*, Philadelphia: Fortress, 1988.

McNicoll, A., R. H Smith and B. Hennessy,, *Pella in Jordan I.* An interim report on the joint University of Sydney and The College of Wooster Excavations at Pella, 1979–1981, Canberra: Australian National Gallery, 1982.

Maddox, R., *The Purpose of Luke-Acts*, Göttingen: Vandenhoeck and Ruprecht, 1982.

Malina, B. J., 'Christ and Time: Swiss or Mediterranean?', *CBQ* 51 (1989), 1–31.

Marshall, I. H., *Eschatology and the Parables*, London: Tyndale, 1963.

'Slippery Words: I. Eschatology', *ExpTim* 89 (1977), 264–9.

Marxsen, W., *Mark the Evangelist: Studies on the Redaction History of the Gospel*, Nashville TN: Abingdon Press, 1969.

Massaux, E., 'L'Influence littéraire de l'évangile de Saint Matthieu sur la Didachè', *ETL* 25 (1949), 5–41.

Massingberd Ford, J., 'The Parable of the Foolish Scholars (Matt. xxv 1–13)', *NovT* 9 (1967), 107–23.

Meinertz, M., 'Die Tragweite des Gleichnisses von den zehn Jungfrauen', in J. Schmidt and A. Vögtle, ed. *Synoptische Studien [für] Alfred Wikenhauser zum 70. Geburtstag*, Munich: Karl Zink Verlag, 1953, 94–106.

' "Dieses Geschlecht" im Neuen Testament', *BZ* 1 (1957), 283–289.

Metzger, B. M., *A Textual Commentary on the Greek New Testament*, London and New York: United Bible Societies, 1971.

Milavec, A. A., 'The Pastoral Genius of the Didache: An Analytical Translation and Commentary' in J. Neusner, E. S. Frerichs, A. J. Levine, ed. *Religious Writings and Religious Studies* II, *Christianity*, Atlanta: Scholars Press, 1989, 89–125.

Mohrlang, R., *Matthew and Paul: A Comparison of Ethical Perspectives*, SNTSMS 48, Cambridge: Cambridge University Press, 1984.

Moore, A. L., *The Parousia in the New Testament*, Leiden: E. J. Brill, 1966.

Mounce, R. H., *The Book of Revelation*, NICNT 17, Grand Rapids: Eerdmans, 1977.

Murphy-O'Connor, J., 'The Cenacle – Topographical Setting for Acts 2:44–45', in R. Bauckham, ed. *The Book of Acts in Its First Century*

Setting, 4, *Palestinian Setting*, Grand Rapids: Eerdmans, 1995, 303–21.

Mussner, F., *Christ and the End of the World: A Biblical Study in Eschatology*, Notre Dame, IN: University of Notre Dame Press, 1965.

Myers, C., *Binding the Strong Man: A Political Reading of Mark's Story of Jesus*, Maryknoll, NY: Orbis, 1988.

Nardoni, E., 'A Redactional Interpretation of Mark 9:1', *CBQ* 43 (1981), 365–84.

Neirynck, F., 'Marc 13. Examen critique de l'interprétation de R. Pesch', in J. Lambrecht, ed. *L'Apocalypse johannique*, 369–401.

Duality in Mark: Contributions to the Study of the Markan Redaction, rev. edition, BETL 31, Leuven: Leuven University Press, 1988.

Nepper-Christensen, P., *Das Matthäusevangelium: Ein judenchristliches Evangelium?*, Aarhus: Universitetsforlaget, 1958.

Neville, G., *The Advent Hope: A Study of the Context of Mark 13*, London: Darton, Longman and Todd, 1961.

Newport, K. G. C., *The Sources and* Sitz im Leben *of Matthew 23*, Sheffield: Sheffield Academic Press, 1995.

Nickelsburg, G. W. E., *Jewish Literature Between the Bible and the Mishnah*, Minneapolis: Fortress, 1981.

Niederwimmer, K., *Die Didache*, Kommentar zu den apostolischen Vätern, Band 1, Göttingen: Vandenhoeck und Ruprecht, 1989.

Nützel, J. M., 'Hoffnung und Treue: Zur Eschatologie des Markusevangeliums', in P. Fiedler and D. Zeller, ed. *Gegenwart und kommendes Reich: Schülergabe Anton Vögtle zum 65. Geburtstag*, Stuttgart: Verlag Katholisches Bibelwerk, 1975, 79–90.

Ong, W. J., *Orality and Literacy: The Technologizing of the Word*, London and New York: Methuen, 1982.

'Text as Interpretation: Mark and After', *Semeia* 39 (1987), 7–26.

Orton, D. E., *The Understanding Scribe: Matthew and the Apocalyptic Ideal*, Sheffield: Sheffield Academic Press, 1989.

Patte, D., *The Gospel According to Matthew: A Structural Commentary on Matthew's Faith*, Minneapolis: Fortress, 1987.

Patten, P., 'The Form and Function of Parable in Select Apocalyptic Literature and Their Significance for Parables in the Gospel of Mark', *NTS* 29 (1983), 246–58.

Perelmuter, H. G., *Siblings: Rabbinic Judaism and Early Christianity at Their Beginnings*, New York and Mahwah, NJ: Paulist Press, 1989.

Perrin, N., *Rediscovering the Teaching of Jesus*, London: SCM, 1967.

'The Evangelist as Author: Reflections on Method in the Study and Interpretation of the Synoptic Gospels and Acts', *BR* 17 (1972), 5–18.

Perrin, N. and D. C. Duling, 'The Gospel of Mark: The Apocalyptic Drama', in N. Perrin and D. C. Duling, ed. *The New Testament: An Introduction*, 2nd edition, New York: Harcourt Brace Jovanovich, 1982, 233–62.

Perrot, C., 'Essai sur la Discours eschatologique (Mc. XIII, 1–37; Mt. XXIV, 1–36; Lc. XXI, 5–36)', *RSR* 47 (1959), 481–514.

Pesch, R., *Naherwartungen. Tradition und Redaktion in Mk 13*, Düsseldorf: Patmos-Verlag 1968.

'Eschatologie und Ethik. Auslegung von Mt 24:1–36', *BibLeb* 11 (1970), 223–38.

'Markus 13', in J. Lambrecht, ed. *L'Apocalypse johannique*, 355–68.

Das Markusevangelium. II Teil. Kommentar zu Kap. 8,27–16,20, HTKNT II,2, 2. Aufl. Freiburg: Herder, 1980.

Petersen, N. R., *Literary Criticism for New Testament Critics*, Philadelphia: Fortress, 1978.

Peterson, E., 'Die Einholung des Kurios', *ZST* 7 (1929/30), 682–702.

Pfleiderer, O., 'Über die Komposition der eschatologischen Rede. Matth. 24', in *Jahrbücher für Deutsche Theologie* 13 (1868), 135ff.

Das Urchristentum, seine Schriften und Lehren, 2nd edition, Berlin: Georg Reimer, 1902.

Pritz, R. A., *Nazarene Jewish Christianity, from the End of the New Testament Period until its Disappearance in the Fourth Century*, Jerusalem: Magnes Press, 1988.

Puig i Tàrrech, A., *La Parabole des dix vierges (Mt 25,1–13)*, AnBib 102, Rome: Biblical Institute Press, 1983.

Reicke, B., 'Synoptic Prophecies on the Destruction of Jerusalem', in D. E. Aune, ed. *Studies in New Testament and Early Christian Literature, Essays in Honor of Allen P. Wikgren*, Leiden: E. J. Brill, 1972, 121–34.

Reimarus, H. S., *Von dem Zwecke Jesu und seiner Jünger*, ed. G. E. Lessing, Berlin: Sander, 1778.

Rengstorf, K. H., 'σημεῖον', *TDNT*, VII, 200–69.

Ricoeur, P., 'Biblical Hermeneutics', *Semeia* 4 (1975), 29–148.

Robbins, V. K., '*Dynameis* and *Semeia* in Mark', *BR* 18 (1973), 5–20.

Jesus the Teacher: A Socio-Rhetorical Interpretation of Mark, Philadelphia: Fortress, 1984.

Robinson, J. A. T., *Jesus and His Coming*, 2nd edition, London: SCM, 1979.

Robinson, J. M., *The Problem of History in Mark*, London: SCM, 1957.

'The Problem of History in Mark, Reconsidered', *USQR* 20 (1965), 131–47.

Roloff, J., 'Das Kirchenverständnis des Matthäus im Spiegel seiner Gleichnisse', *NTS* 38 (1992) 337–56.

Rordorf, W., 'Le Problème de la transmission textuelle de *Didachè* 1,3b. – 2,1', in F. Paschke, ed. *Überlieferungsgeschichtliche Untersuchungen*, TU 125, Berlin: Akademie Verlag, 1981, 499–513.

'Does the Didache Contain Jesus Tradition Independently [sic] of the Synoptic Gospels?', in H. Wansbrough, ed. *Jesus and the Oral Gospel Tradition*, JSOTSup 64, Sheffield: JSOT Press, 1991, 394–423.

Rordorf, W. and A. Tuilier, *La Doctrine des douze Apôtres*, Paris: Cerf, 1978.

Rousseau, F., 'La Structure de Marc 13', *Bib* 56 (1975), 157–72.

Rowland, C., *The Open Heaven: A Study of Apocalyptic in Judaism and Early Christianity*, New York: Crossroad, 1982.

Christian Origins, London: SPCK, 1985.

Rowley, H. H., *The Relevance of Apocalyptic: A Study of Jewish and Christian Apocalypses from Daniel to the Revelation*, London: Lutterworth Press, 1963.

Russell, D. S., *The Method and Message of Jewish Apocalyptic*, London: SCM, 1964.

Apocalyptic: Ancient and Modern, London: SCM, 1978.

Sabatier, P., ΔΙΔΑΧΗ ΤΩΝ ΙΒ' ΑΠΟΣΤΟΛΩΝ: La Didachè ou L'enseignement des douze apôtres, Paris: Charles Noblet, 1885.

Safrai, S., *Pilgrimage at the Time of the Second Temple*, Tel Aviv: Am Hasseler Publ., 1965.

Sanders, E. P., ed. *Jewish and Christian Self-Definition*, I, London: SCM, 1980.

Jesus and Judaism, Philadelphia: Fortress, 1985.

Schenke, L., ed. *Studien zum Matthäusevangelium, Festschrift für Wilhelm Pesch*, Stuttgart: Verlag Katholisches Bibelwerk, 1988.

Schmithals, W., *The Apocalyptic Movement: Introduction and Interpretation*, Nashville, TN: Abingdon Press, 1975.

Schmoller, O., *Die Lehre vom Reiche Gottes in den Schriften des Neuen Testaments*, Leiden: E. J. Brill, 1891.

Schnackenburg, R., 'Kirche und Parusie', in H. Vorgrimler, ed. *Gott in Welt. 1, Festgabe für K. Rahner*, Freiburg: Herder, 1964, 551–78.

Schoeps, H.-J., 'Ebionitische Apokalyptik im Neuen Testament', *ZNW* 51 (1960), 101–11.

Schöllgen, G., 'Miszellen: Die Didache – ein frühes Zeugnis für Landgemeinden?', in *ZNW* 76 (1985), 140–3.

Schottroff, L., 'Die Gegenwart in der Apokalyptik der synoptischen Evangelien', in D. Hellholm ed. *Apocalypticism in the Mediterranean World and the Near East*, 707–28.

Schüssler Fiorenza, E., '*Apokalypsis* and *Propheteia*. The Book of Revelation in the Context of Early Christian Prophecy', in J. Lambrecht, ed. *L'Apocalypse johannique*, 105–28.

Schuster, H., 'Die konsequente Eschatologie in der Interpretation des Neuen Testaments, kritisch betrachtet', *ZNW* 47 (1956), 1–25.

Schweitzer, A., *Das Messianitäts- und Leidensgeheimnis: eine Skizze des Lebens Jesu*, vol. II of *Das Abendmahl im Zusammenhang mit dem Leben Jesu und der Geschichte des Urchristentum*, Tübingen: J. C. B. Mohr, 1901.

Out of My Life and Thought, NY: Mentor, 1953 (German original *Aus mein Leben und Denken*, Leipzig: Meiner, 1932).

The Quest of the Historical Jesus: A Critical Study of Its Progress from Reimarus to Wrede, 3rd edition, London: A. and C. Black, 1954.

Schweizer, E., 'Eschatology in Mark's Gospel', in E. E. Ellis and M. Wilcox, ed. *Neotestamentica et Semitica: Studies in Honour of Matthew Black*, Edinburgh: T. and T. Clark, 1969, 114–18.

The Good News According to Mark, Atlanta, GA: John Knox Press, 1970.

The Good News According to Matthew, Atlanta, GA: John Knox Press, 1975.

Das Evangelium nach Markus, 17. durchges. Aufl., Göttingen: Vandenhoeck and Ruprecht, 1989.

Seeberg, A., *Didache des Judentums und der Urchristenheit*, Leipzig: A. Deichert (Georg Böhme), 1908.

Seeliger, H. R., 'Erwägungen zu Hintergrund und Zweck des apokalyptischen Schlusskapitels der *Didache*', in E. A. Livingstone, ed., *Studia
Patristica*, XXI, Leuven: Peeters, 1989, 185–92.

Segal, A. F., 'Matthew's Jewish Voice', in D. L. Balch, ed. *Social History
of the Matthean Community: Cross-Disciplinary Approaches*, Minneapolis: Fortress, 1991.

Segbroeck, F. van, C. M. Tuckett, G. van Belle and J. Verheyden, ed. *The
Four Gospels 1992, Festschrift F. Neirynck*, II, Leuven: Leuven University Press, 1992.

Selby, D. J., 'Changing Ideas in New Testament Eschatology', *HTR* 50
(1957), 21–36.

Senior, D., 'The Struggle to be Universal: Mission as Vantage Point for
New Testament Investigation', *CBQ* 46 (1984), 63–81.

Sherriff, J. M., 'Matthew 25:1–13. A Summary of Matthean Eschatology?',
in *StudBib 1978*, II, Sheffield: JSOT Press, 1980, 301–5.

Simon, M., 'La Migration à Pella: légende ou réalité?', *RSR* 60 (1972),
37–54.

Sibinga, J. Smit, 'The Structure of the Apocalyptic Discourse, Matthew 24
and 25', *ST* 29 (1975) 71–9.

Smith, R. H., 'An Early Roman Sarcophagus of Palestine and its School',
PEQ 105 (1973), 71–82.

Pella of the Decapolis I, The 1967 Season of The College of Wooster
Expedition to Pella, Wooster: College of Wooster, 1973.

Smith, R. H. and L. P. Day, *Pella of the Decapolis* II, Final Report on The
College of Wooster Excavations in Area IX, The Civic Complex,
1979–1985, Wooster: College of Wooster, 1989.

Sowers, S., 'The Circumstances and Recollection of the Pella Flight', *TZ*
26 (1970), 305–20.

Spicq, C., 'L'Amour de charité se refroidira (Mt. XXIV, 12)', in E.
Lucchesi, ed. *Mémorial A.-J. Festugière*, Cahiers d'Orientalisme 10,
Geneva: Patrick Cramer, 1984, 113–17.

Stanton, G. N., ' "Pray that your Flight may not be in Winter or on a
Sabbath" (Matthew 24.20)', *JSNT* 37 (1989), 17–30.

A Gospel for a New People: Studies in Matthew, Edinburgh: T. and T.
Clark, 1992.

Stein, R. H., 'The Proper Methodology for Ascertaining a Markan
Redaction History', *NovT* 13 (1971), 181–98.

Stommel, E., 'Σημεῖον ἐκπετάσεως (Didache 16,6)', *RQ* 48 (1953), 21–42.

Stone, M. E., 'Reactions to Destructions of the Second Temple: Theology,
Perception and Conversion', *JSJ* 12, 2 (1982), 195–204.

Features of the Eschatology of IV Ezra, HSS 35, Atlanta: Scholars Press,
1989.

Fourth Ezra, Minneapolis: Fortress, 1990.

Strack, H. L. and P. Billerbeck, *Kommentar zum Neuen Testament*, I, *Das
Evangelium nach Matthäus*, Munich: C. H. Beck, 1986.

Strauss, D. F., *The Life of Jesus Critically Examined*, trans. G. Eliot
(republished), Philadelphia: Fortress, 1972.

Strecker, G., *Das Judenchristentum in den Pseudoclementinen*, Berlin:
Akademie Verlag, 1958.

Der Weg der Gerechtigkeit: Untersuchung zur Theologie des Matthäus, FRLANT 82, 3. durchges. u. erweit. Aufl., Göttingen: Vandenhoeck and Ruprecht, 1971.

Eschaton und Historie, Göttingen: Vandenhoeck and Ruprecht, 1979.

Strobel, F. A., 'Zum Verständnis von Mt XXV 1–13', *NovT* 2 (1958), 199–227.

Stuhlmann, R., *Das eschatologische Mass im Neuen Testament*, FRLANT 132, Göttingen: Vandenhoeck and Ruprecht, 1983.

Stuiber, A., 'Die drei ΣΗΜΕΙΑ von Didache XVI', in JAC 24, Münster: Aschendorff, 1981, 42–4.

Tannehill, R. C., 'The Disciples in Mark: The Function of a Narrative Role', in W. Telford, ed., *The Interpretation of Mark*, Philadelphia: Fortress, 1985, 134–57.

Taylor, J., 'The Love of Many will Grow Cold: Matt. 24:9–13 and the Neronian Persecution', *RB* 96 (1989), 352–57.

Taylor, V., 'The Apocalyptic Discourse of Mark xiii', *ExpTim* 60 (1948/49), 94–8.

The Gospel According to St. Mark: The Greek Text with Introduction, Notes and Indexes, London: Macmillan, 1952.

Theissen, G., *The Gospels in Context: Social and Political History in the Synoptic Tradition*, Minneapolis: Fortress, 1991.

Thompson, J. W., 'The Gentile Mission as an Eschatological Necessity', *ResQ* 14 (1971), 18–27.

Thomson, W. G., *Matthew's Advice to a Divided Community. Mt. 17,22–18,35*, AnBib 44, Rome: Biblical Institute Press, 1970.

Thüsing, W., 'Erhöhungsvorstellung und Parusieerwartung in der ältesten nachösterlichen Christologie', *BZ*, NS, 12 (1968), 54–80, 223–40.

Tolbert, M. A., *Sowing the Gospel: Mark's World in Literary-Historical Perspective*, Minneapolis: Fortress, 1989.

Towner, W. S. 'An Exposition of Mk 13.24–32', *Int* 30 (1976), 292–6.

Trilling, W., *Das wahre Israel: Studien zur Theologie des Matthäusevangeliums*, 3rd edition, SANT 10, Munich: Kösel/KNO, 1964.

Der zweite Brief an die Thessalonicher, EKKNT XIV, Zurich and Neukirchen-Vluyn: Benziger und Neukirchener Verlag, 1980.

Trotti, J. B., 'Mark 13.32–37', *Int* 32 (1978), 410–13.

Tuckett, C. M., 'Synoptic Tradition in the Didache', in J.-M. Sevrin, ed. *The New Testament in Early Christianity*, Leuven: Leuven University Press, 1989, 197–230.

Van Unnik, W. C., 'Flavius Josephus als historischer Schriftsteller', in K. H. Rengstorf, ed. *Franz Delitzsch Vorlesungen*, Neue Folge, Heidelberg: Verlag Lambert Schneider, 1978.

Vassiliadis, P., 'Behind Mark: Towards a Written Source', *NTS* 20 (1974), 155–60.

Verheyden, J., 'The Flight of the Christians to Pella', *ETL* 66 (1990), 368–84.

'Persecution and Eschatology, Mk 13,9–13', in F. van Segbroek *et al.*, ed. *The Four Gospels* 1141–59.

Vermes, G., 'The Use of נש בר/נשא בר in Jewish Aramaic', in *An Aramaic Approach to the Gospels and Acts*, ed. M. Black, 3rd edition, Oxford: Clarendon Press, 1967, 310–30.

Vielhauer, P., 'Apocalyptic in Early Christianity', in E. Hennecke and W. Schneemelcher, ed. *New Testament Apocrypha*, II, 608–642.

'Zum "Paulinismus" der Apostelgeschichte', *EvT* 10 (1950/51), 1–15.

Vokes, F. E., 'The Didache and the Canon of the New Testament', in *SE*, III, Berlin: Akademie Verlag, 1964, 427–36.

Waetjen, H. C., *A Reordering of Power: A Socio-Political Reading of Mark's Gospel*, Minneapolis: Fortress, 1989.

Walter, N., 'Tempelzerstörung und synoptische Apokalypse', *ZNW* 57 (1966), 38–49.

Weber, T., *Pella Decapolitana: Studien zur Geschichte, Architektur und Bildenden Kunst einer hellenisierten Stadt des nördlichen Ostjordanlandes*, Abhandlungen des Deutschen Palästinavereins 18, Wiesbaden: Harrassowitz, 1993.

Weeden, T. J., 'The Heresy That Necessitated Mark's Gospel', *ZNW* 59 (1968), 145–58.

Mark: Traditions in Conflict, Philadelphia: Fortress, 1971.

Weiss, J., *Jesus' Proclamation of the Kingdom of God*, London: SCM, 1971.

Wellhausen, J., *Das Evangelium Marci*, Berlin: G. Reimer, 1909.

Einleitung in die ersten Evangelien, Berlin: G. Reimer, 1911.

Wendt, H. H., *The Teaching of Jesus*, Edinburgh: T. and T. Clark, 1892.

Wengst, K., ed., *Schriften des Urchristentums: Didache (Apostllehre), Barnabasbrief, Zweiter Klemesbrief Schrift an Diognet*, Munich: Kösel-Verlag, 1984.

Wenham, D., 'Paul and the Synoptic Apocalypse', in R. T. France and D. Wenham, ed. *Studies of History and Tradition in the Four Gospels*, Gospel Perspectives 2, Sheffield: JSOT Press 1981, 345–75.

'"This generation will not pass . . ."; A Study of Jesus' Future Expectation in Mark 13', in H. H. Rowden, ed. *Christ the Lord: Studies in Christology, Presented to Donald Guthrie*, Leicester: Inter-Varsity Press, 1982, 127–50.

The Rediscovery of Jesus' Eschatological Discourse, Gospel Perspectives 4, Sheffield: JSOT Press, 1984.

'The End is Near. In What Sense?', *Themelios* 13, 3 (1988), 75–8.

Wenham, D., ed., *The Jesus Tradition Outside the Gospels*, Gospel Perspectives 5, Sheffield: JSOT Press, 1984.

Werner, M., *Der protestantische Weg des Glaubens*, I and II, Berne: Verl. P. Haupt, 1955.

The Formation of Christian Dogma: An Historical Study of its Problem, London: A. and C. Black, 1957.

Winandy, J., 'Le Logion de l'ignorance (Mc, XIII, 32; Mt, XXIV,36)', *RB* 75 (1968), 63–79.

Windisch, H., *Der Sinn der Bergpredigt*, 2. Aufl., Leipzig: Hinrichs, 1937. Translated as *The Meaning of the Sermon on the Mount*, Philadelphia: Westminster, 1951.

Witherington III, B., *Jesus, Paul and the End of the World: A Comparative Study in New Testament Eschatology*, Downers Grove, IL: Inter-Varsity Press, 1992.

INDEX OF MODERN AUTHORS

INDEX OF BIBLICAL AND OTHER ANCIENT TEXTS

Old Testament

Genesis
19:12ff, 89
49, 70

Exodus
9:18, 94

Leviticus
24:4, 43

Deuteronomy
6:5, 149n.18
7:3, 170n.54
30:4, 95
32–3, 70

2 Samuel
6:15, 35
(= LXX 2 Kings) 22:7, 45

1 Chronicles
28–9, 70

2 Chronicles
15:6, 94
24, 163

Job
16:18, 35

Psalms
5:1, 35
17(18):6, 35
48:6, 94
101(102):1, 35
110:1, 68

Proverbs
17:3, 196

Isaiah
1:9–10, 204n.39
2:9–21, 89
8:21, 94

13:10, 95
13:10a, 95
13:13, 94
13:22, 39n.45
19:2, 94
23, 204n.38
25:6ff, 38n.43
29:6 (*variant*), 35
30:19, 35
34:3, 89
34:4, 95
62:5, 38n.44
65:19, 35
66:6, 35
66:66, 35n.33

Jeremiah
4:19, 35
4:31, 94

Lamentations
4:6, 204n.39

Ezekiel
16:50, 204n.39
32:5–6, 89
37:9, 194
47:12, 64

Daniel
7:13, 68, 95
8:11ff, 122–3n.38, 124
8:11–13, 122–3n.38
8:13, 122–3n.38
8:17, 123
9:27, 115, 122–3n.38, 124
11:29ff, 122–3n.38
11:31, 115, 122–3n.38
11:32, 122–3n.38, 124
11:33ff, 122–3n.38
12:1, 90, 94
12:10, 144n.13

SUBJECT INDEX

theodicy, 15, 16, 23, 176–8, 208
two-sequence interpretation/technique,
 153–62, 165–7, 169–73, 179, 207

two-source hypothesis, 2, 22n.42, 175

Zealots, 124–33, 164